Mornings with JESUS 2024

DAILY ENCOURAGEMENT *for Your* SOUL

366 DEVOTIONS

Guideposts

Mornings with Jesus 2024

Published by Guideposts Books & Inspirational Media
100 Reserve Road, Suite E200
Danbury, CT 06810
Guideposts.org

Acknowledgments

Every attempt has been made to credit the sources of copyrighted material used in this book. If any such acknowledgment has been inadvertently omitted or miscredited, receipt of such information would be appreciated.

Scripture quotations marked (AMP) are taken from the *Amplified Bible*. Copyright © 2015 by The Lockman Foundation, La Habra, California. All rights reserved.

Scripture quotations marked (CEV) are taken from *Holy Bible: Contemporary English Version*. Copyright © 1995 by American Bible Society.

Scripture quotations marked (CJB) are taken from the *Complete Jewish Bible* by David H. Stern. Copyright © 1998. All rights reserved. Used by permission of Messianic Jewish Publishers, Clarksville, Maryland. messianicjewish.net.

Scripture quotations marked (CSB) are taken from *The Christian Standard Bible*. Copyright © 2017 by Holman Bible Publishers. Used by permission.

Scripture quotations marked (ERV) are taken from *Easy-to-Read Version Bible*. Copyright © 2006 by Bible League International.

Scripture quotations marked (ESV) are taken from the *Holy Bible, English Standard Version*. Copyright © 2001 by Crossway Bibles, a division of Good News Publishers. Used by permission. All rights reserved.

Scripture quotations marked (GNT) are taken from the *Holy Bible, Good News Translation*. Copyright © 1992 by American Bible Society.

Scripture quotations marked (GW) are taken from *God's Word Translation*. Copyright © 1995 by God's Word to the Nations. Used by permission of Baker Publishing Group.

Scripture quotations marked (ISV) are taken from the *Holy Bible, International Standard Version*. Copyright © 1995–2014 by ISV Foundation. All rights reserved internationally. Used by permission of Davidson Press, LLC.

Scripture quotations marked (KJV) are taken from the *King James Version of the Bible*.

Scripture quotations marked (MSG) are taken from *The Message*. Copyright © 1993, 1994, 1995, 1996, 2000, 2001, 2002 by Eugene H. Peterson.

Scripture quotations marked (NASB and NASB1995) are taken from the *New American Standard Bible*. Copyright © 1960, 1962, 1963, 1968, 1971, 1972, 1973, 1975, 1977, 1995 by The Lockman Foundation, La Habra, California. Used by permission.

Scripture quotations marked (NCV) are taken from the *New Century Version*. Copyright © 2005 by Thomas Nelson.

Scripture quotations marked (NIV) are taken from *The Holy Bible, New International Version*. Copyright © 1973, 1978, 1984, 2011 by Biblica, Inc. Used by permission of Zondervan. All rights reserved worldwide. zondervan.com.

Scripture quotations marked (NKJV) are taken from *The Holy Bible, New King James Version*. Copyright © 1982 by Thomas Nelson.

Scripture quotations marked (NLT) are taken from the *Holy Bible, New Living Translation*. Copyright © 1996, 2004, 2007 by Tyndale House Foundation. Used by permission of Tyndale House Publishers Inc., Carol Stream, Illinois. All rights reserved.

Scripture quotations marked (NLV) are from the *New Life Bible*. Copyright © 1969 by Christian Literature International. Used by permission. All rights reserved.

Scripture quotations marked (RSV) are taken from the *Revised Standard Version of the Bible*. Copyright © 1946, 1952, 1971 by the Division of Christian Education of the National Council of the Churches of Christ in the United States of America. Used by permission.

Scripture quotations marked (TLB) are taken from *The Living Bible*. Copyright © 1971 by Tyndale House Publishers, Inc., Carol Stream, Illinois. All rights reserved.

Scripture quotations marked (TPT) are taken from *The Passion Translation*. Copyright © 2016 by Broadstreet Publishing Group, Savage, Minnesota. All rights reserved.

Cover design by Müllerhaus
Cover photo by iStock Photo
Indexed by Matthew MacLellan
Typeset by Aptara, Inc.

ISBN 978-1-959634-02-7 (softcover)

Printed and bound in the United States of America
10 9 8 7 6 5 4 3 2 1

Dear Friends,

We are thrilled to encourage your walk with Jesus with the 2024 edition of *Mornings with Jesus*. The theme of this year's volume is "Hope," as found in Romans 5:5 (NIV): "And hope does not put us to shame, because God's love has been poured out into our hearts through the Holy Spirit, who has been given to us."

The 366 all-new devotions in *Mornings with Jesus 2024* are infused with hope anchored in Jesus. As in years past, our beloved writers share how Jesus is essential to their life, and this year, they write about the many ways they've put their hope and trust in Jesus—in times of joy and thankfulness, sorrow and grief, doubts and fears, strife and hardship, and many more.

You'll recognize many of our returning *Mornings with Jesus* writers, including Becky Alexander, Susanna Foth Aughtmon, Jeannie Blackmer, Isabella Campolattaro, Pat Butler Dyson, Grace Fox, Heidi Gaul, Tricia Goyer, Sharon Hinck, Jeanette Levellie, Ericka Loynes, Erin Keeley Marshall, Dianne Neal Matthews, Claire McGarry, Cynthia Ruchti, Emily E. Ryan, Karen Sargent, Cassandra Tiersma, Suzanne Davenport Tietjen, and Barbranda Lumpkins Walls. We are also thrilled to welcome back Pamela Toussaint Howard and welcome newcomers Susan Downs, Jennifer Anne F. Messing, and Brenda L. Yoder to the fold.

It is our prayer that as you read each day's scripture, followed by the writer's powerful reflection, you will recognize how you can connect moments in your own life with the wisdom and insights of others. And as you continue to mull over the day's lesson, let the "faith step" encourage you to praise and thank our Savior as you, too, put your hope and trust in Him.

Faithfully yours,
Editors of Guideposts

Especially for You!

Sign up for the online newsletter *Mornings with Jesus* at guideposts.org/newsletter. Each week, you'll receive an inspiring devotion or personal thoughts from one of the writers about her own devotional time and prayer life and how focusing on Jesus influenced her relationship with Him and others.

New Year's Day, Monday, January 1

The LORD will guide you continually, giving you water when you are dry and restoring your strength. Isaiah 58:11 (NLT)

DECADES AGO, I READ THAT people who write out their goals are forty-two times more likely to achieve them than those who don't. So I went crazy—making and writing down lifetime goals, bucket list dreams, and yearly and monthly objectives. I tacked the lists to my bedroom wall where I saw them often.

Some goals are impressively spiritual: learn to meditate, talk to God constantly, memorize Psalm 37. Others seem earthier: exercise five times a week, declutter my office, find a pair of orange pants like the ones I lost on vacation (you don't want to know).

I've achieved many of those goals. But I haven't succeeded by my own wimpy willpower or my puny pea brain. Every item on my list that has a red check mark beside it became a reality because of the power of Jesus Christ in me.

When I gave my life to Jesus, He in return gave me His Spirit—the Holy Spirit, who guides and helps me continuously. He's the person who gives me writing and preaching ideas. He helps me say no to sweets and gossip. He pokes my conscience when I'm thinking mean thoughts.

He hasn't brought me those orange pants yet, but I'm not giving up! —JEANETTE LEVELLIE

FAITH STEP: *Write down five goals. Now ask Jesus for the power of His Holy Spirit to help you achieve them.*

TUESDAY, JANUARY 2

Is anything too hard for the LORD? No! I will return to you at the right time a year from now, and Sarah will have a son. Genesis 18:14 (NCV)

THE WEATHER TODAY IS DISMAL. The rain is melting off the remaining snow from what had been a white Christmas. Not exactly spirit lifting. Although keeping a hopeful, positive outlook when things look bleak and gray can be challenging, Jesus reminds me in His Word that nothing is too hard for Him. No matter how bleak, dismal, or gray the weather—or my outlook—He's always at work in nature and in me.

Even though the new year has only begun, I'm feeling adventurous in this time of fresh beginnings and do-overs. I'm daring to pick up discarded dreams, brush them off, and start acting in faith to see Jesus bring those dreams into fruition. I recently read somewhere that "faith is an act." Not play-acting but *action*. While present circumstances may appear bleak as previous hopes and plans are seemingly melting away, that doesn't mean I can't still act in faith—faith that Jesus has brighter things in store for me this year.

Jesus can certainly breathe sweet new life into my little dreams and aspirations if I let Him. While Jesus is renewing my hope for the new year ahead, my job is to take action. —CASSANDRA TIERSMA

FAITH STEP: *Think about what Jesus-honoring aspirations you've left behind from previous years. Write down ways you can take action as you ask Jesus to renew your hope and faith.*

WEDNESDAY, JANUARY 3

To put off your old self, which belongs to your former manner of life and is corrupt through deceitful desires, and to be renewed in the spirit of your minds, and to put on the new self, created after the likeness of God in true righteousness and holiness. Ephesians 4:22–24 (ESV)

THOUGH I WAS RAISED NOMINALLY Catholic, it wasn't until I was thirty-three that I really recognized Jesus. I'd had a challenging childhood and left home as soon as I could, aiming to start what I thought was a new life. Turns out, it wasn't as new as I'd hoped. I carried some of the same old, familiar patterns that had made my childhood so difficult. As the saying goes: wherever you go, there you are!

Throughout my twenties, I lived a faithless life, certainly not righteous or holy. When I met Jesus, some things changed promptly. I was empowered to quit drinking, smoking, and reckless dating. My ambitions changed too. I stepped off the corporate ladder and pursued more meaningful work. Yet, notwithstanding all of that sudden and spontaneous change, old habits, thinking, and ways of being lingered.

The Apostle Paul implores believers to *put off* the old self to *put on* the new self. This isn't passive! Just as I remove my clothes to put on my pajamas, I have to remove my corrupt self to put on my new holy self. Of course, I can't do this alone. By the power of the Spirit of Christ, I'm doing this in partnership with Jesus.

What will you put on in this new year? —ISABELLA CAMPOLATTARO

FAITH STEP: *Use a fashion magazine to select clothes you really like. Cut them out, glue them into your journal, and label each article with a holy virtue you'd like to wear.*

THURSDAY, JANUARY 4

The LORD your God is with you, the Mighty Warrior who saves. He will take great delight in you; in his love he will no longer rebuke you, but will rejoice over you with singing. Zephaniah 3:17 (NIV)

JESUS HAS BEEN TEACHING ME to pay attention to my self-talk. It's been a valuable lesson because it has revealed pet phrases that are far from the truth. One of the degrading thoughts is *you're not enough*.

I've caught myself thinking this phrase within the context of being a sister, wife, mother, and grandmother. It creates the fear of inadequacy and hinders transparency in my relationships with my loved ones.

I struggle with it within the context of podcasting and writing for publication. It causes me to compare my skills with others in the same field and makes me feel as though I fall short.

I wrestle with it when I don't maintain health-related goals or when I set new goals and don't reach them as fast as I want. Before long, I feel like throwing those goals to the wind because I'll never achieve them anyway. *Why bother? You're not enough.*

Self-talk matters. The words I speak about myself, either aloud or silently in my thoughts, carry power to bring hope or breed discouragement. Now, when I catch myself speaking a lie, I immediately reject it and replace it with truth. *You're not enough* becomes *Jesus is with me. He loves me, saves me, delights in me, and rejoices over me with a song.* Self-talk based on truth reminds me that Jesus thinks I'm special. That's enough for me. —GRACE FOX

FAITH STEP: *Identify a self-talk pet phrase that's untrue. Now find a Bible verse that speaks truth into your life, write it on a note card, and memorize it.*

FRIDAY, JANUARY 5

For sin shall no longer be your master, because you are not under the law, but under grace. Romans 6:14 *(NIV)*

I STARTED A DIET A few days ago, limiting my portions and counting calories. I recorded every mouthful of food that passed through the trapdoor of my lips. I already have results. I've gained a pound. I'm not surprised. Whenever I concentrate on eating less, my attention instead turns to eating in general. Anything. Everything.

The most effective approach to weight reduction I've found—for me, that is—is through exercise. Activity and hard workouts remove some of the excess weight. My shape changes as fat is replaced by healthy muscle.

The same holds true for sin. Days spent in self-absorption, my mind wallowing in regrets, weaken my witness as a Christian. The problem isn't just the sin but my obsession with it. I make it all about me. During those periods, I allow a tsunami of shame to overwhelm me.

When I exercise the hope and power I possess through Jesus, my faith muscles grow and shift. As a result, I become more effective. My hands and heart share more love for Him, with Him, and through Him.

Just as my clothes drape nicely after several trips to the gym, looking upward instead of inward helps my faith fit better, and it shows.

It's time for another workout. Now, where's my Bible? —HEIDI GAUL

FAITH STEP: *Move your focus away from sins and inadequacies. On a sheet of paper, list some of your achievements—ways your body, mind, and spirit have gotten healthier. Think of one new way you can exercise your faith today too.*

SATURDAY, JANUARY 6

He has made everything beautiful in its time. Ecclesiastes 3:11 (NIV)

WHEN I PACKED AWAY CHRISTMAS decorations, I kept out my newest candle purchase. The crackling wood wick soothes me, but the best part is the effect the flame has on the candle holder. Unlit, the vase looks solid red, but the fire reveals pretty, glowing designs in the glass. At first, snowflakes appeared around the top; as the wax melted farther down, I saw pine trees in the middle. When I bought the candle, I had no idea that designs were etched into the silver interior of the glass, waiting to be revealed as the heat burned away the wax.

The candle makes me think about how fire transforms us too. In the Bible, fire symbolizes trials and afflictions that purify our faith, but it's also used to represent the Lord's presence. The past few years have been filled with an extra measure of difficulties, yet when I look back, I can see Jesus was there through it all. Trials reveal the beautiful ways my character has been changed by knowing and following Jesus. The more I tend and nurture His flame glowing within me, the more transforming work He can do in my heart and my life.

As my candle burns, it becomes more beautiful. I can't wait to see what designs the flame will reveal over the coming weeks in what is now blank space around the bottom of the glass. I also can't wait to see what beauty Jesus will reveal in the blank spaces of my life this year. —DIANNE NEAL MATTHEWS

FAITH STEP: *Light a candle and remind yourself of the ways Jesus is always present in your life, even when you go through fires of trouble and hardship.*

Sunday, January 7

Give, and it will be given to you. A good measure, pressed down, shaken together and running over, will be poured into your lap. For with the measure you use, it will be measured to you. Luke 6:38 (NIV)

As a youngster, I watched the offering basket get passed around at church each Sunday. Almost everyone gave, and we dutifully put our family's envelope in too, with my mom's perfect penmanship indicating name, address, and amount. I grew up understanding I was supposed to give in the offering plate, but as a young adult in the work world, I got stingy. I had learned about biblical tithing, giving one-tenth of my income to the local church, but it took me a while to get on board. I loved to travel and eat out and accumulated a good amount of credit card debt to prove it. I ran out of money by the end of the month. How could I give away 10 percent?

My transformation around tithing was gradual but effective. As I grew in my relationship with Jesus, I was struck by the depth of His sacrifice for me on the cross. I realized that I prospered personally because I acknowledged that Jesus ordered my steps and orchestrated my success—not me. Once I understood this, I knew I could not withhold support for the church—a place where I watched people answer altar calls and give their lives to Him.

Through tithing and giving with a grateful heart, I play a part in advancing Jesus's kingdom on earth. There's no better investment!
—Pamela Toussaint Howard

Faith Step: *Pray about the possibility of giving financially to your local church regularly and cheerfully. If you already tithe, ask Jesus to show you new opportunities to give.*

MONDAY, JANUARY 8

I will celebrate before the LORD. I will become even more undignified than this, and I will be humiliated in my own eyes. 2 Samuel 6:21–22 *(NIV)*

MY SON SAVED HIS MONEY to buy a high-quality virtual-reality headset, and the first time I played with it, he secretly recorded me with his phone. He showed me the video when I was done, and I couldn't help but laugh. I looked ridiculous! I swatted at unseen enemies, dodged invisible obstacles, and ducked under barriers that seemed not to exist. With the headset on and my senses absorbed in the world only I could see, my movements and actions made sense. But from the outside looking on, I could admit that I looked like a fool.

It made me think of how King David looked to his wife, Michal, when he celebrated what the Lord had done for Israel by dancing with all his might (2 Samuel 6:12–22). She said he looked undignified. He said it didn't matter how he looked because his eyes were on his Lord.

I've done a lot of silly things for Jesus over the years. I've worn a pink wig, ridden a unicycle, and wrestled a goat when serving in the children's ministry at church. But I've also taken jobs with small salaries and followed the Bible's standards for purity in marriage with the intent of honoring Him. In many cases, my actions probably looked foolish from the perspective of others. But when I keep my eyes on Jesus, I remember to follow Him no matter how foolish or undignified I may look to others. —EMILY E. RYAN

FAITH STEP: *Is Jesus asking you to do something that might not make sense to others? Stop hesitating and do it.*

TUESDAY, JANUARY 9

My peace I give to you; not as the world gives do I give to you.
John 14:27 (NKJV)

"ADJUST YOUR OXYGEN MASK AND breathe normally. If you don't know how to breathe normally, just breathe as you normally would."

The passengers erupted in laughter as the flight attendant sprinkled his standard safety speech with humor. Air travel can sometimes produce anxiety, and his comedic comment cut the tension.

I was stuck, though, on the tongue-in-cheek line, "Just breathe as you normally would." Too often I've caught myself holding my breath over a crisis or strained moment. A grown child hovers close to a bad decision. A pinch point of pain causes me to conclude that I will receive a horrible diagnosis. I even hold my breath when friends are at odds with one another and my peacekeeping efforts fail. But Jesus tells me—in all seriousness: "Just breathe as you normally would."

If the airplane's little yellow plastic cup and tubing drops from overhead, is "breathe normally" going to be my instinct? No. And it's not automatic when I face in-life rather than in-flight emergencies, either.

"Peace I give to you," Jesus says. Today I'm considering how those words serve as a reminder to breathe normally, no matter what. "I've provided an oxygen mask for you in the likely event of loss of emotional cabin pressure. Breathe, child of Mine."

The pilot of my soul has my life's flight plan well under control. With Jesus, I need not fear. —CYNTHIA RUCHTI

FAITH STEP: *Is there a spot in your home, car, or office where you need peace? Write an O (the chemical symbol for oxygen) on a sticky note and place it wherever you need to claim Jesus's peace and be reminded to breathe normally.*

WEDNESDAY, JANUARY 10

Simon answered, "Master, we've worked hard all night and haven't caught anything. But because you say so, I will let down the nets." Luke 5:5 (NIV)

"BECAUSE I SAID SO." If I had a dollar for every time I've uttered that nonnegotiable statement as a parent, my children's college savings would have been fully funded. A debate always preceded my frustrated declaration, my daughters arguing their side and me arguing mine, until we reached an impasse and I made that final, authoritative announcement.

"Because I said so" could mean two things: No, you can't do what you want. Or, yes, you have to do what I want you to do.

When my quiet time took me to Luke 5 this morning, Simon's response to Jesus reminded me of the well-worn phrase from my parenting days. Exhausted after a failed night of fishing, Simon did not want to cast his nets one more time as Jesus instructed. But instead of arguing, he replied, "Because You say so."

Similar to my voice, I hear Simon's weariness. But our statements, which also sound similar, are vastly different. "Because I said so" is a response to disobedience. "Because You say so" is a response of obedience. *I don't want to do what You're asking of me, Lord, but I will do it anyway. Because You say so.*

When my heart feels resistant, Simon's words, now written on the whiteboard in my office, will be my reminder to tell Jesus, "Because You say so." —KAREN SARGENT

FAITH STEP: *Have you been arguing with Jesus about something He wants you to do or not to do? Write "Because You say so" on a note card and place it where you will see it often. When Jesus asks, do it.*

THURSDAY, JANUARY 11

Dear friends, this is now my second letter to you. I have written both of them as reminders to stimulate you to wholesome thinking. 2 Peter 3:1 (NIV)

YOU'D THINK WE'D WON THE lottery at my house when my friend's letter arrives in the mail. My excitement in receiving the fat envelope of handwritten pages rivals that of a child receiving a Christmas stocking stuffed with surprises. Patty and I used to visit in person when we lived in the same state, but since I moved two states away, our visits have been replaced by infrequent "snail mail" correspondence. Good old-fashioned handwritten letters—epistles, as they're called in the Bible.

Reading my friend's candid, heartfelt letter from afar feels like a chatty heart-to-heart visit. I love reading her handwritten words, bringing me up to date on the events of her life since our last correspondence. The experience is further enriched by the faith we share, being able to speak freely about Jesus and what He's doing in our lives.

My other favorite letter writer is the Apostle Paul, who composed four famous epistles called the Prison Letters while under house arrest for preaching the gospel. I can just imagine the joy and excitement of the early Christians upon receiving a personal letter from their beloved spiritual mentor, Paul.

I may not get a lengthy letter in the mail every day, but I can turn to the Bible—God's love letter for a heart-to-heart visit with Jesus, who stimulates my wholesome thinking, reminding me about the wonderful things He's done and the promises of what He's going to do. —CASSANDRA TIERSMA

FAITH STEP: *Are you overdue in corresponding with a long-distance friend? Write a letter today about what Jesus has been doing in your life.*

FRIDAY, JANUARY 12

*Call to me and I will answer you and tell you great and unsearchable
things you do not know. Jeremiah 33:3 (NIV)*

I LOVE TO TRAVEL. I even love the research involved in finding places
to explore and sites to see. My family is dreaming of a European
vacation, and we are currently narrowing down the countries we'd
like to visit. England, Ireland, France, Germany, Italy, Greece...how
do we choose? They all sound fascinating.

This enjoyment of new-to-me locations has always been part of
who I am, and it has evolved as I've grown. Before I could drive, I
liked bike riding because I could expand my horizons across town.
When I got a driver's license, I was excited to explore the bigger
world of other towns. And the freedom of my first road trip with
friends felt like an IV of energy coursing through my soul as we
crossed state lines.

Jesus created me with a unique spirit of adventure, a longing
beyond the routine. That desire doesn't mean I only want to go
to faraway places, though. Adventure can take the form of a new
hobby, job, relationship, or growth step. But most of all, my unique
spirit for adventure provides a pathway to experience the vast
character of Jesus. I've traveled through many decades with Him,
and He always has more to show me about Himself—great and
unsearchable things I haven't yet known or discovered about Him.

Do you have dreams to get away and desires for new adventures?
Maybe it's time for an adventure with Jesus—abroad or right in
your own home. —ERIN KEELEY MARSHALL

FAITH STEP: *Journal about a trip you want to take or a desire you have. Ask
Jesus to show you one new thing about His character.*

SATURDAY, JANUARY 13

The faithful love of the LORD never ends! His mercies never cease.
Great is his faithfulness; his mercies begin afresh each morning.
Lamentations 3:22–23 (NLT)

I GOT A NEW CAR. Reluctantly. I loved my old car. I don't particularly like new things, but my husband, Jeff, thought I needed a car with the latest safety features since I haul around the grandkids. I couldn't argue with that.

This new car doesn't even have an ignition switch. It starts by pushing a button. I have no idea what most of the dials indicate. And it beeps at me at random times, but I can't figure out what I'm doing wrong. Plus, there's a button above the console that Jeff warned me not to touch.

The only new thing I feel comfortable with, even adore, is Jesus's mercy. Recently, I was grateful for His mercies after I got up and the house was freezing. The repairman had supposedly fixed the heater the week before but apparently not. The day swiftly headed downhill from there, taking me with it. I griped at Jeff for not picking up his clothes. I snapped at my daughter for being late. I fumed at a driver who cut in front of me. I slammed the door on the dryer and banged the dishes around in the sink. I was so grouchy I couldn't stand myself. Later that night, I climbed into bed, relieved the day was finally over.

I asked Jesus to forgive me for being awful, and I knew He would. Thank goodness His mercies are new each day! Tomorrow, I promised Him, I'd do better. —PAT BUTLER DYSON

FAITH STEP: *Put a sticky note on your bedside table or bathroom mirror to remind yourself to thank Jesus for the gift of a new day.*

SUNDAY, JANUARY 14

In him was life, and that life was the light of all mankind. The light shines in the darkness, and the darkness has not overcome it. John 1:4–5 (NIV)

TOMORROW IS BLUE MONDAY. THOUGH not proven through science, the third Monday in January is often tagged as the saddest day of the year. New Year's resolutions have proven challenging, Christmastime bills have started to arrive, and the weather is dark and dreary. For those of us suffering from seasonal affective disorder (SAD), this non-holiday comes as no surprise. We get it. Like a gas tank running on empty, we're low on hope. And yet the words in Emily Dickinson's poem "Hope Is the Thing with Feathers" ring true: "Hope is the thing with feathers, That perches in the soul, And sings the tune without the words, And never stops at all."

As a Christian, my hope never ends, even when things seem impossible. I am not alone, ever, because Jesus is with me (Matthew 28:20), and I don't need to be anxious (Isaiah 41:10). Jesus guides me and gives me rest (Exodus 33:14). He comforts me as I encourage others (2 Corinthians 1:3–4).

Candles, special SAD "happy" lights, adjusting my diet, and getting outdoors every day—even in foul weather—help combat my moodiness. So does daydreaming about my garden or planning future trips and new adventures. And talking with friends is a huge help.

But my greatest comfort comes from my friend Jesus (John 15:15). He sits in silence with me through my sorrow. His presence lights my soul and drives out the darkness, no matter what the weather. —HEIDI GAUL

FAITH STEP: *Sit under a bright light and let your thoughts focus on Jesus. Be comforted as His light overcomes the darkness.*

MARTIN LUTHER KING JR. DAY, MONDAY, JANUARY 15

You intended to harm me, but God intended it for good to accomplish what is now being done, the saving of many lives. Genesis 50:20 (NIV)

ONE OF DR. MARTIN LUTHER King Jr.'s first experiences of segregation happened when he was about six years old. He was told by the parent of a white friend that they couldn't play together anymore. It's no surprise, then, that in his famous "I Have a Dream" speech, he says he dreams of a nation where black and white children can hold hands. Where someone else might have used a traumatic experience and blow to the heart to fuel the fire of hatred and division, Dr. King used his to unite people.

In the book of Genesis, Joseph's brothers are so jealous of their father's extravagant love for him that they sell Joseph into slavery. When Joseph becomes the second most powerful man in Egypt, and his brothers come begging for help in the famine, Joseph graciously provides for them. He uses his traumatic experience and blow to the heart for good, saving his brothers' lives and those of the people of Egypt.

Like all of us, I've had traumatic experiences and blows to my heart. But I mustn't ever forget these two powerful examples. They're wonderful reminders that Jesus can still use me to make the world a better place—not despite my hardships, but because of them and the goodness He can draw forth from them. —CLAIRE MCGARRY

FAITH STEP: *Identify a hardship from your life and recognize the good that has come from it. How can you use that goodness to bless others?*

TUESDAY, JANUARY 16

I am the good shepherd; I know my sheep and my sheep know me.
John 10:14 (NIV)

I WASHED YARN FROM LONG ago today—wool from one of our own flock that I'd spun in the grease, full of lanolin. Most of the lanolin drained away, but some remained, leaving a sweet scent and softness behind.

This is #208's yarn, according to the index card in the bag. I'd forgotten to record the sheep's name alongside her number. That disappoints me.

We enjoyed naming our lambs. Many recognized their names and came when called. We had naming themes, like flowers, games, or colors, for the lambs born each year. I knew my sheep by name and remembered their individual stories that way—certainly not by number alone. Our registry book listing names beside numbers was lost during our move, so I can't look up #208's name.

Her wool is unusually lovely, a soft, deep brown with no sheen at all. Like a black hole, the yarn absorbs every bit of the light that touches it, reflecting nothing back. Her scent is on my fingers today, these many years later.

Even though I'm curious about her name, I don't need to know who grew this wool. Being anonymous doesn't lessen the worth of the wool that will edge the shawl I'm knitting.

But it's different with the Good Shepherd. No one is anonymous. Jesus never forgets any of us, including me. He calls me by name. He forgives me by name. And He will welcome me to eternity by name. Because He is my Shepherd, I listen to Him and give off His scent. —SUZANNE DAVENPORT TIETJEN

FAITH STEP: *Sing "I Am Jesus' Little Lamb" to end your time with Jesus. If you don't know or remember this childhood song, listen to it online.*

WEDNESDAY, JANUARY 17

Now listen, you who say, "Today or tomorrow we will go to this or that city, spend a year there, carry on business and make money." Why, you do not even know what will happen tomorrow. What is your life? You are a mist that appears for a little while and then vanishes. James 4:13–14 (NIV)

I AM NOT A SPONTANEOUS person. I love to plan, and seeing my calendar full makes me happy. But as a mom of ten children, my days rarely go as planned. I've made arrangements with friends only to have my children become ill. I've designed a relaxing evening only to hear about a significant school project due the next day. Flat tires, drop-in visitors, and serious late-night talks often surprise me. Each day seems to bring something different.

Unlike me, your life may not be full of family interruptions, yet my guess is your days rarely go as planned either. The only thing we can know for sure about tomorrow is that Jesus will be there with us. We may not know where we'll be tomorrow or next year. We may have unexpected losses or extraordinary surprises, but we can have hope knowing Jesus will be there. As fragile as life can sometimes be, Jesus cares greatly for each of us. While we may not control our calendar, we can continue to turn our hearts to the One who will be with us, no matter what tomorrow holds.

After all, nothing surprises Him. —TRICIA GOYER

FAITH STEP: *Take out your calendar and write these words in the spaces of upcoming days: "Jesus is not surprised." Then thank Jesus for the hope you can have every day as you trust in Him.*

THURSDAY, JANUARY 18

I press on toward the goal to win the prize for which God has called me heavenward in Christ Jesus. Philippians 3:14 (NIV)

I ENJOY WATCHING ALL TYPES of game shows. *Who Wants to Be a Millionaire?*, *The Price Is Right*, *Deal or No Deal*, *Wipeout*, *Family Feud*. But my all-time favorite game show is *Wheel of Fortune*, a competition in which three players spin a huge roulette-type wheel and guess one letter at a time to solve hidden words or phrases on a gigantic light-up board. In one magical thirty-minute segment of television, I set my sights on a contestant through whom I can vicariously win life-changing amounts of cash, beyond-my-wildest-dreams vacations, and sometimes even a car!

With each spin of the wheel, I play "with" my chosen contestant and rack up cash and prizes. As letters to the puzzle are revealed, I guess at the words and phrases by yelling my answers at the television set—hoping and praying that "we" don't spin and land on the bankrupt slot and lose the game.

Thanks to Jesus, my outcome is not a guessing game. I don't have to live vicariously through someone else to win in this life. Jesus lives inside of me, so it's not luck, my good guessing, or a strong spin of the wheel that makes me a winner. Jesus has already solved the toughest puzzle on earth—how to win over death—by putting Himself in my place to give me the ultimate prize package—eternal life with Him. And that's something I can never lose. —ERICKA LOYNES

FAITH STEP: *What wheels do you keep spinning, trying to land on that one thing you really want in life? Stop trying to solve the puzzle alone. Ask Jesus, the longest-winning Champion, to help you.*

FRIDAY, JANUARY 19

I have told you these things, so that in me you may have peace. In this world you will have trouble. But take heart! I have overcome the world.
John 16:33 *(NIV)*

I OFTEN TRAVEL WITH MY husband, a minister and district superintendent in our denomination, as he visits churches under his jurisdiction across the West Texas Panhandle and the High Plains Desert region. The arid landscape has a beauty all its own, with fields of cotton white unto harvest and oil derricks instead of trees. Frequently, abandoned homesteads dot the horizon, the skeletal remains of houses that once held families. Places I imagined were filled with love, laughter, and hope. But when hard times hit, the people who lived in these dwellings were forced to move on.

Recently, when we passed one of these crumbling houses, I asked David to stop so I could snap a picture of the melancholy scene. "It's just so sad," I said, getting out of the car. "All the hopes and dreams these people had when they built this home died when they left."

"Maybe so," he replied. "But I'd like to think they were carrying their hopes with them as they sought a better future."

I, too, have had seasons when the landscape of my life looked abandoned and crumbled. Jesus never promised His followers an easy life—just the opposite. Situations may not have turned out the way I expected, but I confidently put my hope and trust in Jesus, knowing a better future is in store for me. —SUSAN DOWNS

FAITH STEP: *Make a list of those hard times in your life when you might be tempted to give up hope, then seek out a scripture verse for each one that encourages you to keep your hope alive.*

SATURDAY, JANUARY 20

The LORD God is my strength; He will make my feet like deer's feet, and He will make me walk on my high hills. Habakkuk 3:19 (NKJV)

I HAVE QUITE THE COLLECTION of flat shoes. They're comfortable and cute, and I can find a style that is appropriate for almost any occasion. I marvel at how women can walk in sky-high pumps. To me, that goes against the law of gravity. But I received a new perspective on walking with God one morning as I opened my Bible and my eyes landed on a familiar verse.

The prophet Habakkuk says the Lord will "make my feet like deer's feet, and He will make me walk on my high hills." As I meditated on those words, an image immediately came to mind of me trying to walk in stilettos. The thought made me chuckle. I've seen footage of fashion models—who should be pros at prancing around in high heels—falling flat on their faces as they sashayed down the runway.

Like those unfortunate models, I've fallen down many times in my life. Disappointment when a "sure thing" didn't come through. Hurt after a relationship ended. Disbelief when the unexpected happened. But after each fall, I eventually was able to get back up and continue walking. I know I cannot glide down the runway of life on my own, but with Jesus's help and strength, I will be able to walk upright as I take on the hills and valleys—in high heels or flats. —BARBRANDA LUMPKINS WALLS

FAITH STEP: *What high hills are you facing? Put on your walking shoes and step outside for a stroll. Pray for Jesus to guide and strengthen you wherever you go today.*

SUNDAY, JANUARY 21

His divine power has given us everything we need for a godly life through our knowledge of him who called us by his own glory and goodness.
2 Peter 1:3 (NIV)

"DO YOU LOVE ME?" MY friend Pam playfully asked her husband one night. After Henry answered yes, she wanted to know how much. Henry paused for a moment and responded with one word: "Enough." At first Pam was taken aback, but after thinking about it, she decided she liked that answer just fine.

When Pam shared that conversation, I remembered how I felt taken aback when our pastor introduced a new sermon series called "The Adequate Life." *Adequate?* I thought. *Who wants to settle for that?* But as we dug into the book of Colossians, I understood the word choice. In a world of superlatives, we've lost our appreciation for the concept of *enough*. Our culture's distorted standards and marketing efforts can breed discontent with my possessions, my relationships, and myself. I'm constantly urged to chase after something better, newer, improved—something more.

But Jesus gives me everything I need for a meaningful, godly life. The Bible promises that He will supply all our needs (Philippians 4:19). Even more, His grace is sufficient during times of pain and trouble (2 Corinthians 12:9). The entire book of Ephesians focuses on all the spiritual riches we have in Christ. In light of such generous provision and promises, our relationship with Jesus makes it easy to live out the truth of an old proverb I cross-stitched years ago: "Enough is as good as a feast." —DIANNE NEAL MATTHEWS

FAITH STEP: *Make a list of things you feel discontentment with. One by one, pray over each item. After you've prayed, cross it out and write "Jesus is enough."*

MONDAY, JANUARY 22

See what great love the Father has lavished on us, that we should be called children of God! And that is what we are! The reason the world does not know us is that it did not know him. 1 John 3:1 (NIV)

THIS PAST WEEKEND, OUR COLLEGE friends Lance and Tina came to stay with us. They were taking a much-needed sabbatical as lead pastors of their church. Our weekend together was full of laughter, mostly because Tina has the best laugh ever. Tina and I decided to pamper ourselves with a morning of sipping delicious coffee and getting a pedicure. I told Tina that I wanted to treat her.

Tina's manicurist finished her toes first and sent her to the front of the shop. When I joined her a few minutes later, I saw Tina putting her wallet away. I asked, "Did you just pay for your pedicure? I wanted to treat you." She started laughing and said, "Oh, well." Then the receptionist told me that she had paid for my pedicure too. My shock gave Tina a great deal of joy. She had out-treated and out-loved me. I had to join her in laughing. Her generosity was overwhelming. All I could do was say, "Thank you."

Jesus finds great joy in out-treating and out-loving me on a regular basis. He loves overwhelming me with His goodness and generosity. I don't deserve His mercy or His grace. But there He is, meeting me at every turn, lavishing His love on me. All I can do is say, "Thank You." —SUSANNA FOTH AUGHTMON

FAITH STEP: *Spend some time journaling about how Jesus has "out-treated" you this past week. Say a prayer of thanks for all the ways He has overwhelmed you with His love and grace.*

TUESDAY, JANUARY 23

My help comes from the LORD, the Maker of heaven and earth.
Psalm 121:2 (NIV)

I FELT HELPLESS AS I read proposed legislation that would adversely affect students with whom I work. As a school counselor, I wondered how to advocate for vulnerable children and situations that lawmakers might not fully understand. I considered ranting on social media. Comments, likes, and shares are empowering when you lack control.

Deep in my heart, though, I knew the Internet was not the place to respond. A friend encouraged me to contact key lawmakers. I was skeptical that my input would make a difference. I spent hours reading the bill, taking notes, emailing concerns, and calling legislative offices. I was exhausted after staying up late doing this for two consecutive nights while working all day at school.

There was no response from those I contacted, and I felt defeated. I wrestled with Jesus about what to do next. *Is it time to write that post? Take matters into my own hands?*

As I started crafting a social media post, Jesus impressed upon me to pray about the situation. Restraint, rather than rant, felt contradictory to the immediate gratification of online validation, but I refrained from commenting about the bill on social media.

Eventually, the legislation was defeated. I don't know if the energy I used petitioning lawmakers helped, but I do know that when I feel helpless, prayer, obedience, and faith in Jesus are the best actions to take. I took that message to my online account—finally something to post about. —BRENDA L. YODER

FAITH STEP: *What is an area in which you feel helpless? Ask Jesus what you should do as you step forward in prayer and obedience, trusting the results to Him.*

WEDNESDAY, JANUARY 24

Come near to God and he will come near to you. James 4:8 *(NIV)*

OUR YOUNGEST CAT, PRINCESS DI, is a mixture of loving and mean. And when she's mean, she's a bully. Dr. Phibes, the old man of my four kitties, loves to snooze on the back of my brown recliner. If Princess Di sees him, she'll leap onto the seat, stand up, and swat him in the face. When Dr. Phibes tries to escape her, she chases him around the house.

There's only one place Dr. Phibes can sit that's safe from this naughty cat. On my lap. If Dr. Phibes is curled up on my lap as I read at night or pray in the morning, Princess Di will walk over, see that I am holding the old cat, and quietly saunter away.

This is much like my relationship with Jesus. The closer I stay to Jesus, the more peaceful my life remains. I come near Him by reading His love letter (the Bible) and by talking to Him throughout my often-hectic days. I draw near to Him when I sing songs of praise and worship. I trust Him to hold me and keep me safe when danger approaches.

Just as Dr. Phibes is endangered by Princess Di, my faith in Jesus is endangered by the sharp claws of a mean word, the hissing of doubt, and the lurking worries that chase me. I can run, even try to hide from all that threatens to upset my serenity. But the best way to escape the enemy's tactics is to stay near to Jesus. He is my safe place. —JEANETTE LEVELLIE

FAITH STEP: *Envision yourself snuggled in Jesus's lap, safe, secure, and at peace.*

THURSDAY, JANUARY 25

---

*By this everyone will know that you are my disciples,
if you love one another. John 13:35 (NIV)*

I LIKE TO WEAR WHAT I call my unity sweater. It's a cozy, V-neck sweater that is half light gray and half chocolate brown. The colors are split straight down the middle in the front and the back. I bought it because of the heightened division in today's world: racial rifts, differing political views, and even the little disagreements about parenting practices or puppy training.

I'm conflict-averse and desire peace, so this has been a difficult season for me. It helps to wrap myself in a cozy sweater that reflects division yet is still attractive—unified despite its divided design. I wear it as a reminder that as believers we can carry differing opinions but still be unified in our faith.

Jesus knew unity would be a struggle. He prayed that those who followed Him would live in harmony: "… that they may become perfectly one, so that the world may know that you sent me and loved them even as you loved me" (John 17:23, ESV).

Unity and love go hand in hand. Love is the glue that holds us together and can create a unity that will impact the world. We will face disagreements, but despite our differences, we can remain unified in our faith if we keep our focus on living as Jesus did and loving each other as He loved us. Like my sweater, differences can come together to be beautifully unified. —JEANNIE BLACKMER

FAITH STEP: *Think of a way you can promote love and unity today. Deliver flowers, make cookies, call and pray with someone, or write an encouraging note to show the love that reflects Jesus's love for you.*

FRIDAY, JANUARY 26

Do not judge, or you too will be judged. For in the same way you judge others, you will be judged, and with the measure you use, it will be measured to you. Matthew 7:1–2 (NIV)

IT HAD BEEN A TOUGH week: work pressures, health challenges, and a whole lot of discouragement. By the time Friday rolled around, the only comfort measure I craved was a juicy cheeseburger from a local restaurant.

My husband and I had been trying to eat healthy, but a kale salad just wouldn't do the trick. I grappled with whether to take him up on his offer to make a cheeseburger and French fry run.

My daughter looked at me with compassion and said, "No judgment, Mom." A weight lifted from my shoulders. Her approval reminded me that I didn't need to beat myself up for an occasional slip.

The relief of not being judged made me ponder how often I'd judged someone else in the past week. The friend pursuing alternative health ideas that I didn't trust. The parents struggling with an unruly child. Or the time I rearranged the dishes in the dishwasher after my husband loaded it. Critiquing the choices of others comes far too easily.

When Jesus invites me to step away from judgment, He isn't saying that my moral choices don't matter or that I can't have an opinion. But He is calling me to examine being unduly critical of people who do things in a different way. He invites me to recognize the freedom that comes from being accepted and accepting others—especially when an occasional Friday night cheeseburger is involved.
—SHARON HINCK

FAITH STEP: *Think about a time you found fault in someone else's choices. Ask Jesus to give you a heart of love and understanding.*

SATURDAY, JANUARY 27

I have fought the good fight, I have finished the race, I have kept the faith.
2 Timothy 4:7 (NIV)

EVERY DECADE, I UPDATE MY final wishes. The original document, prepared in my forties, included an outline of funeral details—preferred speaker, message theme, songs, and scriptures. A later version loosened the instructions a bit and focused more on keeping the service brief and simple. Recently, I rewrote the guidelines once again.

"There is no need for an expensive burial. Let someone who loves me talk about Jesus, and then scatter my ashes where the wildflowers grow on the farm. Mark the spot with a small sign that reads: 'I have fought the good fight, I have finished the race, I have kept the faith.'"

These words from 2 Timothy say it all: no sadness; no regrets; I did my best; I'm moving on to heaven.

The older I get, the less my official end on the earth matters to me. I don't desire fanfare or recognition. A marble headstone with two attached flower vases isn't necessary. Of greater importance is the hope of eternal life and the promise of a forever future. For now, I must run the race. I want to teach my grandkids about Jesus, help people who are hurting, and share the Gospel with those who haven't heard. But when I reach the finish line, I plan to quietly close my eyes in this world and triumphantly open them anew in my everlasting home. —BECKY ALEXANDER

FAITH STEP: *You have a race to run too! List three things you'd like to accomplish for the Kingdom before you reach the finish line, then choose one to work on this week.*

SUNDAY, JANUARY 28

He heals the brokenhearted and binds up their wounds. Psalm 147:3 (NIV)

WHEN MY CHURCH WAS CLOSED during COVID-19, I'd park my car in the back parking lot and sit inside, having breakfast with Jesus. It brought me so much peace to commune with Him away from the chaos of my home. There was one thing, however, that interrupted my tranquility and irked me to no end.

As my gaze wandered over the church building, I surveyed the foundation wall. Years ago, the concrete was painted a deep beige to match the clapboards on the rest of the church. Apparently, someone ran out of paint about 6 feet before they completed the task, and they never circled back to finish. Worse yet, within that unpainted expanse, the wall had been broken to install a pipe. The patch job was obvious and unsightly. If the contractor had just painted over it, that area would have blended right in.

That wall is me. Jesus has painted over my rough spots with His grace so I can relate to other believers in a concrete and foundational way. But He's not finished yet. I have struggles and challenges that still break me. Nonetheless, Jesus is always there to patch me back together. The resulting scars are mine to keep, though. I need to recognize that those scars turn from unsightly to beautiful when I witness to the world that in my weakness Jesus is my strength, whether I'm perfectly completed or not. —CLAIRE McGARRY

FAITH STEP: *Meditate on your scars, blemishes, or other areas in need of repair. Bring those things to Jesus, knowing He can finish them perfectly.*

MONDAY, JANUARY 29

Jesus replied: "Love the Lord your God with all your heart and with all your soul and with all your mind." This is the first and greatest commandment.
Matthew 22:37–38 *(NIV)*

MY FRIEND SHARON CARED FOR her husband, Larry, in his final stages of Alzheimer's disease. For more than forty years, Larry taught third graders about Jesus at church. Just before he was moved into hospice care, Sharon found Larry giving what appeared to be his final Bible lesson. His shirt was inside out. His message was jumbled and hard to follow. And his "audience" was an upright vacuum cleaner parked in the corner of their foyer. Nevertheless, the passion behind Larry's voice was evident. In his mixed-up mind broken with disease and confusion, he believed he was telling children about Jesus.

Sharon grabbed her phone to record the memory and captured the moment at the end of Larry's lesson when his voice became strong and his message clear. He faced the camera and said boldly, "One more thing. I can't let you leave without it. Jesus loves you. And you ought to keep reading His book. It's the best book there is that you can read. Thank you."

Larry died about a week later, but I'll never forget the passion with which he shared his love for Jesus in his final days. Even though his earthly body and mind were breaking down, he was still able to fulfill the greatest commandment. He loved his Lord with all his heart, soul, and mind.

I want to be fully devoted to Jesus like Larry was and use every last day to let others know that Jesus loves them. —EMILY E. RYAN

FAITH STEP: *As you go about your day, make it a point to tell someone, "Jesus loves you."*

TUESDAY, JANUARY 30

*In peace I will lie down and sleep, for you alone,
LORD, make me dwell in safety. Psalm 4:8 (NIV)*

EACH MORNING WHEN MY HUSBAND, Jeff, and I wake up, we say the same three words to each other—and they aren't "Good morning, darling!" Nope. We say, "Did you sleep?" Sleep is an elusive prize in the Dyson household.

Jeff has trouble sleeping because of aches and pains in his feet, knees, and legs from old football injuries and forty years of tramping across concrete floors at his family's hardware store. My aches and pains start a bit higher up—in my head.

The minute I turn out the light and close my eyes, I'm treated to an instant replay of all the ways I messed up during the day. Next, my mind transports me to all that can potentially go wrong the following day. And when I finish with that, I worry about my family, all sixteen of them, one by one. By then, it's time to get up.

"Have you ever thought about turning your worries over to Jesus?" my friend Sue suggested.

Of course I'd thought about it. Easier said than done.

Nonetheless, I decided it was worth a try. I knelt by my bed and asked Jesus if I could cast my cares on Him. I felt His assent. He led me to read Psalm 4:8. I've memorized that verse, and when I turn out the light, I repeat those soothing words as I drift off to sleep and rest peacefully with Jesus. —PAT BUTLER DYSON

FAITH STEP: *If worry keeps you up at night, memorize Psalm 4:8. Then imagine resting peacefully beside Jesus.*

WEDNESDAY, JANUARY 31

He tends his flock like a shepherd: He gathers the lambs in his arms and carries them close to his heart; he gently leads those that have young.
Isaiah 40:11 (NIV)

YESTERDAY, I LEARNED SOMETHING NEW from a Wyoming shepherd about the instincts of very young lambs. In the high country, large flocks of sheep graze unenclosed by fences. Shepherds and dogs keep them safe day and night. The sheep rest near the herders' wagons, sometimes within a lantern-lit circle. If the very youngest lambs are sleeping soundly, then awakened suddenly, they jump up, bleating loudly, then follow anything in motion. This instinct is what helps lambs stay with their mother and the herd. But if the motion is from an ATV or the predator that woke them, following could cost them their lives.

Later, as they get older, lambs will learn to follow their mother's voice as well as their shepherd's.

I like to think this may be why the shepherd in Isaiah 40:11 was carrying the littlest lambs in his arms, close to his heart. This description points to Jesus, the Good Shepherd, who knows His own and whose own know Him (John 10:14).

Too often, like these lambs, I give in to knee-jerk reactions. I might praise someone without knowing very much about them. Or share something on social media that I haven't fully read or considered. I need to react less like a startled lamb, foolishly following whatever moves, and instead listen to my Shepherd's voice and follow Him. In Jesus's arms is the safest place for me.
—SUZANNE DAVENPORT TIETJEN

FAITH STEP: *Watch some sheep in person or on YouTube. Contemplate why we're compared to them. Then talk to the Shepherd and thank Him for His love and protection.*

THURSDAY, FEBRUARY 1

---

*A new commandment I give to you, that you love one another: just as
I have loved you, you also are to love one another. John 13:34 (ESV)*

I OPENED MY EMAIL SPAM folder to clear it out, and this message
header greeted me: "Let eHarmony show you what real love looks
like today!" Later I opened my music library to choose some house-
cleaning accompaniment and noticed how many songs had "love"
in the title. I wondered how many of the untold numbers of books,
poems, and songs that have ever been written about love are focused
on feelings and emotions rather than on the real thing.

Jesus didn't just teach about love; His entire life defined it—
encouraging, healing, building up, raising the dead, and most
importantly, giving up His life on our behalf. The New Testament
is filled with His followers' encouragement and instructions to help
us love as Jesus did. They urge us to put others' interests ahead of
our own (Philippians 2:4), love each other deeply since love covers
many sins (1 Peter 4:8), and love with our actions, not just words
(1 John 3:18). The thirteenth chapter of 1 Corinthians beautifully
describes what a lifestyle of Christlike love looks like.

Jesus didn't command us to feel love but to live it out. Isn't it inter-
esting that just a single letter differentiates the words "live" and "love"?
Come to think of it, the more I take "I" out of the way I live, the more
I will be able to love others as Jesus did. —DIANNE NEAL MATTHEWS

FAITH STEP: *Are you satisfied with how well you're following Jesus's example to
love? Read through 1 Corinthians 13 and ask Him to show you any areas where
you can improve.*

FRIDAY, FEBRUARY 2

*But the L*ORD* said to Samuel, "Do not consider his appearance or his height,
for I have rejected him. The L*ORD* does not look at the things people look at.
People look at the outward appearance, but the L*ORD* looks at the heart."*
1 Samuel 16:7 *(NIV)*

I TRY TO MAINTAIN A healthy body image, but because I'm just under
5 feet tall, it's hard not to notice extra pounds when they collect on
my waistline and squeeze out the top of my jeans. The older I get,
the more my clothes seem to shrink.

I shared my weighty concerns with Jesus while driving down the
freeway recently. I confessed it sometimes bothers me even though
I think it shouldn't. I know what the Bible says. I'm created in His
image (Genesis 1:27). I am His masterpiece (Ephesians 2:10). I am
fearfully and wonderfully made (Psalm 139:14). Yet I struggled to
accept the parts of me that don't measure up to the world's standards
of beauty. "What do I do, Lord?" I whispered as I exited the freeway.
"Do I work harder to lose weight or just accept myself as I am?"

That's when I noticed a breakfast diner ahead with a bold, flashing
sign that proudly proclaimed its special of the day: "Mega muffin
tops!"

I burst out laughing at Jesus's sense of humor. I'd never before had
a prayer answered in such a comical way. Jesus both acknowledged
and lightened my concerns with the blatant reminder that it doesn't
matter how many pounds or inches I have around my middle. He's
looking at my heart, not my waistline. —EMILY E. RYAN

FAITH STEP: *Look in the mirror and ask Jesus to help you focus less on your
outward appearance and more on your heart.*

SATURDAY, FEBRUARY 3

Therefore encourage one another and build each other up, just as in fact you are doing. 1 Thessalonians 5:11 (NIV)

LAST FALL WHILE MY DAD was out of town, we sisters decided to have one of our girls' weekends. My mom and I, my sisters, Erica and Jenny, and my sister-in-law, Traci, all got together at my parents' house. We kept up our usual traditions of shopping, eating chocolate, and drinking hot beverages—tea for Mom and Erica and coffee for me, Traci, and Jenny. There was some lazing around, nap-taking, and reading.

But the thing we did most was talk. We talked about our kids. We chatted about work. We discussed our physical ailments *at length*—this is how we know we are getting older! And we encouraged each other.

Life can be confusing and difficult. Sometimes it's cuckoo crazy. So, we reminded each other of the truth—hard seasons come and go, our kids are in Jesus's capable hands, and we have each other's backs no matter what.

Like my family, Jesus encourages me too. He tells me to take heart or have courage so that I'm not afraid or overwhelmed (John 16:33). He is omniscient and knows the ins and outs of my days (Job 28:24). He never leaves me when life is confusing, difficult, and cuckoo crazy (Matthew 28:20). He puts people in my life to remind me who He is and encourage me, not only on a girls' weekend but every day. Jesus has my back—no matter what.
—SUSANNA FOTH AUGHTMON

FAITH STEP: *Text a good friend today and offer her encouragement. Remind her of your friendship and that she is in Jesus's capable hands. Let her know Jesus has her back too.*

SUNDAY, FEBRUARY 4

*And I will ask the Father, and he will give you another advocate to help
you and be with you forever—the Spirit of truth. The world cannot
accept him, because it neither sees him nor knows him. But you know
him, for he lives with you and will be in you. I will not leave you
as orphans; I will come to you. John 14:16–18 (NIV)*

OUR YOUNGEST DAUGHTER HAD INVITED my husband and me to her
home for Sunday lunch. I always try to be fully present wherever
I go, but my mind was elsewhere this time.

A close family member had been hospitalized with COVID-19
two days prior, and his condition had deteriorated rapidly. Doctors
had just placed him on a ventilator in the ICU. The news made me
want to rush to the hospital, but it was a twelve-hour drive away
and besides, no one was allowed in his room. I felt helpless.

I broke the news to my daughter and her husband, unaware that
my two-year-old granddaughter listened from nearby. Suddenly, I
felt her little hand slip into mine. "It's OK, Grandma," she whispered. "Don't worry. I'm here."

Her reassurance seemed heaven-sent. It reminded me of Jesus's
words to the disciples before He returned to heaven. Jesus knew their
future held hardships, so He promised to be with them through the
indwelling presence of the Holy Spirit. No matter what challenges
they might face, they needn't worry because He was with them.

Jesus's words still hold true. "It's OK," He says when I feel afraid.
"Don't worry. I'm here." —GRACE FOX

FAITH STEP: *Draw two stick figures holding hands and put it on your refrigerator. The next time you're worried, imagine Jesus slipping His hand into yours.*

MONDAY, FEBRUARY 5

For we were saved in this hope, but hope that is seen is not hope; for why does one still hope for what he sees? But if we hope for what we do not see, we eagerly wait for it with perseverance. Romans 8:24–25 *(NKJV)*

BIRDS USED TO SWARM THE five feeders outside my office windows year-round. I loved the happy distraction from deep and draining thoughts. Sometimes I took a break, grabbed my bird book, and attempted to identify new fluttering beauties.

Then, all the birds vanished. A week passed...a month...a second month...no birds. I missed my flying friends. I tried everything to entice them back—tossing seed on the ground, washing the feeders in vinegar and water, dumping the old seed and replacing it with fresh. Nothing worked. Still, I hoped and even prayed for their return.

Hope involves a strong desire for something, attached to an expectation of obtaining it. As a believer, I hope for the return of Jesus. The Bible says: "Behold, He is coming with clouds, and every eye will see Him, even they who pierced Him" (Revelation 1:7, NKJV).

As a last effort, I purchased a different brand of birdseed and filled the feeders at work. A few chickadees and nuthatches appeared in the yard and glided over for a snack. A tufted titmouse, a cardinal, and a family of sparrows followed. Though I can't see Jesus yet, I eagerly await the day my eyes will behold Him—the Maker of the birds and the Creator of the universe. —BECKY ALEXANDER

FAITH STEP: *If you're not already a bird-watcher, become one for a week. Try to spot and identify various kinds of birds. Allow them to remind you of the hope you have for Jesus's return.*

TUESDAY, FEBRUARY 6

For our light and momentary troubles are achieving for us an eternal glory that far outweighs them all. So we fix our eyes not on what is seen, but on what is unseen, since what is seen is temporary, but what is unseen is eternal.
2 Corinthians 4:17–18 (NIV)

HAVE YOU HEARD THE EXPRESSION "fake it till you make it"? The idea is to act as if you feel a certain way until you actually do. For instance, acting confident at a new job or pretending to love an unlovable person in your life. By imitating the qualities you want, the slogan implies, eventually those traits will be achieved.

It's a handy tool, but I've found a better one: "*faith* it till you make it." Rather than relying on my feeble, non-Academy Award acting abilities by behaving as an imposter or brainwashing myself to do the opposite, I simply trust Jesus with whatever circumstances or difficulties come my way.

"Faith it till you make it" is a deeper and more powerful eternal approach to navigating the challenges of life. It's not some voodoo faith that conjures miraculous solutions, supernatural protection, or extraordinary favor in the face of disaster. It's fixating my attention on an eternity with Jesus, who is Master of all things and who loves me unconditionally. It is trusting that no matter what happens, even consequences of my own bad choices or those of someone else, in Jesus, I will transcend it.

I can't always fake it till I make it, but faith it till I make it? That's something I can do! —ISABELLA CAMPOLATTARO

FAITH STEP: *Reflect on how your current, temporary troubles may be achieving a greater glory. What do you need to do in order to "faith it till you make it"?*

WEDNESDAY, FEBRUARY 7

One person decides that one day is holier than another. Another person decides that all days are the same. Every person must make his own decision.
Romans 14:5 (GW)

HAPPY FETTUCCINE ALFREDO DAY! DON'T laugh, but I have a quirky way of setting days apart from one another. I incorporate national food holidays into my meal planning. I first adopted this practice while working as an activities assistant in a Christian assisted-living facility. We wanted to give the folks something to look forward to each day, so we celebrated everything we could.

We planned our monthly activities calendars around any possible excuse to bring pleasurable moments to the residents. To this day, I still celebrate as many holidays as possible, whether it's National Fettuccine Alfredo Day or National Strawberry-Rhubarb Pie Day. Small celebrations remind me that every day is special, that life is worth living.

The word *holiday* actually means "holy day." And the word *holy* means "sacred, dedicated to God." One of the ways I dedicate my day to God is by spending my mornings with Jesus—reading His holy Word, talking to Him in prayer, and seeking His guidance and direction. No matter how tough a time I might be going through, I can stay focused on Jesus. He is with me, reminding me that every day is a holy day. And that's something to celebrate!
—CASSANDRA TIERSMA

FAITH STEP: *What can you celebrate today? Ask Jesus to help you appreciate the holiness in each and every day and to show you how you can more fully dedicate your day to Him. If possible, eat fettuccine Alfredo for lunch or dinner as a reminder that every day is a holy day.*

THURSDAY, FEBRUARY 8

If you need wisdom, ask our generous God, and he will give it to you.
He will not rebuke you for asking. James 1:5 (NLT)

THE LIFE OF A TEENAGER preparing for high school graduation is all about taking exams and filling out applications—for college admissions, grants, scholarships, or jobs. One early morning, I drove AJ, my son, to take the SAT for the second time to see if he could improve his score. The air was thick in the car. Although I was outwardly calm, inside I was upset and fearful. He hadn't prepared for this second try any more than he had for the first. And it was not because he didn't have parental prodding!

As I pulled into the parking lot with a zillion other parents, I talked to Jesus silently: *Now Lord, You know he didn't study the way he should have. The half-hearted practice tests he did are just not enough.* Immediately, I heard in my spirit: *No, but I am enough. And I have enough wisdom to take him where he needs to go.* In an instant, Jesus broadened my perspective and brought calm to my frustrated heart.

Jesus sees the end from the beginning (Isaiah 46:10), so He wasn't anxious about the test. Not only would He give my son wisdom during the exam, but He also helped me understand that this was but a tiny part of AJ's journey toward his God-ordained destiny, no matter how he scored on his SAT. —PAMELA TOUSSAINT HOWARD

FAITH STEP: *When you experience a challenge or are not sure what to do, stop what you're doing and ask Jesus for guidance, then wait to hear His answer.*

FRIDAY, FEBRUARY 9

And hope does not put us to shame, because God's love has been poured out into our hearts through the Holy Spirit, who has been given to us. Romans 5:5 (NIV)

TWENTY-EIGHT YEARS AGO, I ATTENDED my first writers' conference with the hope of having a novel published. I only had a seed of an idea that I hadn't spent much time on, and I'd reworked the first twenty pages of my novel dozens of times but hadn't gotten much further than that. While I didn't have a great understanding of plot and characters, being an avid reader, I had a basic idea of the elements of a good story. I yearned to see a book, with my name, in print. But more than that, I felt this book was a dream Jesus had put in my heart.

Now, as a published author, it's easy to laugh at my feeble efforts. I can even joke about how big my dreams were compared to my skill. The emotion that most fills my heart, as I think back to that first writers' conference, is thankfulness. I'm grateful I dared to hope in a dream, despite my lack of experience.

Hope grows best when we allow Jesus's love to fill us. I dared to believe my dream was possible because I also believed that Jesus had good plans for my life. Hope didn't just fill in the gap where I lacked skill. Hope filled my heart and spirit with the truth that Jesus will fill me with the skills I need to live a life for Him. —TRICIA GOYER

FAITH STEP: *Has Jesus given you a dream beyond your skill? With hope, write down one first step you can take to follow His plan and turn that dream into a reality.*

SATURDAY, FEBRUARY 10

If I speak in the tongues of men or of angels, but do not have love, I am only a resounding gong or a clanging cymbal. 1 Corinthians 13:1 (NIV)

LAST SATURDAY, I WAS INTERVIEWED on a podcast. I subscribe to quite a few, so I was excited to participate. I remained at home and borrowed my husband's headset, but his microphone didn't have a "sock" on it. The audio technician said the sound quality wasn't great. Too much popping and sibilant interference. My husband quickly created a foam cap to pull over the mic and filter out the noise. Sound quality is important because the podcaster doesn't want listeners to be distracted from the message.

The Gospel records many conversations that Jesus had while on earth. He exhorted. He explained. He joked. He shared beautiful word pictures. He taught. He sometimes chided. But everything in Jesus's life reflected love. Because of that, His message comes through loud and clear.

I'm a lot like that unbuffered microphone. I love to talk. I process my thoughts by babbling about them. Sometimes my words slide into whining or frustration. Other times my ego demands that my opinions are heard, even when I should be listening instead. As I ponder the example of Jesus, I realize how important it is for my speech to be filtered through a foundation of love. Thoughts shared in love can be more readily heard without distortion and distraction. They can encourage, reassure, and unite. Love gives the sound quality that conveys the message I want people to hear. —SHARON HINCK

FAITH STEP: *Notice sounds today, especially interference that makes it hard to hear. Ask Jesus to fill your speech with love and eliminate attitudes that would distort your words.*

SUNDAY, FEBRUARY 11

*LORD, you have examined me and know all about me. You know when
I sit down and when I get up. You know my thoughts before I think them.*
Psalm 139:1–2 (NCV)

DURING A FEBRUARY VISIT WITH my mom, we stopped inside the
church doors as I admired the beautiful new light fixtures that had
recently replaced the old ones from my childhood. Then we carried our contributions for the Valentine's Day lunch to the kitchen.
I glanced at a bowl of conversation hearts, familiar pastel heart-
shaped candies stamped with short messages—the ones that taste
chalky to me. Back in the sanctuary, an old friend and I chatted
about Valentine candy. As I turned around, Pastor J.B. asked, "You
don't like them?" I assured him that I hated them. I wondered
why he looked surprised and maybe even hurt, until he glanced
up toward the ceiling. Then it dawned on me: I was talking about
candy; he was talking about the new chandeliers.

Human communication is not perfect; there's always a risk that
someone will misinterpret our words or misunderstand our actions.
The results may be comical, or they may be disastrous and can even
damage a relationship. I'm so thankful to know that Jesus always
understands me perfectly; as a matter of fact, He understands me
better than I do myself. Some days, I might prefer that He didn't
understand my thoughts or motives. That's when I remember that
despite His intimate knowledge of my good, bad, and ugly, His love
for me is unchanging and unconditional—sweeter than any candy.
—DIANNE NEAL MATTHEWS

FAITH STEP: *Think about a time when someone misunderstood your words,
behavior, or intentions. Read through Psalm 139 and thank Jesus for the assurance you find there.*

MONDAY, FEBRUARY 12

Because your love is better than life, my lips will glorify you.
Psalm 63:3 (NIV)

ONE OF MY FAVORITE GADGETS is the remote garage door opener. It comes in handy, especially when it's dark or rainy. With just the push of a button, the heavy door slides up. When I'm safely inside, I push the button again and the door slides down. Years ago, I had to muster all my strength to lift and lower the door myself. I don't ever want to go back there.

These days, my garage door opener works intermittently. The fact that it works part of the time keeps me from calling the repairman. I hold my breath when I press the button. Usually when I'm running late, it doesn't work. But on the days it works, I'm thrilled. Until I get to the end of the driveway and see the closed door slowly rising.

Why would a sensible person live with this uncertainty? I can't trust that unfaithful garage door opener to work for me every time.

I adore Jesus every minute of every day, but I wonder if my dedication to Him is intermittent like my garage door. Some days, I'm overscheduled and I skip my devotional time. Some nights, I fall into bed, neglecting to pray. Occasionally, I don't always love others the way He commanded.

Thank goodness Jesus's love is reliable and certain. It doesn't depend on anything I can do, have done, or will do (John 3:16). I trust He will always be there anytime I need Him.

Today, I'm pledging to be more dependable and consistent in my relationship with Jesus. Then I'll call the repairman. —PAT BUTLER DYSON

FAITH STEP: *Think of ways you can be more consistent with Jesus as you go through the week.*

TUESDAY, FEBRUARY 13

Above all, love each other deeply, because love covers over a multitude of sins. 1 Peter 4:8 (NIV)

TOMORROW IS MY FORTY-NINTH WEDDING anniversary. Kevin and I decided to get married on Valentine's Day in 1975 so we could be special valentines. Of course, our marriage hasn't been perfect. Before you think, *Wow, they need large trophies for staying together this long,* I'll tell you a secret. I still don't understand Kevin.

God wired our brains differently, and my husband often says things that make no sense to me. Once as we sat on the couch and watched reruns of *The Andy Griffith Show,* Kevin suddenly said, "I think I did a good job today."

I looked at him quizzically. *Where did that come from?* Kevin went on to explain that his weekly sermon at a local nursing home had gone well.

I asked what that had to do with Andy, Barney, and Aunt Bee.

"They're sitting on the front porch, singing. It reminded me of church."

I shook my head. After forty-nine years, I decided I didn't need to identify with Kevin's sense of logic to stay in love with him. I suspect that Kev came to that same conclusion about me—perhaps while we were on our honeymoon! We simply made a decision to love each other.

Jesus never needed to decide to love us in spite of our sometimes-wacky selves. Jesus loves us by His very nature. He is love. Even better, Jesus understands all of us, including me. He is the most special and perfect valentine. —JEANETTE LEVELLIE

FAITH STEP: *Sing the children's song "Jesus Loves Me" and bask in His perfect love, even when it's not Valentine's Day.*

Ash Wednesday, February 14

He is the atoning sacrifice for our sins, and not only for ours but also for the sins of the whole world. 1 John 2:2 (NIV)

I CAN TELL A LOT about a person by their tattoos—birds, flowers, words, or Asian characters. I enjoy learning the stories behind the ink crawling up an arm or leg or blanketing a chest or back. Tattoos reveal an individual's mindset, what they choose to represent.

Though I sport no tattoos of my own, there is one marking I identify with. I wait for it all year long and relish the moment I receive it. At Ash Wednesday service, our pastor marks my forehead with the sign of the cross. I wear it with a mixture of gratitude and humility, for these dusty ashes represent my public penitence for sin.

The next forty days and six Sundays will be filled with reflection. Often, I choose a fast to honor Jesus. Usually, it's a daily block of time spent in serving others. There are also years I decide to sacrifice a favorite food or activity.

But it's of greater importance to me, during this extended period, to meditate on His vast forgiveness. The ashes of shame I wear today have been washed clean by His sacrifice. Now I endeavor to forgive others with the same generosity He's offered me.

By tomorrow, the ashen cross will have disappeared from my face, but I will remember it. Though others won't see that holy symbol anymore, I pray they'll recognize Jesus in me. After all, He is tattooed on my soul. —HEIDI GAUL

FAITH STEP: *Today, imagine you have a cross tattooed on your forehead. Represent Jesus well in your words and deeds.*

THURSDAY, FEBRUARY 15

Do not give the devil a way to defeat you. Ephesians 4:27 *(NCV)*

IT WAS THE FIRST DAY of our church's three-week corporate time of prayer and fasting, and I woke up early with great anticipation. My husband, Hal, and I had committed to an intermittent fast during that period: no food or caffeine between 6 a.m. and 6 p.m. We also decided to participate in the daily seven o'clock prayer call led by our pastor each morning of the fast, a wonderful way to be encouraged and connect with other believers on the journey.

When I got up to prepare for the prayer call, Hal asked me if I had cooked something after dinner because he'd smelled food all night long. I hadn't.

"That's just the devil trying to discourage you," I said.

I then dialed the number for the prayer call and a recording said the line was at capacity. *What?* I'd never known one of our church's prayer calls to be at capacity. I couldn't believe it.

I immediately recognized that my failure to be part of the prayer call was the enemy trying to discourage me. However, those devilish distractions just strengthened our resolve to do what we believed the Lord wanted us to do. So, Hal and I prayed together, and we made it through the first day. From then on, we stuck to our commitment and successfully completed the fast with Jesus's help. Although the devil tried to discourage me, Jesus always wins in the end. —BARBRANDA LUMPKINS WALLS

FAITH STEP: *Look for ways the devil might be tempting or trying to discourage you. Ask Jesus to help you defeat the enemy.*

FRIDAY, FEBRUARY 16

---

*Shout for joy to the L*ORD*, all the earth, burst into jubilant song with music; make music to the L*ORD *with the harp, with the harp and the sound of singing, with trumpets and the blast of the ram's horn—shout for joy before the L*ORD*, the King. Psalm 98:4–6 (NIV)*

I LOVE LISTENING TO MUSIC and singing along. Loudly. This morning, after dropping off my fifteen-year-old son, Addison, at school, I cranked up "God Will Work It Out" in the car. I launched into a full-voice vehicular praise-and-worship session on my way to get coffee. I wait to sing until after drop-off; otherwise, Addison gives me his you-need-to-calm-down look. Anything that draws attention is off-limits, as far as he is concerned.

I turned down the volume to order in the Starbucks drive-thru, but I turned it back up as I moved forward in line to pick up my coffee. Because it was the good part of the song, I thumped my hand on the steering wheel and sang along—until I realized that the barista was holding my cup of coffee out the pickup window and staring at me. Addie would have died. I smiled, paid, grabbed my coffee, and drove away.

Jesus deserves all the loud singing I can give Him. He works on my behalf every day with His grace, His love, and His forgiveness (Hebrews 7:25). Singing about Him and His goodness is one way I can honor Him. I'm thinking of keeping a tambourine in my glove box, but don't tell Addison! —SUSANNA FOTH AUGHTMON

FAITH STEP: *Crank up your favorite worship song and spend time praising Jesus. Praise Him for working things out on your behalf every day of your life.*

SATURDAY, FEBRUARY 17

Will it be well when He searches you out?... Job 13:9 (NKJV)

I STARED AT THE UGLY lumps in the muffin tin. What went wrong?

My body needed a reset, so I'd been avoiding sugar, grains, dairy, and a few other things to promote gut healing. I'd been experimenting with unique ingredients like cassava flour often used in special diets. The restrictions had been manageable, but my taste buds wanted something sweet.

The muffins had smelled delicious as the timer ticked, then rang. But when I opened the oven door, my appetite felt as dull as the muffins looked—a lackluster, noncommittal gray. I watched as they sagged and hardened and gave up in shame. Their flavor matched their appearance. A review of the recipe revealed I had halved the eggs and doubled the cassava flour. I hadn't paid enough attention.

My heart is like a recipe in that way. I can think I have the ingredients for a healthy spiritual life that reflects Jesus. But He searches my motives and intentions and misses nothing.

Those unappetizing muffins convinced me to check my heart regularly lest it not be as healthy as I think. Unchecked pride, unforgiveness, self-condemnation, people-pleasing, dishonesty, and other unsavory ingredients can taint my character.

Job follows up today's passage by asking, "Can you deceive him, as one deceives a man?" (Job 13:9, ESV).

That would be a humbling *no*. The muffin mishap couldn't hide, and neither can my humanity. Transparency with Jesus leads to wholeness. His convictions lift me toward His heart without shame.

I think I'll have a sweet healing heart check with Jesus.

—ERIN KEELEY MARSHALL

FAITH STEP: *Enjoy a sweet treat and healing conversation with Jesus. Invite Him to check your heart.*

SUNDAY, FEBRUARY 18

First of all, then, I counsel that petitions, prayers, intercessions and thanksgivings be made for all human beings. 1 Timothy 2:1 *(CJB)*

I PRAY FOR STRANGERS. SOMETIMES when I'm sitting in a crowd, I silently pray, *Jesus, who needs Your love and help today?* Then I scan the backs of the people's heads and trust Him to help me settle on one person. Praying like this seems a little like spiritual fishing—casting a line out to connect that person's needs to Jesus, who loves them more than anyone could imagine.

I don't know what their specific issue is for that particular day other than, like me, the stranger needs Jesus. Even if the person I'm praying for already knows Jesus, she may have some other situation, great or small, that I could pray about. I never know what her circumstances are, and I don't have to. Jesus does—that's what Jesus's omniscience (the state of knowing everything) is all about. He is fully aware of everyone's hearts and struggles, their hopes, joys, and sorrows.

I don't make a show of praying. I just silently talk to the Father in Jesus's name. Occasionally, the person turns around, as if looking for a friend. Or hearing someone speak their name. *Was it because of my prayers?* I hope this practice of secret intercessory prayer will make me more like Jesus, who noticed and cared about the people around Him. —SUZANNE DAVENPORT TIETJEN

FAITH STEP: *The next time you go to a public place, try praying for a stranger. Trust Jesus to give you the words as you secretly send up prayers on behalf of another person.*

PRESIDENTS' DAY, MONDAY, FEBRUARY 19

The blessing of the LORD makes one rich, and He adds no sorrow with it. Proverbs 10:22 (NKJV)

"YOU ARE SO RICH. I envy you," our Airbnb guest gushed as her husband packed their car. The comment caught me off guard. As new empty nesters, we enjoy hosting guests in our now-vacant spaces, but our home is not grand. It's a modern farmhouse with no-frills amenities, less-than-perfect paint jobs, and scratches on the doors.

Our guests weren't the first ones who remarked about the richness of our surroundings after sitting on the front porch and watching horse-and-buggy travel by as they often do in our neighborhood. The nearby cornfields and pastures with Holstein cows and fainting goats must appear idyllic to a visitor. To us, it's just home.

I didn't admit to her that for years I'd envied others who had fancier homes and more lucrative lifestyles. For most of our married life, my husband, Ron, and I have lived modestly as we've raised four kids on a limited budget. Simple living is the norm for our rural, Amish and Mennonite community. Our family grows a big garden and preserves vegetables, and we do lots of things the old-fashioned way. It was eye-opening to hear another person's viewpoint about a life I've often wanted to escape.

It was also a wake-up call from Jesus. He allowed me to see my possessions with a perspective not tainted by jealousy or discontentment. I had taken the simplicity of our lifestyle for granted rather than embracing its richness. It took the envy of another to see the wealth I had all along. —BRENDA L. YODER

FAITH STEP: *Thank Jesus for the simple provisions He has given you. Rather than focusing on what you don't have, embrace the wealth and goodness Jesus provides.*

TUESDAY, FEBRUARY 20

Be strong and courageous. Do not be afraid; do not be discouraged, for the LORD your God will be with you wherever you go. Joshua 1:9 (NIV)

I ATTENDED A CHRISTIAN WOMEN'S conference a couple of years ago, and one particular phrase from its theme jumped out at me: Be Brave. "Uh-oh," I said. I immediately knew Jesus had a message for me that day. I have problems letting go.

I'm what some experts call a *multipotentialite*—a person who has many different interests and creative pursuits in life. Aside from not wanting to disappoint people who invite me to participate in an event or volunteer for a specific task, I am often interested in the mission or vision behind the work and find fulfillment in dabbling in all aspects. The concerning part for me is that once I'm involved, I find it hard to move on when my part is finished.

Sometimes it's scary for me to move forward and not know what will happen to the work I'm leaving behind. It's even scarier to not know exactly what lies ahead. But when I grip an event or task I'm supposed to let go of, I'm not allowing Jesus to replace what I have. That's where bravery comes in. Jesus can't put something else in my hands because they are already full. By opening my hands and letting go, only then can He give me more or lead me to the next place in my life.

Letting go can be scary at times, but I feel brave knowing that when I open my hands, Jesus will be there to hold them. —ERICKA LOYNES

FAITH STEP: *Will you do what Jesus asks you to? Write down the words "Be Brave" and then do what He says.*

WEDNESDAY, FEBRUARY 21

Since, then, you have been raised with Christ, set your hearts on things above, where Christ is, seated at the right hand of God.
Colossians 3:1 (NIV)

MY HUBBY AND I ARE preparing for a vacation. Minnesota winters are bitter cold, and we're traveling to Florida to stroll on a beach and collect seashells. I've been checking my weather app frequently. Even southern states have been unusually cold and cloudy this year, but I keep hoping that by the time we fly south, the sun will show up and it will be warm enough to toss aside our coats. Part of the fun of a vacation is the preparation and wondering what lies ahead.

Just as planning our vacation gives me a chance to practice waiting and hoping for delightful adventures, Jesus has given me the opportunity to practice waiting and hoping for my future with Him. When I was welcomed into His kingdom, He didn't instantly take me into eternity. I continue to journey through life, sometimes skipping and sometimes trudging. The daily challenges, interactions with others, and glimpses of the home Jesus has prepared allow me to deepen my hope and learn patience.

Because I'm traveling with my favorite human—my husband—I have even more reason to hope that our vacation will be fun and refreshing. Likewise, because Jesus is traveling with me through life, I can enjoy a sure hope that eternity with Him will be glorious.
—SHARON HINCK

FAITH STEP: *List a few of Jesus's promises of what the future holds and ask Him to provide patience while you wait for that hope to unfold.*

Thursday, February 22

After he was raised from the dead, his disciples recalled what he had said.
Then they believed the scripture and the words that Jesus had spoken.
John 2:22 *(NIV)*

This year, I challenged myself to look at all the 2:22s in the Bible—the second chapters and twenty-second verses, since those are the first numbers in my February 22 birthdate. (The last four numbers shall remain a secret!)

Today, I considered John 2:22. The part about remembering sounded familiar to me at my stage in life, since both my husband and I frequently ask, "What did we decide about that again?" or "Do you know where I left my garden gloves?" or "Help me remember to change that battery, will you?" Each of us relies on the other to boost our memories.

Jesus told His disciples a lot of things they forgot, didn't fully understand, ignored, or didn't think to explore further while He was alive. After Jesus was resurrected, the disciples suddenly remembered everything He had said. These were young men, for the most part. It wasn't their memories that caught them off guard. It was their humanness that prevented them from flat-out believing the amazing and inconceivable things Jesus had taught and told them.

As I turn another year older today, I realize that I sometimes have problems remembering. But I do recall that I've been provided with a powerful gift to help me remember what Jesus said—the Bible. Now that's something to celebrate! —Cynthia Ruchti

Faith Step: *Using the month and date of your birthday, search the Scripture. Write a verse on a note card that you feel Jesus wants you to remember and celebrate Him!*

FRIDAY, FEBRUARY 23

All Scripture is inspired by God and is useful to teach us what is true and to make us realize what is wrong in our lives. It corrects us when we are wrong and teaches us to do what is right. 2 Timothy 3:16 (NLT)

I'M NOT A FAN OF reading instructions. After all, I've earned a college degree, published six books, and raised two children into adulthood. I should be able to figure out how to install a light-therapy lamp. Or so I thought.

I inserted the plug into the wall just dandy. I placed the cord into the lamp. And then turned it on. But the doohickey that swivels the lamp's bulb to face me would not cooperate. No matter what I did, I couldn't get it to work. I surrendered and took the silly thing to my handyman husband, Kevin.

Kevin grabbed the lamp, twisted a couple times, and presto, just like the photo on the box, it was perfect. I rolled my eyes, smiled, and thanked him.

When it comes to life, my approach is the exact opposite. I read the instruction manual—the Bible—every day. I realize I'll never thrive—or survive—based on my education, innate talents, or past experience. I need the wisdom that only God's Word can provide.

And if I don't get something? I talk to Jesus. "What does this mean, Lord? I can't figure it out." If I listen deep and long enough—not all Jesus's answers come immediately—He shows me what He meant. Jesus can make everything in my life work. —JEANETTE LEVELLIE

FAITH STEP: *Write down a scripture or biblical concept you don't understand. Pray daily until Jesus helps you make sense of it.*

SATURDAY, FEBRUARY 24

Your word, LORD, is eternal; it stands firm in the heavens.
Psalm 119:89 (NIV)

FOUNDED IN 1848, OUR TOWN, Albany, Oregon, has more than 700 historic structures—including our home. Out of respect to the original craftsmanship, the historic society encourages homeowners to retain as many of the original features as possible. Consequently, our 110-year-old historic home has no insulation, so on some wintry mornings, I indulge in a bath. As I soak in the luxurious hot water, I gaze at the skylight above. A glittery ceiling of frost twinkles on the curved plexiglass, forming a prism in soft shades of pink, green, blue, and white. The below-freezing weather taking place just 10 feet above me seems distant from my reality. I'm safe, warm, cozy, and secure in the tub. Nothing—not the phone, the front door, or daily concerns—can disturb the serenity enveloping me. Instead, I breathe in the steamy air and let the bubbly water ease my tense muscles as my mind empties.

Later, dressed and better ready to greet the day, I pause in prayer. I may encounter interpersonal conflicts, financial challenges, or illness. Only God knows what the hours ahead will hold. But I have a buffer for the anxieties that make up daily life, one much more effective than a toasty tub. Jesus.

Jesus doesn't need bubbles or fragrant oil to calm me. He is the Prince of Peace (Isaiah 9:6). Knowing I can place my trust in Him to guide me through anything and everything, I am bathed in an unshakable sense of serenity. —HEIDI GAUL

FAITH STEP: *When was the last time you took a luxurious bath? Set aside some time to relax in the tub. Feel the serenity that Jesus brings.*

SUNDAY, FEBRUARY 25

He guides me along the right paths for his name's sake. Even though I walk through the darkest valley, I will fear no evil, for you are with me; your rod and your staff, they comfort me. Psalm 23:3–4 (NIV)

As I SAT IN MY car after church, warming up the engine, I watched an older couple walk across the parking lot. Their hands were linked, and I noticed their feet moved in perfect unison, seemingly without conscious thought, naturally and rhythmically. They came to a curve where the parking lot turned the corner. It meant their distance would vary; the outside person would have a fraction more to walk. For three or four steps, their cadence broke as the husband lengthened his stride to compensate. When they got to straight ground, he seamlessly adjusted his pace to match hers again. It was clear to me that this couple had been together a long time, partnering with each other through thick and thin. It's the only way they could be so in sync, without words or even apparent awareness.

As I watched them, it felt as if I were seeing Jesus's walk with me. His steps always match mine in perfect rhythm, partnering with me through every minute of every day. Whenever I come to a twist or turn in my life, He's the One who lengthens His stride, going the distance to do whatever it takes to get me through. Even when I'm not aware, Jesus is right there beside me, walking in step with me no matter where I go. —CLAIRE MCGARRY

FAITH STEP: *Go for a walk today and imagine Jesus walking beside you. As you encounter twists and turns in your path, know that He will always be the one to bridge the distance.*

MONDAY, FEBRUARY 26

Yet you do not know what your life will be like tomorrow. For you are just a vapor that appears for a little while, and then vanishes away.
James 4:14 *(NASB)*

I WAS SHOCKED TO RECEIVE word recently that one of my college roommates had suddenly passed away. It had been more than twenty years since I'd seen or talked to Debbie. But I remembered her beautiful eyes, friendly smile, quick-cadence speech, and unshakable faith in God. After thinking about Deb for a couple of days, I opened a bookcase where I keep old photo albums and pulled out a few to look for pictures of her.

The photographs, more than forty years old, were fading. The colors were nowhere near as vibrant as they used to be. But I could still see images of Debbie taken in our dorm room, on campus, and outside the church we attended. Some of my other classmates in the pictures have also departed this earth. Even though they are gone, they've not faded from my memories.

Now that I'm older, it seems each day goes by faster than the one before. So much can happen in a blink of an eye, let alone in twenty-four hours or twenty years. How I wish I could have seen or talked to Debbie one last time. I know I will see her in heaven, but it would have been nice to say goodbye.

While life is just a vapor in God's grand plan, I have hope, comfort, and peace in knowing that in eternity Debbie and I will be roommates once again. —BARBRANDA LUMPKINS WALLS

FAITH STEP: *Pull out some photo albums and thank God for the people who've come into your life. Reconnect with those you've lost touch with, if possible.*

TUESDAY, FEBRUARY 27

Rejoice in the Lord always. I will say it again: Rejoice!
Philippians 4:4 (NIV)

RECENTLY MY DAUGHTER WAS VISITING our home with her toddler and baby. Just before bedtime, my three-year-old granddaughter, Amelia, hurt herself while playing. It wasn't anything serious, but since she was already tired, she couldn't be consoled. That's when Nana came to the rescue. In a moment, I swooped her up. I rocked her and gently spoke to her. I suggested reading stories, and she settled to listen. My granddaughter's joy returned as she snuggled in bed with her blanket, favorite toy, and me curled by her side. My calm, steady presence was exactly what Amelia needed.

Can you relate? I can! Often, I desire the same from Jesus when I am hurt, exhausted, and overwhelmed. To rejoice in the Lord is to be calmed and delighted in His presence. When I am hurting, it's not as if all the pain immediately goes away. Instead, a quiet joy comes from the fact that Jesus is there.

As I come to understand that the Lord is near, I find comfort in Him. I also find hope when I give Jesus my concerns in prayer. Then calmness settles in, and peace comes. The situation doesn't always change, but I'm grateful that my heart does. Just as Amelia needed Nana, it's only with Jesus that I find tiny slivers of joy in challenging situations. Thankfully, I can turn to Jesus again and again, always rejoicing in Him. —TRICIA GOYER

FAITH STEP: *Consider a situation that has you worried, anxious, or in pain. Picture yourself as a child with Jesus beside you. Find comfort in His nearness and rejoice at His calm, steady presence.*

WEDNESDAY, FEBRUARY 28

Therefore, as God's chosen people, holy and dearly loved, clothe yourselves with compassion, kindness, humility, gentleness and patience.
Colossians 3:12 *(NIV)*

THE POST OFFICE PARKING LOT was so congested that I almost didn't stop. But I needed stamps, so I joined the long line of disgruntled patrons and waited impatiently. As I reached the front of the line, it was almost closing time.

A diminutive older couple ahead of me juggled two large boxes. They spoke in another language. Chonda, the postal clerk, gently told them the boxes they chose to mail their items were incorrect. I expected her to point to a shelf and let them locate and repack their boxes. Instead, Chonda went to the shelf, selected the right boxes, and brought them back to the counter.

In halting English, the gentleman asked her if she could open the incorrect boxes and help them put their things into the new boxes. To my surprise and frustration, Chonda did just that. She taped the boxes and gave the couple two mailing labels to address. When the couple hesitated, Chonda addressed the labels for them. I blinked hard so I wouldn't roll my eyes. The couple ahead of me finally went on their way, all smiles. But I was not smiling.

As I stepped to the counter to get my quick book of stamps, the peacefulness I saw on Chonda's face dissolved my impatience.

"I just love helping people," Chonda said dreamily.

I went in for stamps and walked out with a lesson in compassion, kindness, humility, gentleness, and patience. —PAT BUTLER DYSON

FAITH STEP: *Ask Jesus to place someone in your path to whom you can show patience, compassion, humility, gentleness, and kindness. Be prepared to love people as Chonda does.*

THURSDAY, FEBRUARY 29

Jesus replied, "Blessed are you, Simon son of Jonah, for this was not revealed to you by flesh and blood, but by my Father in heaven. And I tell you that you are Peter, and on this rock I will build my church, and the gates of Hades will not overcome it." Matthew 16:17–18 (NIV)

A FEW YEARS AGO, A *Mornings with Jesus* reader wrote me a letter. She noticed that my married name (Aughtmon) was like hers (Altman). She wondered if there might be a connection. I decided to do a little research. I discovered that five generations back, my husband, Scott's, great-great-great-grandfather's name was Thomas Altman. There were four different last-name spellings across a 200-year span: Altmann. Altman. Aughtman. Aughtmon.

This past week, Scott and I were discussing his family name again. We wondered why Scott's ancestors changed the spelling. Then I looked up the meaning of *Altman* in German. I had to laugh. *Alt mann* means "old man." Susanna Foth Old Man has quite a ring to it. Maybe Scott's many grandpas didn't like being called "old man." Maybe they wanted to be seen in a different light. Maybe they wanted their name to reflect who they truly were.

Jesus likes changing people's names. Abram to Abraham. Sarai to Sarah. Saul to Paul. Simon to Peter. A name change can reflect a new way of life. Or a promise of all that He sees in that person's heart. When Jesus came into my life, my name changed too. He gives me many names to choose from. Beloved. Child of God. Disciple. Friend. —SUSANNA FOTH AUGHTMON

FAITH STEP: *Look up the meaning of your name. Does it reflect your potential? Spend time meditating on the names that Jesus has given you.*

FRIDAY, MARCH 1

Forget the former things; do not dwell on the past. See,
I am doing a new thing! Isaiah 43:18–19 (NIV)

MY ROLES AND RESPONSIBILITIES IN life have expanded, and I've allowed other people's perceptions of my work and style, as well as my own self-doubt, to lead me to question who I am and what I'm capable of doing. One day when I was particularly discouraged, my mind went back to a *VeggieTales* episode my son, DJ, used to watch. "A Snoodle's Tale" featured a teardrop-shaped, Smurf-blue character named Snoodle Doo with white wings, a tuft of white hair, and white gloves. This little guy carried a backpack that contained a kazoo and palette—clues to help him discover his skills and talents. However, his low-level flying and elementary drawings were ridiculed by mean-spirited Snoodles. They drew pictures of Snoodle Doo's shortcomings and stuffed them in his backpack to remind him of his limitations. But when he stumbled upon his Maker, Snoodle Doo was given a new drawing. It was a picture of him fully developed and completely competent. That is how his Maker saw him, and soon, Snoodle Doo saw himself that way too.

DJ and I watched "A Snoodle's Tale" thirteen years ago, yet the moral of the story stayed with me. I need to tune out the mean-spirited voices (including my own) that try to keep me down. Because of Jesus, my past does not define my future. Just like Snoodle Doo, I must listen to my Maker and see myself the way He sees me too.
—ERICKA LOYNES

FAITH STEP: *Do you let the words or opinions of others discourage you? Close your eyes and ask Jesus to give you a vision of how He sees you.*

SATURDAY, MARCH 2

He replied, "If you have faith as small as a mustard seed, you can say to this mulberry tree, 'Be uprooted and planted in the sea,' and it will obey you."
Luke 17:6 (NIV)

I LOVE THE HERB TARRAGON. I have a chicken, rice, and carrot recipe that tastes bland until I go to my French tarragon plant in the garden, cut off a branch, and snip its leaves into the pot.

This particular plant traveled more than a thousand miles when we moved from our home in Michigan's Hiawatha Forest to our new place in Wyoming. A hot, windy summer last year nearly sucked it dry. I brought it in for the winter to nurse it along in our sunny bay window, where it appeared to die.

Every time I tried to uproot this little crispy-leafed plant to throw it away, something stopped me. So, I talked to it like my green-thumbed Grandma May had done with her ferns. I even prayed for it, in Jesus's name. Maybe there was some hope left. Some faith.

When the disciples asked Jesus to increase their faith, He didn't. Maybe faith being present was all that mattered; maybe the size of faith wasn't important. After all, Jesus said that faith as tiny as a mustard seed could uproot a mulberry tree and cast it into the sea.

One late winter morning, I watered all my plants as usual, feeling a little silly to be watering the dead French tarragon. As I looked closer, I saw three small sprouts peeking out of the soil—healthy and green.

Although my faith in that dying plant was as small as it gets, it was there, growing too. —SUZANNE DAVENPORT TIETJEN

FAITH STEP: *Pray for something you need that, until now, has seemed too big to believe in. Muster up a little faith as you trust Jesus.*

SUNDAY, MARCH 3

I have told you this so that my joy may be in you and that your joy may be complete. John 15:11 (NIV)

TWO SUNDAYS AGO, A LITTLE girl—two or three years old—wandered through the sanctuary at the end of the service. She looked lost but happily so. The child gazed up into every passing face, as if hoping to see one she recognized. I stooped to her eye level and asked if she knew where her mommy or daddy was. She said no but smiled.

I took her hand. Together, we made our way through the crowded foyer. A woman about my age approached. "Ellie! There you are!" Grandma said the little one was fearlessly "prone to wander." We all smiled with relief and joy.

It happened again this past Sunday during the opening worship set. This time, a small boy strolled in mid-service. He peered at all the faces. Again, too young to wander alone, he obviously needed to be reunited with someone. I left my seat and took him by the hand. Soon parents and child joyfully reconnected.

I apparently hadn't gotten the lesson the first time. Now, though, I more fully understand what Jesus might have meant when He said His "joy" could be ours. Could it be this—reuniting a wandering, lost child with the Father? It explains how Jesus could talk about joy so close to His upcoming crucifixion. Inexpressible joy overflows in the simple task of reuniting people with the Father, as Jesus spent His whole life—and death—doing. After all, we're all prone to wander. —CYNTHIA RUCHTI

FAITH STEP: *Watch for ways Jesus might invite you to rise from your chair to do some small thing to help reconnect a wanderer with His Father.*

MONDAY, MARCH 4

---

*For whatever things were written before were written for our learning, that
we through the patience and comfort of the Scriptures might have hope.*
Romans 15:4 (NKJV)

VIRGINIA AND I SHARED A special friendship—and a boss with a quick
temper. When our supervisor was triggered, his face turned red, the
veins in his neck protruded, and his voice blasted through the halls of
our workplace. At twenty-two, I was utterly terrified of him.

He didn't scare Virginia, though. His outbursts concerned her,
and she wanted to help him by introducing him to Jesus. She wrote
a calming Bible verse on a small square of paper and carried it daily
in her pocket, waiting for just the right opportunity.

One day, our boss began screaming at a helpless coworker. Virginia reached for his hand and gently placed the scripture in it. I
watched in fear, expecting his rage to shift to her. But instead, he
stopped yelling, read the paper, and walked away.

Virginia gave our boss a Bible verse during each episode of anger
after that. Surprisingly, he always accepted them. The words of
Jesus, delivered through my friend, seemed to settle his spirit, offering him healing and hope.

What a great role model Virginia provided for me at such a young
age. She demonstrated a unique way to share Jesus with another
person, even a difficult one. I learned about the power of scriptures
in teaching patience and self-control and supplying comfort. And I
learned how Jesus's words could change a life, including mine, one
verse at a time. —BECKY ALEXANDER

FAITH STEP: *Try Virginia's method of sharing Jesus this week. Write a Bible
verse of hope on a square of paper, and look for a chance to slip it into somebody's
hand.*

TUESDAY, MARCH 5

But our citizenship is in heaven. And we eagerly await a Savior from there, the Lord Jesus Christ. Philippians 3:20 *(NIV)*

I BECAME A NATURALIZED AMERICAN citizen in 1996. To become a citizen, I completed two important steps. First, I studied for and passed a forty-question multiple-choice test about American history and government. Second, after successfully passing the examination, I attended an event to be sworn in as a new citizen. During this oath-taking ceremony, I renounced any allegiance to a foreign country (in my case, the Philippines) and promised to always defend the government of the United States.

Years ago, as a young teenager, I became a born-again Christian. After confessing Jesus as my Lord and Savior, I acquired a new citizenship—a heavenly citizenship. I cannot help but see a similarity between the steps I took to become an American citizen and the steps I take to be a responsible citizen of heaven.

I must diligently study Jesus's Words to learn about Him and the history of God's people, as well as understand and obey His laws and commands.

As a Christian, I have also had to give up any sinful habits that are not in conformity with the nature of Jesus. To continually engage in a sinful practice is like maintaining allegiance with my old world. But that's not what I want anymore—I want my lifestyle, actions, and words to truly reflect my loyalty to Jesus. Though I live in this world, I can be encouraged by remembering that my true home—my real citizenship—lies with Jesus and His heavenly kingdom. —JENNIFER ANNE F. MESSING

FAITH STEP: *Ask for Jesus's help to give up any worldly desires and for His forgiveness for any wrongdoings. Aim to positively represent your heavenly citizenship everywhere you go.*

WEDNESDAY, MARCH 6

A cheerful heart is good medicine, but a crushed spirit dries up the bones.
Proverbs 17:22 (NIV)

WHEN MY FRIEND HANNAH FOUND me sitting in the church lobby with my computer open during Wednesday evening services, I told her I was working. But really, I was hiding. Hiding from people. Hiding from small talk. Hiding from anyone who might notice my sour mood bubbling below my fresh makeup and fake smile.

I forgot that Hannah is not a surface-level friend. Within five minutes, I'd shared my burden. I cried and she prayed for me. Her words and hugs were just what I needed to realign my emotions with the infinite love of Jesus.

Then she caught me off guard. "You need something fun on your calendar," she said. "Plan something, and I'll ask you about it when I see you next."

A few weeks later, it was her first question. "Have you done anything fun yet?" she asked with a smile that was equal parts best-friend-at-a-sleepover and schoolteacher-asking-for-homework. I knew then that her challenge had been more than a flippant remark. It was a reminder from Jesus that a cheerful heart is good medicine, and I hadn't been taking my medicine lately. As a result, my lack of fun and laughter were partly to blame for my perpetual gloom. I needed a dose of the joy of Jesus in my life.

I started with an afternoon of guaranteed enjoyment—an outing with my family. My smile returned, and I thanked Jesus for the healing power of laughter and fun. —EMILY E. RYAN

FAITH STEP: *What is something fun you can put on your calendar? How can you add the joy of Jesus into your life?*

THURSDAY, MARCH 7

It is of the LORD's mercies that we are not consumed, because his compassions fail not. They are new every morning: great is thy faithfulness. Lamentations 3:22–23 (KJV)

I LOVE MY WRITING AND editing work and the mental and emotional energy that goes into it. But I've learned that after time in deep thought at a computer, I need to unwind my mind by doing something active. Often that means freshening up spaces in our home. A lovely, cozy room refuels my creative bucket.

After a recent stint at my desk, the guest room was calling my name. Over several wintery days, I'd caulked trim and prepped the walls for paint.

Today, I went to reassess my work. The room was clearly still in process, but I bypassed the upheaval and crossed to the window to look out over skeletal branches reaching toward the backyard sky. Winter was fading. Spring's breath hovered with rejuvenating freshness, much like the almost-there refreshment of this guest room.

And then I heard it. A bird chirped cheerfully from those trees. It had been many weeks since I'd heard birds. It called again and I leaned toward the glass. My heart lifted and my head cleared, and the unfinished mess of the room looked full of potential beauty.

That little bird was thriving in Jesus's faithfulness through the winter months. Its voice heralded the Savior's provision and care, for itself and, I felt, for me too. Its sound felt like a gentle smile from heaven. No matter how wearying winter may seem, Jesus is faithfully working refreshment in my spirit. —ERIN KEELEY MARSHALL

FAITH STEP: *Today, look for a reminder of Jesus's faithfulness. When you spot it, write a prayer of thankfulness and trust in Him.*

FRIDAY, MARCH 8

Bear in mind that our Lord's patience means salvation. 2 Peter 3:15 (NIV)

AFTER DECADES OF SERVICE, OUR range stopped working. It's old and missing many pieces, so it needed replacing. Our historic home's layout is awkward, requiring the range to vent through the basement, be all-electric, and somehow fit the space provided in our kitchen island. After shopping several used and new appliance stores, we learned there were two models left in the entire country, one of which was currently unavailable. The other was on back order for several months. On the way home, we purchased a toaster oven to get us through.

I'm ultra-klutzy when it comes to mastering new skills. Appliances are especially challenging. So far, I've burnt a loaf of bread and incinerated a batch of cookies. Today, I'll try my hand at a casserole. I trust that in time incredible edibles will once again come forth from my kitchen, but for now, I'm scraping off the blackened bits and salvaging what little is left. It's that or toss the mistakes and start over.

Jesus does the same for me. He sees the mistakes I make, the moments sin overtakes me, and allows me to start over. He knows my intentions are good but that I haven't mastered life yet, and I probably never will.

But I trust He'll accept my pathetic efforts and love me just the same. He'll scrape off the bad and savor what's good in me. He always has. —HEIDI GAUL

FAITH STEP: *On the left side of a sheet of paper, list a column of mistakes you've made recently. Pray for clarity, then on the right side, list the goodness you salvaged from those very mistakes.*

SATURDAY, MARCH 9

*But the pot he was shaping from the clay was marred in his hands; so the
potter formed it into another pot, shaping it as seemed best to him.*
Jeremiah 18:4 (NIV)

TAKING A POTTERY CLASS IS on my retirement list of fun things to
do, so when my daughter enrolled in a pottery class where she lived,
I was jealous in the best way. We were both excited, until the first
evening.

The clay was difficult to mold. She added water and worked it
with her hands, but by the end of class, she'd produced only one
unsatisfactory piece compared to several lovely pieces each of the
other students had created. She accepted the instructor's offer to
come to the studio on Saturday to practice.

That's when the instructor discovered the problem. "This is bad
clay," he said and gave her a new bag. When she placed a ball on the
wheel and began spinning, the clay was pliable and obedient. She
texted me a picture of her first successful piece—a ceramic bowl.

Although I wasn't in the class, I learned clay can be bad. I thought
clay was clay, and if a project didn't turn out, the potter's skill was
to blame. My daughter's instructor tossed aside that rebellious lump
that failed her.

I'm so thankful the Master doesn't give up on bad clay! Sometimes I refuse to be shaped, or I try to take on a form of my own.
But Jesus doesn't throw me away. He patiently continues shaping
me, smoothing my cracks, refusing to give up on His work in progress, molding me as He sees best. —KAREN SARGENT

FAITH STEP: *How pliable are you in Jesus's hands? Think of one way He is
molding you now and surrender to His gentle direction.*

SUNDAY, MARCH 10

Indeed, we all make many mistakes. James 3:2 (NLT)

IT HA'D BEEN A SOMEWHAT restless night as I anxiously anticipated leading my church's morning prayer call, which attracts hundreds of people from around the country. It would be the first time for me to have that awesome responsibility.

Leading the call involved muting and unmuting participants and, most importantly, recording the call so that those who couldn't join us would have the opportunity to listen to the prayer later. I was a little nervous about remembering to do everything at the proper time, so I made a cheat sheet with the various codes to use for each call function. I prayed before I opened the phone line, asking the Lord to guide me and let everything go smoothly.

I started the call by greeting everyone. I shared a short scripture reading and began to pray. The words flowed and the time passed before I knew it. I ended with "Amen," relieved that everything had gone well. And then the big revelation came: I hadn't recorded the call! I was mortified. And I was angry at myself for making such a silly mistake.

As I began to beat myself up over the error, a text came in from a friend. "Beautiful prayer; thanks so much!" I thanked her and admitted I'd forgotten to record the call. "You'll remember next time," was the simple and much appreciated reply.

I thought about what happened and decided that Jesus wanted to teach me a lesson. Mistakes happen even with the best-laid plans and cheat sheets. They keep me humble and dependent on Him.
—BARBRANDA LUMPKINS WALLS

FAITH STEP: *What mistake have you made? Are you still stewing over it? Ask Jesus to help you let it go and reveal what you can learn from it.*

MONDAY, MARCH 11

Blessed be the God and Father of our Lord Jesus Christ, the Father of mercies and God of all comfort, who comforts us in all our affliction, so that we may be able to comfort those who are in any affliction, with the comfort with which we ourselves are comforted by God. 2 Corinthians 1:3–4 (ESV)

WHEN THE PANDEMIC STARTED IN 2020, I found myself calm. I believe this was partly due to having just emerged from another crisis: the failure of my business and subsequent bankruptcy with scant support. During that intensely trying time, I depended on Jesus as never before.

I sensed it was the perfect opportunity to share the hope of Christ with others. I asked the Lord, "How can I leverage my serenity, faith, and gifts to be of service?" The answer came swiftly. I started blogging and sharing daily afternoon messages of hope during the height of quarantine online—*4 O'Clock Faith.*

I'd never done videos and was clueless about setting up the equipment. I was self-conscious and felt unworthy, but at the same time, I was compelled to share God's message. Jesus led me to themes and scriptures. I enjoyed getting dressed up and having a purpose every day. Eventually, I relaxed and gained a little following. People told me how much it helped them.

It helped me too. As an ambassador for Jesus, I am called to be calm in the face of chaos so I can encourage and comfort others. My *4 O'Clock Faith* is not just for four o'clock—I need it all the time.
—ISABELLA CAMPOLATTARO

FAITH STEP: *Set an alarm on your phone for four o'clock and pray about how you can be intentional about seeking out people or ministries to share your experience, strength, and hope to comfort others.*

TUESDAY, MARCH 12

Let the morning bring me word of your unfailing love, for I have put my trust in you. Show me the way I should go, for to you I entrust my life.
Psalm 143:8 (NIV)

HAVE YOU EVER SPENT A night in worry and distress? I have. As the mother of ten children, there is always one of them with a concern that keeps me up at night. Although I try to turn my worries over to Jesus in prayer, the darkness around me makes the situation seem heavier and more oppressive. Yet after a night of discouragement, it's often with the light of dawn that my heart fully understands that Jesus is present and can help in every situation.

Over the years, I've made a habit of meeting with Jesus with an open Bible in the morning. With the first rays of light, my soul rejoices at spending time with the Son of God. Because this is my very first act at the beginning of my day, I'm able to bring all the burdens I've carried through the night and drop them at the feet of Jesus. No matter how many concerns weighed on me in the dark, I'm able to take them to Jesus and leave them there, knowing He will intercede for me (Romans 8:34).

After all, Jesus has many more children than even I do.
—TRICIA GOYER

FAITH STEP: *What burdens do you carry? At this moment, make a list and take them to Jesus. Leave them with Him, asking Him to intercede and bring new light and hope into your heart for every concern.*

WEDNESDAY, MARCH 13

Our God, will you not judge them? For we have no power to face this vast army that is attacking us. We do not know what to do, but our eyes are on you. 2 Chronicles 20:12 *(NIV)*

I STROKED MY MOTHER'S HAND. The emergency room staff proposed surgery to remove the clot that caused Mom's stroke, but they also offered the option of no intervention. I prayed for Jesus to guide my choices, feeling the heavy weight of uncertainty. I OK'd the surgery, and when she didn't improve, more difficult choices followed. Each step of the way, I glimpsed what King Jehoshaphat must have experienced when he prayed, "We do not know what to do, but our eyes are on You." His words held both the pain and hope of that moment.

Many times when life is difficult, I don't know where to turn. I look at the circumstances and feel overwhelmed. I look to friends and family, but they are only human, and while they offer support, they don't have all the answers. I look to my own wisdom and strength and shake my head at my puniness.

What a comfort that I can turn my eyes toward Jesus, the source of true wisdom and strength. He gently steers my decisions and pours out His grace on whatever choice I make.

We eventually brought Mom home and cared for her with the support of hospice. I turned my gaze toward Jesus day by day. Weeks later, when my mother met Him face-to-face, He was not a stranger. Her eyes had been on Jesus all her life. I'm striving to do the same. —SHARON HINCK

FAITH STEP: *Pray King Jehoshaphat's prayer in 2 Chronicles 20:12 and set your eyes on Jesus.*

THURSDAY, MARCH 14

Even after Jesus had performed so many signs in their presence,
they still would not believe in him. John 12:37 (NIV)

"WILL YOU HELP ME UPDATE my résumé?" my daughter asked. She had completed her first year in an entry-level position and was ready for her next career step. The one-page résumé she had prepared right out of college had a lot of white space, listing basic skills, part-time jobs, and no work history in her career field.

She updated her employment information and added new skills to the résumé. She briefly described major projects she'd completed and the computer programs she'd mastered. Very quickly, the white space disappeared as she presented evidence to convince a future employer that she was qualified for the job she desired.

I wonder how often Jesus has to convince me He is qualified for the job. *Remember that time you prayed for direction? Or when you asked Me to walk with you through that illness? What about the relationship I healed? That time the finances came through? Or when you needed to be rescued?* Perhaps I'm too focused on the problem in front of me to look back at Jesus's history and qualifications. Sometimes, in spite of my Savior's impressive résumé, I doubt He can or will do the job. Or I foolishly think I can do it better myself.

When I shift my eyes onto Jesus and consider the work He has done for me and in me, I have no doubt He is the only one qualified, if not overqualified, to fulfill every need I will ever have. —KAREN SARGENT

FAITH STEP: *Make a résumé for Jesus by listing everything He has done in your life. When you face uncertainty, review His work history and trust Him to do the job.*

FRIDAY, MARCH 15

Therefore, if anyone is in Christ, he is a new creation. The old has passed away; behold, the new has come. 2 Corinthians 5:17 (ESV)

WHILE REORGANIZING MY OFFICE, I found my name tag from the first writing conference I attended. I picked it up and remembered how I'd covered it with my notebook whenever I got near the editor who had been assigned to evaluate the manuscript I'd submitted. Up until the last day, an inner voice whispered to me: *When he reads it, he'll wonder why you even came to a writers' conference. You don't belong here. If these people knew you had zero writing talent, they would kick you out.*

More than twenty years later, I still hear that nagging voice sometimes. I think most of us struggle with circumstances, places, or people that make us feel as though we don't measure up. Our insecurity can make us afraid to let others see who we truly are. Self-doubt can cause us to miss wonderful opportunities that God intends for us. That's why I need to focus on who Jesus says I am.

Once I became a new creation in Christ, He gave me a new identity based on His sacrifice for me. Now I'm God's adopted child, accepted and unconditionally loved even when I fail miserably. Regardless of what other people think about me or how I feel about myself on any given day, Jesus has written a new set of name tags for me: *Forgiven, Free, Beloved, Esteemed.* There's never any need to cover those up. —DIANNE NEAL MATTHEWS

FAITH STEP: *Pray and ask Jesus who He says you are. Then make a name tag for yourself with those words. Pin it to your shirt and wear it as a reminder to see yourself as He sees you.*

SATURDAY, MARCH 16

She had a sister called Mary, who sat at the Lord's feet listening to what he said. Luke 10:39 (NIV)

I MET A LOVELY WOMAN the other day. Debbi is the owner of a Christian retail store and spends long days doing all the work by herself. Thinking about all the tasks on her list, I asked if she were more like busy Martha or serene Mary, the sisters who visited with Jesus in Luke 10. Debbi said she's definitely a Martha. Yet, the minute she goes home and takes off her shoes, she's a Mary through and through. She may have to keep her shoes on for a few hours when she gets home, tackling whatever tasks are waiting for her there. But the minute she slips off whatever's on her feet, she declares her tasks done and clicks over to a stance of Sabbath rest to be restored by Jesus.

Her concept had a profound impact on me. I began to wonder what triggers I have that are like Debbi's shoes. What action or items do I equate with sacred time with Him? When I sit in my prayer chair each morning, I feel an automatic connection with Jesus. Like exercise is to muscle memory, my time in that chair creates a spiritual reflex connecting me directly to Him. But I lack an evening ritual that signals it's time to rejuvenate in Jesus again.

Rest assured, I'm experimenting with my own taking-off-my-shoes trigger that signals it's time to be restored at His feet.
—CLAIRE MCGARRY

FAITH STEP: *Develop your own taking-off-your-shoes ritual that signals it's time to be rejuvenated by Jesus.*

SUNDAY, MARCH 17

When they had all had enough to eat, he said to his disciples, "Gather the pieces that are left over. Let nothing be wasted." John 6:12 (NIV)

THE BIBLE STORY ABOUT THE loaves and fishes fascinates me. To witness Jesus feeding the multitudes with just a young boy's lunch must have been life-changing. Did the food replenish itself in the baskets as they were passed or in the recipient's very hands? I can only guess at the awed expressions as the crowd received this divine gift. Each of those people, stomachs filled, passed the blessing along. Not one clasped the basket tight in his grip, unwilling to share. Afterward, the twelve gathered the remnants, so as not to waste a bit.

Today, my refrigerator and pantry are so empty they nearly echo. Yet as I rifled through veggie compartments and canned goods, I discovered enough ingredients to prepare a tasty "from scratch" pasta sauce. But who ever heard of a tiny pot of spaghetti? I'll share this dish with my neighbors. Come summer, I'll find bags of juicy pears on my porch, just waiting to be bitten into. Or perhaps, an invitation to dinner.

Like most of us, I receive everyday miracles made no less remarkable by their common nature. When I give, I will receive—from Him directly or through others' actions. Not just a belly full of food but a heart full of trust. Because even the fragments of everyday miracles are precious. They were touched by His hand, and in Him nothing is ever wasted. —HEIDI GAUL

FAITH STEP: *Bake a double batch of cookies. Step out of your comfort zone to share your abundance with someone new.*

MONDAY, MARCH 18

Listen and hear my voice; pay attention and hear what I say.
Isaiah 28:23 (NIV)

I WAS RECENTLY DOUBLE-BOOKED FOR two morning meetings at work. One was an in-person department meeting I knew would provide timely information I needed in my position. I wanted to be at that meeting. The second, however, was a virtual meeting I knew would be a large waste of time. Unfortunately, it was required.

I hopped online early and explained my situation to the moderator. I asked if I could give my input quickly and log out, but she didn't like that idea. Instead, she suggested I put in a single earbud so I could listen to the online meeting while attending the other one in person. Since I had no other way to be in two places at once, I agreed.

What I found once both meetings ended was that I hadn't been able to concentrate on either. With noise from one source pouring into my right ear while noise from another poured into my left, I couldn't truly hear anything. Listening, I discovered, cannot be multitasked.

This memory comes to mind whenever I read Jesus's commands to listen, hear, and pay attention to what He says. I want to listen to what Jesus says through His Word and prayer, but sometimes I catch myself only half listening. It's as if I have one ear tuned to Jesus and one ear tuned to the world. I need to remember that to listen to Jesus means to listen *only* to Jesus. To truly hear Him, I must pay attention. —EMILY E. RYAN

FAITH STEP: *Use an audio version of the Bible today and listen closely to Jesus's message to you.*

TUESDAY, MARCH 19

*What a wretched man I am! Who will rescue me from this body
that is subject to death? Thanks be to God, who delivers me through
Jesus Christ our Lord! Romans 7:24–25 (NIV)*

WHILE TRYING TO EDUCATE MYSELF on nutrition, I recently came across an article that encouraged readers to eat foods that would give life to their bodies. That particular wording stung. I know I need to eat healthier, but my favorite foods are often salty, creamy, chocolatey, buttery, fluffy, and caffeinated. I know that pure water and raw fruits and vegetables are good choices, and when I choose them, I'm completely satisfied. But I give in to eating what's not so healthy for me more often than I would like. My lack of willpower leaves me feeling defeated.

The Apostle Paul captured his feelings of hopelessness in Romans 7. Instead of doing the good things he wanted to do, he did the evil things he didn't want to do (Romans 7:19). He described this struggle as an internal war between his mind that so desperately wanted to follow the Spirit and his body that was destined to sin and death (Romans 7:23). But even in the midst of that deep despair, Paul had hope in Jesus Christ. No amount of willpower, attitude adjustments, or nutrition advice will compel me to make the right food choice all the time. Each day, I battle between what I want to eat and what I know I need to eat. No matter how much I try to change my bad choices, I can only get so far on my own. My real hope for healthy change is through the life-giving Spirit of Jesus Christ within me. —ERICKA LOYNES

FAITH STEP: *Next time you have to make a choice, consider all of the options you have and what you really want to achieve. Then, ask Jesus to help you make the healthy, life-giving choice.*

WEDNESDAY, MARCH 20

A time to rend, and a time to sew; a time to keep silence,
and a time to speak. Ecclesiastes 3:7 (KJV)

"HOW'S YOUR MOM DOING AFTER her gallbladder surgery?" I asked the grocery store cashier.

"Recovering well," she replied. "We appreciate your prayers."

I was about to say more when my daughter Melissa elbowed me in the ribs—my signal to stop talking and move on.

"Mom, didn't you see the line behind you?" Melissa scolded as we left the store. Over the years, my kids have voiced their annoyance and embarrassment about me chitchatting with most everyone I meet. I like people and am interested in their lives, but Melissa thinks it's inappropriate and nosy.

At my devotional time the next morning, I consulted the One I knew would be honest with me. *Jesus, do I talk too much? Am I being nosy?*

For the next several days, I practiced silence. I simply thanked the cashiers when they rang my purchases. I refrained from telling the mother pushing the stroller how cute her baby was. I even talked less around the house. My husband, Jeff, asked me if I was sick!

At a department store as I searched the shelves for my size, a clerk came up to me, a huge smile on her face. She reminded me I'd promised to pray for her daughter, who was experiencing a high-risk pregnancy. And I had.

"My grandson was born yesterday, and he and my daughter are fine," she said. Then she gave me a hug and thanked me for praying for her family. And I thanked Jesus for showing me it's OK to be chatty. —PAT BUTLER DYSON

FAITH STEP: *Ask Jesus to lead you when to speak and when to keep silent.*

THURSDAY, MARCH 21

Hear my voice when I call, LORD; be merciful to me and answer me.
My heart says of you, "Seek his face!" Your face, LORD, I will seek.
Psalm 27:7–8 (NIV)

MY HUSBAND, SCOTT, AND I have been married for more than two decades. That seems crazy to me. Wasn't it just yesterday that I was looking for him in our college cafeteria?

Before we started dating, I used to get my lunch tray and search for him. I hoped he was there, having lunch at the same time. If he was, I would make my way toward his table and try to catch his eye. He was nice, funny, and cute. He would have everyone at the table laughing. I knew that I liked him. I hoped he liked me too. Luckily, he did. All these years later, I still like sitting next to Scott. I like talking through my day with him or just sitting together on the couch. It is comforting to know he is always nearby.

Long ago, I started looking for Jesus too, and I used to think that finding Him was daunting. *What would I have to do to seek His face? How would I know if He heard my prayers? How could I find my way into His presence?* The truth is, Jesus is always near, always in my presence. When I draw near to Him, He will draw near to me (James 4:8). He hears my cries and He answers my prayers. And He loves me more than I could ever hope or imagine.
—SUSANNA FOTH AUGHTMON

FAITH STEP: *Set aside time today to draw near to Jesus and seek His face. Go to a quiet spot and have a meal or snack while you talk to Him.*

FRIDAY, MARCH 22

Therefore, my dear friends, flee from idolatry. 1 Corinthians 10:14 (NIV)

I USED TO THINK THE Old Testament Bible prohibition against idols in the Ten Commandments (Exodus 20:4) was all about actual statuary. Carved icons, totem poles, golden calves—no problem. I wasn't bowing down to any statue hewn from human hands.

Or was I?

Turns out, idols are sometimes disguised as good things: a significant other, children, jobs, money, friends, parents, church, a particular lifestyle...and yes, sports figures and other celebrities. Potentially less-friendly idols include items that can turn into addictions, such as food, alcohol, sex, or gambling. Bowing to them means submitting, or as *Merriam-Webster* bracingly puts it, "agreeing to the demands of" this or that, him or her. Ouch.

Unfortunately, I've had a lifetime of idols to which I freely gave precedence over seeking Jesus, bowing deeply to their demands. What I've learned is that idols break, tarnish, disappoint, and sometimes destroy. They fail to deliver the promised satisfaction in the long run. The persistent expectation that they were enough left me feeling bitter, depressed, disillusioned, and longing for something more substantial to make me feel whole. Meanwhile, Jesus waited patiently for me to figure out that what I was really after was Him.

The idol prohibition isn't about Jesus's vanity or denying me any good things. It's about reorienting my priorities to what guarantees fulfillment over the long haul when the things I've made into idols fail. —ISABELLA CAMPOLATTARO

FAITH STEP: *Draw or use magazines to collage a totem pole of the different things you've made into idols. Ask Jesus to help you regain perspective and priorities. Then burn the page.*

SATURDAY, MARCH 23

Even the hairs of your head have all been counted. So do not be afraid;
you are worth much more than many sparrows! Luke 12:7 (GNT)

MY HAIR WAS COMING OUT in clumps. This disappearing act began a couple of months after my recovery from a monthlong bout with a life-threatening illness and continued for weeks. Horrified at the alarming rate my waist-length hair was falling out, I blinked back tears as I looked at a handful that seemed like enough to knit a sweater. I consoled myself with the knowledge that Jesus was constantly with me, counting and recounting the swiftly changing number of hairs on my head. Powerless to stop the rapid hair loss, I considered the scripture in 1 Corinthians 11:15 (NLT): "And isn't long hair a woman's pride and joy? For it has been given to her as a covering."

While I lost my "pride and joy," I wondered about losing my "covering." Jesus put my heart and mind at rest, constantly reassuring me that He is my covering (Psalm 91:4). That promise made the transition from having a full head of long hair to experimenting with wigs and hairpieces easier to take in stride. Although my long hair may be a temporal source of pride and joy, my true source of lasting pride and joy is Jesus. Whether wearing a head wrap, wig, hairpiece, or my own natural hair, Jesus has me covered.
—CASSANDRA TIERSMA

FAITH STEP: *What changing circumstances are you experiencing? Run a comb or brush through your hair and thank Jesus that no matter what is happening, He's got you covered.*

PALM SUNDAY, MARCH 24

*They took palm branches and went out to meet him, shouting,
"Hosanna!" "Blessed is he who comes in the name of the Lord!"
"Blessed is the king of Israel!" John 12:13 (NIV)*

I AM RESERVED BY NATURE. As a child, I took to heart the now-frowned-upon adage "children should be seen and not heard." I've continued to practice that motto throughout these many decades of my adulthood, preferring to write my thoughts rather than speak my mind.

As the spouse of a district superintendent in our denomination, I often travel with my husband on Sundays as he visits and preaches in one of the more than 100 churches in his jurisdiction. While I put my best effort into being friendly and an encouragement to the pastors and their spouses, I suspect there are many parishioners across our district who have never heard my voice. As I consider the crowd that surrounded Jesus when He made his way into Jerusalem that first Palm Sunday, I wonder what kind of participant I would have been in this scene. I'd like to think I'd be one of those enthusiastically shouting loud hosannas to our long-awaited King as I waved high a palm branch or draped my cloak on the road to serve as a red-carpet welcome for my Lord. Knowing myself, I fear I'd hang back, quiet and reserved, while the throng celebrated His arrival.

But Jesus knows that although I might be low-key on the outside, I, too, would be celebrating His arrival, whispering silent prayers and enthusiastic praise, thanking Him for the sacrifice He was making for me. —SUSAN DOWNS

FAITH STEP: *Picture yourself in the Jerusalem crowd. How do you think you would have participated in Jesus's arrival?*

Monday, March 25

Do not be like them, for your Father knows what you need before you ask him. Matthew 6:8 (NIV)

AFTER RAISING FIVE CHILDREN TO adulthood, my husband and I now have the privilege of raising one of our grandsons. As a preschooler, just like his aunts and uncles before him, Kai's conversations with me were full of adoration and affection. "Look what I made for you, Grandma!" "When I grow up, can I marry you?" "I love you T-H-I-S much," Kai would say with his arms open as wide as he could stretch them.

Now that he's a middle schooler, those words of adulation are, more often than not, replaced with phrases like, "Can you drive me to…" or "Can you buy me…" And while I love him just as much in these more-demanding days as I did when he was an expressively affectionate preschooler, I do miss the way he trusted me so completely to meet his needs that he seldom felt it necessary to ask.

In the early days of Jesus's life, the magi sought out the Christ child to worship Him and bring Him precious gifts. In His final earthly days, the crowds sought Him out, not for what they could do for Him, but rather for what miracle they might witness or receive.

Like that affectionate preschooler, I want to come to Jesus with words of worship and adoration, trusting Him so completely to meet my needs that I don't ask for anything. Instead, I want to offer Jesus what He wants most—my heart. —SUSAN DOWNS

FAITH STEP: *Spend some quality time today in prayer with Jesus. Rather than bringing a list of needs and wants, give Him your heart as you express your love and adoration to Him.*

TUESDAY, MARCH 26

So the chief priests made plans to kill Lazarus as well,
for on account of him many of the Jews were going over to
Jesus and believing in him. John 12:10—11 (NIV)

"RILEY! WHAT DID YOU DO?" I hollered at our younger of two York-shire terriers. The stuffing from one of their toys covered my office floor. One-year-old Riley looked up at me with those precious puppy-dog eyes that seemed to say, *I don't know. What* did *I do?*

As I sentenced Riley to his crate and surveyed the messy room, I spied his big brother, Sam, hiding under the easy chair. The typi-cally perfect older pup had the squeaker from the destroyed toy in his mouth and the remnants of the chewed toy's outer shell beneath him.

I'd proclaimed Riley guilty. But this time, he was only guilty by association. Sam was the real culprit in this crime. (Well, they may have both had a paw in spreading Sam's destruction far and wide.) Riley was simply in the wrong place at the wrong time—keeping company with the wrong guy.

The religious leaders who plotted to crucify Jesus wanted to kill Lazarus as well. But what had Lazarus done to deserve such a sentence other than serve as living proof of the Messiah's miracle-working power? He was guilty by association.

That made me wonder. Am I so closely associated with Christ that I'm guilty of acting like Him? Can I be accused and convicted of imitating His behavior? Of reflecting His nature? When people look at my life, are they convinced I'm a Christian by the love I express? I hope so. —SUSAN DOWNS

FAITH STEP: *Today, strive to live so much like Jesus that anyone who looks at your life would deem you guilty by association with Him.*

WEDNESDAY, MARCH 27

A woman came to him with an alabaster jar of very expensive perfume, which she poured on his head as he was reclining at the table. Matthew 26:7 (NIV)

WHEN OUR FAMILY OF SEVEN prepared to move to South Korea as missionaries, we got rid of everything we owned, other than what would fit in a 6x6 crate. It all had to go. My collection of Coca-Cola memorabilia, including a still-working antique vending machine. Our sons' *Star Wars* action figures and prized baseball cards. Boxes of our daughters' dolls. My husband's motorbike. Every stick of furniture. All of it priced to sell for pennies on the dollar and carted outside for a huge moving sale.

Folks showed up early to get a good bargain, but there were those among them who seemed genuinely concerned. "How can you do this?" "How can you let all your prized possessions go?" They just didn't get it.

That day, rather than sadness, we felt a joyful sense of release and freedom. We were unencumbered, ready to follow Jesus anywhere. Our sacrifices seemed small in comparison to the rich blessings we received in answering His call.

I believe that Lazarus's sister Mary felt this same sense of release as she offered her most valuable possession to Jesus, her Lord. In an act of overwhelming adoration, she freely poured out costly perfume on Him. What some viewed as a waste of resources, Jesus saw as Mary's act of sacrificial worship. The one who had sat at His feet, had listened (Luke 10:39). She got it and prepared Jesus for His death. —SUSAN DOWNS

FAITH STEP: *As an act of sacrificial worship, consider what you can offer Jesus, even if it means risking the ridicule of those who simply don't get it.*

MAUNDY THURSDAY, MARCH 28

Father, if you are willing, take this cup from me; yet not my will, but yours be done. Luke 22:42 (NIV)

MY HOME IS IN TURMOIL, both inside and out. In celebration of our upcoming fiftieth wedding anniversary, my husband and I decided that, rather than going on a trip, we'd remodel our home. The old is gone, and in its place are all things new. Installers have ripped up all the old carpet and tile and are replacing them with luxury vinyl plank flooring. Our kitchen boasts new light fixtures and countertops. A refreshed backsplash should be installed later today. Painters are busy in every room, while another crew tackles the exterior of the house. With much fear and trepidation, we decided to have the brick painted. Once the primer coat was sprayed on, I turned to my husband and said, "There's no turning back now!"

Jesus knew His fate. He understood what He would soon face. Each day carried Him closer to the cross, where He would give His life as a sacrificial lamb, paying the price for our sins. Humanity had proven itself incapable of keeping the old law. So, Christ willingly instituted a new covenant of redemption—through His blood. As He prayed to the Father on the Mount of Olives and agonized over the realization of what would soon come to pass, He appeared to be looking for another solution. And yet, He overcame his fear by submitting, in faith, to His Father's will. As frightening as the reality was of what He would endure in the coming days seemed, He understood. There was no turning back now. —SUSAN DOWNS

FAITH STEP: *In reckless abandon, commit your life so fully to Christ that there's no turning back now!*

GOOD FRIDAY, MARCH 29

Then he opened their minds so they could understand the Scriptures. He told them, "This is what is written: The Messiah will suffer and rise from the dead on the third day, and repentance for the forgiveness of sins will be preached in his name to all nations, beginning at Jerusalem." Luke 24:45–47 (NIV)

UGH! IT HAS HAPPENED AGAIN! Right now, I'm sitting in the Kansas City airport, four hours into delay upon delay as I try to get home. As it stands, it will be the wee hours of the morning before I land on my home turf—if the flight doesn't end up being canceled altogether. Having spent many a night on an airport floor, with a jacket for a pillow, has made me aware of just how awry my travel itinerary can go. What was supposed to be a quick trip to visit extended family has certainly not gone as planned.

The disciples must have felt that way as they witnessed the events of Holy Week. Instead of seeing the establishment of an earthly kingdom under Jesus's royal reign, as they had expected, all their future hopes and dreams seemed to be crumbling before their eyes. They watched as Jesus was betrayed, suffered humiliation, and was led away to a torturous death. Horror and confusion closed their minds. Their memories were faulty. The depths of their despair so clouded their vision that they had forgotten the words Jesus spoke to them as He promised to rise from the dead.

Jesus's death was *definitely* not their plan, but thankfully, for us, it was His. —SUSAN DOWNS

FAITH STEP: *Think of a time when the future looked bleak. How did Jesus work in the most unexpected of ways to bring about His plan in your life?*

SATURDAY, MARCH 30

The angel said to the women, "Do not be afraid, for I know that you are looking for Jesus, who was crucified. He is not here; he has risen, just as he said. Come and see the place where he lay." Matthew 28:5–6 (NIV)

I DEVELOPED A BAD HABIT as a very young reader that I still practice today. When the suspense of a story gets to be too much for me to handle, I skip to the last chapter and read just enough to assure myself that everything works out OK in the end. Of course, this practice drives everyone crazy, except me. But my nerves can't handle the tension of a well-written suspense scene unless I have the promise of a happy ending.

When the earth began to shake and the angel appeared at the tomb of the resurrected Christ, the rough, tough guards passed out from fear. And yet, the women who had come looking for their Lord, while no doubt scared, as the angel acknowledged, weren't fainting in shock or paralyzed with fear. They had walked with Jesus. They'd sat at His feet. They witnessed Him perform miracles. And though the situation looked bleak on that Saturday, sandwiched between the horror of His Crucifixion and the unrealized glory of what would happen on Sunday, Jesus had shown them enough of the story's ending that those women could face whatever happened next. Little did they know, they were about to experience the happiest ending of all time. —SUSAN DOWNS

FAITH STEP: *As you sit in silence this Saturday, go to a place where you can be alone. Feel the sorrow of not knowing the rest of the story. Then focus on the wonder and joy of knowing the truth—Jesus is alive. He has risen!*

EASTER SUNDAY, MARCH 31

*This is my blood of the covenant, which is poured out for many
for the forgiveness of sins. Matthew 26:28 (NIV)*

WHEN I EXPERIENCED EASTER AS a child and then as a mother of
young children, this holy day was highlighted by egg hunts, candy,
bunnies, and chicks, and accented with Easter finery and spring
flowers. After celebrating the Lord's resurrection at a crowded
church, under the leadership of my pastor-husband, our family
would gather around a food-laden table to share a meal and fellowship. No matter where in the world we commemorated the holiday,
Easter was always a hectic, exhausting event.

But this Easter is different. With our home in the midst of a
remodel, I can't even reach my kitchen, much less cook an Easter
feast. My husband's ministry role is no longer that of a local church
pastor, and all our adult children and their families have other obli-
gations today. Our fourteen-year-old grandson, who lives with us,
declared he was officially too old for egg hunts. So, the three of us
peacefully headed to church without all the usual preservice fanfare.

This year, more than any other, I was able to focus on the true
significance of Christ's sacrifice at Calvary, the redemptive act of
His shed blood, and the life-changing power of His resurrection.
The message of Easter saturated my soul and tears of overwhelming
gratitude dampened my cheeks as I sang songs of praise and heard
the pastor tell the sacred story once again. Hallelujah! He is risen!
He is risen indeed! —SUSAN DOWNS

FAITH STEP: *As you prepare your heart for Easter, regardless of the circumstances surrounding you today, focus on the unfathomable sacrifice Jesus made
for you on Calvary and the divine power He exhibits by overcoming death through
His resurrection.*

EASTER MONDAY, APRIL 1

For I can do everything through Christ, who gives me strength.
Philippians 4:13 (NLT)

STOPPING AT THE MAILBOX TO retrieve a package, I spotted a woman running down the street, pursuing two huge Great Pyrenees dogs. She'd caught one of them by the collar, but the other, collarless, eluded her. For a cat person like me, grabbing that big dog was a daunting proposition, but with cars whizzing by, I had no choice but to tackle the furry critter. I had him, but now what?

"Would you mind putting Moose in your car?" she asked as she made her way to me. "I can help and my house is just down the way."

I glanced at the petite woman. No way could we two lightweights put a struggling dog into the cargo space of my SUV. *Impossible!* I thought. But then I felt Jesus whisper, "You can!" My favorite scripture, Philippians 4:13, came to mind. How many times had that verse sustained me emotionally in times of grief and desperation? But today what I needed was sheer *physical* strength.

I opened the hatch, shoving sports gear aside, as Jesus, the woman, and I hefted Moose into the small space. I drove slowly down the street, praying the hatch wouldn't fly open.

Finally, we reached Moose's house. A man emerged with a leash and ran to retrieve the dog.

"How in the world did you get Moose in here?" he asked.

"Brute strength," I said. "And Jesus." —PAT BUTLER DYSON

FAITH STEP: *Whether it's emotional or physical strength you need, ask Jesus to provide it. Memorize Philippians 4:13 and store it in your heart.*

TUESDAY, APRIL 2

So then, just as you received Christ Jesus as Lord, continue to live your lives in him, rooted and built up in him, strengthened in the faith as you were taught, and overflowing with thankfulness. Colossians 2:6–7 (NIV)

WHEN WE MOVED INTO OUR house two years ago, our backyard was a giant swath of sandy dirt. We hired landscapers to put down 3 inches of topsoil followed by emerald-green sod. I was thrilled. The grass was picture-perfect—lush and green. I loved every inch of it until the winter snow melted away and I noticed tracks of dead grass spread across my lawn. I texted a picture to my mom. She said it looked like I had voles. Voles can destroy a healthy lawn. Under the snow, these tiny meadow mice create pathways in the turf. They gnaw the grass down to the root, killing it. It is hard to love your lawn when it looks like a mini-maze for Stuart Little and his friends. I reseeded the dead patches. Because I love my lawn, I wanted to see it grow.

There are areas in my life, hidden under the cover of busyness or neglect, that are dead or dying. Patches of bitterness. Tracks of envy. Trails of anger. Nothing grows there. Just as I reseeded all the dead patches in my lawn, Jesus wants to sow in these dark places of my heart. He wants to heal and restore me so I can grow.

I will never be picture-perfect like my lawn, but growing in Jesus, I become more beautiful each day. —SUSANNA FOTH AUGHTMON

FAITH STEP: *Sit outside and prayerfully ask Jesus to examine your heart. Are there dying areas that He needs to reseed with His love and grace? Ask Him to heal your heart and help you grow.*

WEDNESDAY, APRIL 3

*You can ask him for anything, using my name, and I will do it,
for this will bring praise to the Father because of what I, the Son,
will do for you. John 14:13 (TLB)*

"DID YOU HEAR WHAT HAPPENED?" the jubilant antiques and collectibles merchant asked. "I couldn't find my wallet and searched everywhere—at home and here in my store for three days." He described how my husband, John, who does odd jobs for him, had also looked for the wallet among furniture, vintage clothing, jewelry, framed art, and books.

With no success, John declared, "We need to *pray* about this!" Stopping straightaway, he earnestly prayed aloud, asking Jesus to help the man find his missing wallet. Finishing the short, spontaneous prayer, he said, "Amen" and left. Before John reached his truck, the shopkeeper threw open the old storefront glass door, shouting, "I found it!" It had fallen into a box of vinyl records.

I rejoiced upon hearing this immediate answer to prayer. I was happy our friend found his wallet. But mostly I was thrilled with the testimony of Jesus's power to answer a simple, ordinary, everyday prayer. More importantly, had John not turned the matter over to Jesus and prayed aloud boldly, our friend would've missed more than his wallet. He would have missed the chance to see how Jesus truly does hear and answer our prayers. —CASSANDRA TIERSMA

FAITH STEP: *Is boldness missing from your prayer life? Pray aloud for a friend in Jesus's name, confident that your petition will be heard.*

Thursday, April 4

Let us acknowledge the Lord; let us press on to acknowledge him. As surely as the sun rises, he will appear; he will come to us like the winter rains, like the spring rains that water the earth. Hosea 6:3 (NIV)

I struggle with seasonal depression between winter and summer with its cloudy skies and frequent rains. I long for sunnier, warmer days when flowers bloom and beautiful things grow rather than the mud and mess of early spring. Last April was worse than usual as I wrestled with grief and loss. My dad passed away a few months earlier and an empty nest was looming ahead. My emotions mirrored the soggy, gray days that seemed endless.

That's why I scoffed when my husband said we desperately needed rain. Hadn't we had enough? Ron was raised a farmer. He knows the importance of spring rains to saturate the soil. Seeds won't grow when there's a drought in early spring. The ground will be desperate for moisture throughout the growing season.

Ron's comment reminded me that the difficult, transitional season I was experiencing was as necessary for me as it was for nature. Emotions, like spring rains, soften hard seasons, especially those filled with loss. My sadness and tears would not last forever. But experiencing them was essential for my soul. Maybe Jesus wanted to grow things from the melancholy and grief. Like the spring soil, my soul needed to be tender. —Brenda L. Yoder

Faith Step: *Are you experiencing a season of loss? Trust what God is growing in you as you wait for brighter days.*

FRIDAY, APRIL 5

Many are the plans in a person's heart, but it is the LORD's purpose that prevails. Proverbs 19:21 (NIV)

ONE DAY, I WAS WORKING on a project I was determined to finish. My silenced cell phone was on my desk. After an hour of productive work, my screen lit up. A friend was calling. *I'll call her later.* But a strong urge to answer tugged at me. I picked up my phone.

Her son had recently lost his job. She shared her concerns and fears and then we prayed together. After hanging up, I went back to work and tried to shake off the interruption.

Jesus, too, was interrupted. While He was speaking in a home, some friends ripped through the roof and lowered a paralyzed man on a stretcher to His feet for healing (Mark 2:1–12). When Jesus sought solitude after finding out about John the Baptist's beheading, He saw the crowds had followed Him. Jesus had compassion on them and put aside His personal pain to heal their sick (Matthew 14:13–14). Another time, Jesus was in a boat with his disciples, napping. When they were frightened by the storm and awakened Him, He calmed the waves (Matthew 8:23–27). Jesus used interruptions as opportunities to let the world know about Him and the Father.

I'd just finished my project when my friend called again. Her son found a new job! I was glad I took the time to pray with her earlier. I said a little prayer of my own to thank Jesus for an interruption that turned out to be an opportunity to witness a miraculous moment for my friend and me. —JEANNIE BLACKMER

FAITH STEP: *Place people above your plans today. Then, tonight, write down how interruptions became meaningful moments in your day.*

SATURDAY, APRIL 6

But whoever looks intently into the perfect law that gives freedom, and continues in it—not forgetting what they have heard, but doing it—they will be blessed in what they do. James 1:25 (NIV)

A FRIEND'S TRAUMATIC BRAIN INJURY left her with innumerable challenges. Swallowing, eating, speaking, sitting, standing, walking— all had to be relearned as her brain healed.

Her type of head injury often brings lingering double vision. Imagine how disorienting that would be, especially for a person who struggles to stand and maintain equilibrium without that added disadvantage.

She was prescribed prism glasses to help break up and realign that second distracting, disorienting image. I wonder what would happen if I had special glasses to help me see hope with more clarity, to recognize the image of Jesus standing in front of me, offering His hand to stabilize me.

Ah, but I *do* have that advantage. The "spectacles" I need are the pages of the Bible, the story of Jesus foretold in the Old Testament and revealed in the New Testament. All distorted images come into focus when I focus my attention on the words and life of Jesus.

I don't know what my friend's special glasses cost her, but I've had a glimpse of what it cost Jesus to provide hope for me. I can either fight the distortion this world hands me or peer intently into the Word that offers clear vision, stability for my faith walk, and sweet resolution of what threatens to frighten or dizzy me. The choice is clear! —CYNTHIA RUCHTI

FAITH STEP: *Have you been squinting to catch a glimpse of hope and peace in your current circumstances? Try looking at life through the pages of Scripture.*

SUNDAY, APRIL 7

Now that I, your Lord and Teacher, have washed your feet, you also should wash one another's feet. I have set you an example that you should do as I have done for you. John 13:14–15 (NIV)

MY HUSBAND AND I DECIDED to treat our children to a nice Chinese food restaurant after church one Sunday. Our party of six gathered around a large circular table and shared egg rolls, fried rice, and a variety of entrées via the fancy rotating tray in the center. Our waiter, a young man named Justin, checked on us often, anticipated our needs, and served us with an infectious smile.

When the check came, we were prepared to spend more than we usually do when we eat out. However, our bill contained an unexpected surprise. The amount due was crossed out in red and "Paid" was written beside it. We scoured the faces of the other restaurant patrons, then called our waiter when we couldn't find anyone we knew. We asked who had paid for our meal, and Justin answered brightly, "I did!" He said it was his custom to choose one table per shift and pay for the meal himself.

I was moved by Justin's generosity, but more than that, I realized how well he had modeled the love of Jesus. Jesus loved others first by serving them, as He did when He washed His disciples' feet. Then He loved others by going to the cross and paying the debt for our sins. The gratefulness I felt when I saw our meal had been paid for pales in comparison to how I feel when I remember that Jesus paid the debt for my sins. —EMILY E. RYAN

FAITH STEP: *Share Jesus's love by serving someone or even by paying their bill.*

MONDAY, APRIL 8

God is love. Whoever lives in love lives in God, and God in them.
1 John 4:16 (NIV)

I HAD PURCHASED A WAFFLE maker at a yard sale and wanted to give it to my aunt, which was weird because while I appreciate a good yard sale find, my aunt preferred new items in unopened packages. When I called to ask if I could visit, she said, "You're a love letter." I didn't understand, so she explained, "I asked Jesus to show me He loved me, and you called."

Then I woke up.

The dream hovered over me the rest of the morning, partly because I missed my aunt, whom I had cared for during her final months of life, but also because the dream felt like an assignment. Was I Jesus's love letter?

I think so…when I weeded and mulched an elderly neighbor's flower beds, or donated to a young woman's mission trip to Paraguay, or made a coffee date with a friend struggling with impossible family issues.

But maybe not…when my husband ignored food splatters in the microwave, or when the delivery person left a package in the rain (again), or when I finally reached a human after convincing a computer voice it couldn't solve my billing issue.

Is being Jesus's love letter different from loving my neighbor as myself? Maybe. The sender is Jesus, not me. A letter from Him carries His love, not mine. I don't want someone to experience my attitude or impatience instead of the love Jesus is trying to deliver through me!

Maybe the whole love letter thing was just a silly dream. But it sure gave me something to think about. —KAREN SARGENT

FAITH STEP: *Call, text, or send a card to remind someone how much you and Jesus love them.*

TUESDAY, APRIL 9

He who was seated on the throne said, "I am making everything new!"
Then he said, "Write this down, for these words are trustworthy and true."
Revelation 21:5 (NIV)

MY FIRST HOUSE WAS A 100-year-old rowhouse in a quaint colonial Maryland town, which was then a tourism hot spot. Sold by a disinterested, faraway daughter after her mother died, it was a real deal for me.

The house had gleaming hardwood floors, an oak banister, a marble fireplace, and probably most important, all new plumbing, wiring, and drywall. Sometime in its history, my new home had been stripped to the studs and everything had been replaced or upgraded to current code.

A friend bought a similar property right up the street, but it had not yet been renovated. She and her husband got to work. As they tore away plaster, they found rotting wood, termites, moldy newspaper insulation, dangerous old wiring, and rodent remains. It was a mess. Once they were done, though, it was gleamingly beautiful. It took a long time.

Just as old houses can be updated, so can I. The Bible tells me that in Christ, I'm a new creation (2 Corinthians 5:17), but the renovation process—sanctification, making me more like Jesus—happens over time. Sometimes this process of spiritual growth feels like gutting an old house. My outside can still look rough, even though there's work in progress on the inside. But no job is too big for Jesus. He makes all things new, including me and my lifetime of debris. —ISABELLA CAMPOLATTARO

FAITH STEP: *Draw a picture of a house and decorate it with words to describe all the ways Jesus has transformed you since your own renovation began.*

WEDNESDAY, APRIL 10

For what good will it do a person if he gains the whole world, but forfeits his soul? Or what will a person give in exchange for his soul?
Matthew 16:26 *(NASB)*

RATS! THERE I WAS IN the shower, soaking wet, about to wash my hair, when I spotted my shampoo on the bathroom counter. I could skate across the slippery tile floor and grab it, but instead, I spied another bottle of shampoo right in front of me—a flea and tick shampoo for dogs. It had been in the shower since our daughter's Chihuahua, Hercules, had visited.

I doubted dog shampoo would enhance my highlights, but it made Hercules's coat shiny. I poured a dab in my hand. It smelled good! And on the off chance I developed a flea infestation, I'd be protected.

Substitutes are iffy. I sometimes substitute ingredients while baking when I'm out of something necessary for the recipe. The results have been mixed. Once I accidentally filled my car with gasoline instead of diesel fuel, with a disastrous outcome.

I thought better about using the dog shampoo, so I gingerly crept across the tile to nab my regular shampoo. As I was drying my hair, I wondered what I'd been thinking.

Although some things can be substituted, some cannot—like living a life with Jesus at the center. Occasionally, I fill my day with frenzied activity, skipping my devotional time. At the end of the day, although I may have accomplished much, I feel empty. There is no material thing, no one, or nothing that can come close to Jesus. Accept no substitutes! —PAT BUTLER DYSON

FAITH STEP: *As you do something mindless today, like showering or drying your hair, ask Jesus if you are substituting anything for Him.*

THURSDAY, APRIL 11

Why, my soul, are you downcast? Why so disturbed within me?
Put your hope in God, for I will yet praise him, my Savior and
my God. Psalm 42:11 (NIV)

LAST WINTER HUNG ON FOR what felt like forever. It began when the sky turned gray in early November. Rain fell nearly every day for nine weeks. Living on a boat presented unique challenges. Mildew grew inside my kitchen cupboards and on the wood paneling in our sleeping berth despite our best efforts to reduce humidity.

January arrived. Showers turned to snow when temperatures dropped below freezing. The river froze, and ice thunked and scraped against our sailboat's hull. My husband rose early every morning to shovel the dock, and I sprinkled salt to melt its frosty glaze. Inside our boat, condensation collected and dripped from the hatches.

The frigid Arctic front lasted two weeks. One day, the temperature rose slightly, and the ice and snow melted into puddles and slush, but then the rain returned. By mid-March, I was emotionally done with overcast skies, damp cold, and mildew wars. I craved sunshine and warmth, flowers, and the freedom to take a long walk without getting soaked.

And then it happened: the clouds parted and the sun appeared. I headed outside for a stroll along the river, and that's when I saw the purple crocus. Its bloom cheered me. The sight was like salve for my weather-beaten soul. The simple flower was a reminder that winter's gray and chill would not last forever. The seemingly endless season that caused distress would pass in God's time. Brighter days, teeming with hope and new beginnings, were ahead. —GRACE FOX

FAITH STEP: *Recall a way in which Jesus has given you a sign of hope in the midst of a difficult season.*

Friday, April 12

Our faith may fail, his never wanes—That's who he is, he cannot change!
2 Timothy 2:13 (ISV)

Significant changes took place around the world in 2020. Even though the pandemic raged, not everything that happened for me was bad. My husband, Michael, who'd been employed full-time at a wholesale hardware firm for thirty-one years, was assigned to work temporarily and later permanently from home.

Frankly, I felt apprehensive. *How will this work-from-home arrangement work out?* Michael was used to, and had enjoyed, reporting to an office. A freelance writer myself, we'd now be home together 24/7.

In years past, Michael usually grabbed a bagel as he hurried out the door, and I often skipped breakfast. After a few days of this new arrangement, Michael and I started having breakfast together. Lingering over coffee, we'd pray, committing our day to Jesus. Sometimes, I read a devotional aloud. We'd chat and share insights.

During these early-morning talks, I got to know my husband in new ways. When we wed thirty years ago, I was the mother of a three-year-old from a previous marriage. We became an instant family—thrown into the pressures of marriage, parenting, and blending our lives. There was little time to stop, talk, or have leisurely meals.

As horrible as the pandemic has been with all the deaths and changes that have occurred, one thing has remained unchanged—Jesus. Even when relationship changes in my life look like endings, He brings hope and new beginnings. —Jennifer Anne F. Messing

Faith Step: *Thank Jesus for His unchanging nature and ability to bring fresh hope in the midst of adversity.*

SATURDAY, APRIL 13

He stretches out the north over empty space; He hangs the earth on nothing. Job 26:7 (NKJV)

ONE MORE BIN OUGHT TO *do it.*

My pantry door was opened wide while I finished a weekend project reorganizing cans, cereal boxes, snack bars, packages of cookies, and other food goods that had overtaken the space. I reached for the last bin, perfect for lunch-box snacks, then slipped it onto a shelf between two other bins.

I stood back and exhaled a sigh of satisfaction. *Everything had a place and everything in its place.*

A memory flashed of when we moved in, when this pantry was empty, void of any sign that a family lived here. There was plenty now. In fact, when I rearranged things, I packed up the overflow to send with my parents, who had just moved into their new home—with empty cabinets that needed filling.

On a much more impactful scale, Jesus takes the empty, unfilled areas of our lives and makes something of them. Whether emptiness comes from loss or conflict or unhealed parts of our hearts, Jesus does not need our resources to fill us. He can rebuild our lives from nothing.

If life feels empty these days, ask Jesus to do it again—to recreate, rebuild, restore, renew. Not just a little but to overflowing so that you can offer the overflow of His love to others who need their empty places filled. —ERIN KEELEY MARSHALL

FAITH STEP: *Ask Jesus to show you if there's an emptiness in you that needs His filling. Then ask Him to help you experience His overflow.*

Sunday, April 14

There is one body and one Spirit, just as you were called to one hope when you were called; one Lord, one faith, one baptism; one God and Father of all, who is over all and through all and in all. Ephesians 4:4—6 (NIV)

ON A NARROW, OLD BOARD, my artist friend painted in a frenzy of inspiration. No careful, definite lines. Only free strokes of varying widths and lengths with uneven edges. Dominant colors of bright yellow and hot pink. Glossy accent shades of blue, turquoise, and red. A dash of glitter across random, overlapping shapes. The final touch, a beloved symbol, created using pearl beads and glue.

I wish you could see the finished masterpiece hanging in my office—an image of a lovely chapel, topped with a pearl cross.

The art blesses me daily by adding light and cheer to my work environment. But bigger than that, the chapel prompts me to reflect on the church of Jesus. As members, we come in many shapes and colors, widths and lengths, uneven edges and all. Some people glitter for the Kingdom in prominent places, while others serve faithfully in accent positions. Yet, we are one body, led by one Spirit, following the one Savior of the world.

We share a common hope too—the hope of heaven. Someday all believers—past, present, and future—will gather in the same glorious place and worship Jesus together. Walls decorated with sapphire, emerald, and amethyst stones. A pure gold street, transparent like glass. Gates of pearl. Perhaps I should ask my artist friend to paint that. —BECKY ALEXANDER

FAITH STEP: *Read the beautiful description of the walls, gates, and street in Revelation 21:19—21. Think about what it will be like there. Thank Jesus for His church and the hope of heaven.*

MONDAY, APRIL 15

When Jesus spoke again to the people, he said, "I am the light of the world. Whoever follows me will never walk in darkness, but will have the light of life." John 8:12 (NIV)

OUR FAMILY ENJOYS GOING ON walks. After dinner, we head outside to make a 1-mile loop around the neighborhood. While most roads have streetlights, one corner's light rarely works. Knowing this, my husband, John, carries a flashlight. As we near the darkened corner, he turns it on. The glow from the flashlight is wide enough for us to see the road and feel safe. Just as important, it also allows approaching cars to see our group.

The light of Jesus came after 400 years of silence from God (Malachi 4:5–6). No prophets spoke for the Lord or led His people during that time. Yet Jesus's arrival declared a change. For all those who had been hoping and waiting for illumination from a man of God, His Son was that light. Those who followed Jesus walked with the Light of the World. Jesus brought God's presence, protection, and guidance back into the world once again.

The same is true for me more than 2,000 years later. The light of Jesus enables me to see myself as I really am—a sinner in need of a Savior. When I stay close to Jesus, His light is a wide enough circle for me to clearly see how to avoid evil and to feel safe with Him. Jesus's light keeps the darkness at bay, no matter where I walk.

—TRICIA GOYER

FAITH STEP: *Tonight, take a flashlight outside after dark or into a darkened room. Notice how that light illuminates the darkness as you thank Jesus for shining His light into your life.*

TUESDAY, APRIL 16

Then Jesus told them this parable: "Suppose one of you has a hundred sheep and loses one of them. Doesn't he leave the ninety-nine in the open country and go after the lost sheep until he finds it?" Luke 15:3–4 (NIV)

I OPENED FACEBOOK ONE MORNING, and my heart sank at the first post that appeared. A missing person report had been filed for one of my former students, a fifteen-year-old girl. She never came home after an evening walk in her neighborhood. I immediately began praying for her and her family but wished there was more I could do.

Not knowing where to begin, I drove aimlessly around her neighborhood before work, knowing even as I weaved through the suburbs that my efforts wouldn't amount to anything. My mind was distracted the entire day, and my heart grieved every time I checked social media for updates and didn't find any.

Thankfully, a day later, the teen was found safe and reunited with her family. Our community praised Jesus for the happy ending. As I celebrated, I couldn't help but process the desperation I'd felt when someone I knew was unaccounted for and the joy I'd felt when she was found. I finally understood Jesus's parable of the lost sheep. I'd been willing to leave everything behind if it meant finding the girl who was missing, like a shepherd in search of a missing sheep. I'm so thankful that my Shepherd, Jesus, pursues me when I stray. I'd wanted to celebrate and party when my former student was found, and Jesus feels the same way when I repent and return to Him.
—EMILY E. RYAN

FAITH STEP: *Have you strayed from Jesus? Return to Him through prayer and repentance, then let the celebration begin!*

WEDNESDAY, APRIL 17

---

*Peter asked, "Lord, why can't I follow you now? I will lay
down my life for you." John 13:37 (NIV)*

WHEN MY STYLIST, ROSIE, SPRAYED the lovely hairdo she'd created, I thanked her for the third time. I had a standing appointment with Rosie. But when surprises popped onto my calendar, she opened her shop on a day she was usually closed. Just for me.

Her answer to my profuse thanks left me speechless. "Jeanette, I'd do anything for you."

No one had ever spoken those six words to me before. I felt so loved. So treasured.

Rosie's statement stayed with me for weeks, playing in my heart like a long-beloved hymn. I knew her words weren't just sweet sentiments from a dear friend. Rosie meant them. Her actions proved it.

As I pondered Rosie's shocking statement, I thought of my relationship with Jesus. Was I willing to tell Him, "Lord, I'd do anything for You"? How risky. What if He asked me to empty my savings and give it to mission work? Or to move to Alaska? (I hate cold weather.) And even more than giving money or relocating, was I willing to give up doing life my own selfish way? That was the true test of whether I could honestly tell Jesus I'd do anything for Him.

I took a deep breath. "Jesus, I don't know if I can wholeheartedly say I'd do anything for You. Please help me to be willing to give up my material goods, my comfort, and mostly my own plans to follow You."

After all, that's what Jesus did for me. —JEANETTE LEVELLIE

FAITH STEP: *Are you willing to do anything for Jesus? Ponder the question for several days and see what Jesus reveals to you.*

THURSDAY, APRIL 18

---

*Can a mother forget the baby at her breast and have no compassion
on the child she has borne? Though she may forget, I will not forget you!*
Isaiah 49:15 (NIV)

DURING A VISIT WITH MY grandchildren, I snuggled with five-year-old Lilah as she showed me the bracelet kit she'd received in her Easter basket. One by one, she held up each tiny, colorful rubber charm with a loop to attach it to the bracelet. Lilah paused as she returned the seahorse charm to the organizer box. Then she handed it to me and spoke softly: "Here, Nana. You keep this one to help you remember me after you leave." As if I ever needed any prompt to remember this darling little girl! Regardless of how much time passes between visits, my children, grandchildren, and other family members are in my thoughts every day.

So is Jesus. How could I ever need a reminder to think about the One who gave His life for me? Each day, I see reminders of Him—in the beauty of creation, the sound of praise music, the nudges in my spirit, and especially in His Word.

What amazes me is that Jesus continuously holds *me* in His thoughts. Every day, He reaches out to offer what I need at any given moment: strength, guidance, encouragement, conviction, peace. Even when I neglect our relationship in ways that make me feel there's a distance between us, Jesus holds me in His loving thoughts while drawing my heart back closer to Him. That is something I could never forget. —DIANNE NEAL MATTHEWS

FAITH STEP: *Take a few breaks during the day to remind yourself that Jesus is thinking about you. Thank Him for His ever-present love and provision.*

FRIDAY, APRIL 19

To this you were called, because Christ suffered for you, leaving you an example, that you should follow in his steps. 1 Peter 2:21 *(NIV)*

I HAVE A GOLDEN POTHOS plant in my office. Because I want the space to look a certain way, it's placed between the window and the heating vent. One side of the plant gets indirect sun from the window. The other side gets direct heat as the furnace blasts to warm the house. Consequently, I have to keep turning the plant every so often so all the leaves get gentle sunlight and only have to tolerate heat for so long.

Sitting on the floor the other day gave me a new angle to view the plant's stems. I noticed that they dip, rise, and turn like the pipes in our plumbing. I've never seen a plant do that before. Apparently, each time I move the plant, it has to adjust, finding a new path away from the scorching heat and back to the gentle sunshine.

When my son was in kindergarten, his teacher would hang a "visual model" for each project on the wall. It gave the students a clear picture of what they were supposed to be working toward.

I think my plant is Jesus's visual model for me. In very concrete terms, He's telling me that no matter how much life spins me in circles and no matter how hot my circumstances get, if I turn and grow gently toward Him, I'll thrive. It may take flexibility and routine pivoting, but feeling the Son shine on me is worth it.
—CLAIRE MCGARRY

FAITH STEP: *Take a few moments to look closely at a plant in your home. Is there anything notable about it that could be a lesson Jesus wants you to learn?*

SATURDAY, APRIL 20

*In all my prayers for all of you, I always pray with joy because of
your partnership in the gospel from the first day until now, being
confident of this, that he who began a good work in you will carry it on
to completion until the day of Christ Jesus. Philippians 1:4–6 (NIV)*

I SHARE A LOVE OF gardening with my parents. When they called
to let me know they'd be coming to Idaho this spring, I got really
excited. I love visiting with my parents, but I also love how they
help me in my yard.

In the past three years, my backyard has gone from a rectangular
patch of hard-packed soil to a lush lawn, four vegetable beds, three
decorative trees, three fruit trees, and two flower beds that hug
the back of the house. This is largely due to my parents. Mom is the
visionary, and Dad is the muscle. Each time they've visited, we've
worked together to add beauty to the space. And we're going to keep
working. As my mom says, "There's always room for more flowers."

Jesus has been working in the hard-packed soil of my life for a
whole lot longer than three years. I have lots of hopes and dreams
and tons of plans for my life. But Jesus is both the visionary and the
muscle when it comes to changing my heart. He has begun good
work in me. And He promises that He will finish what He started
and make all spaces of my life more beautiful. There's always more
room in my life for Jesus. —SUSANNA FOTH AUGHTMON

FAITH STEP: *Think about what Jesus is doing in the soil of your life. Meditate
on Philippians 1:4–6 and be confident knowing He will finish the work He has
started in you.*

SUNDAY, APRIL 21

May the God of hope fill you with all joy and peace as you trust in him,
so that you may overflow with hope by the power of the Holy Spirit.
Romans 15:13 (NIV)

INTERSTATE 57 IS AN IMPORTANT stretch of road for me. A couple of years ago, our family was heading out to Indiana to celebrate my nephew's high school graduation. While my husband drove, I caught a glimpse of a familiar road sign alerting us that we were 73 miles from Kankakee, Illinois. I grinned.

My first job out of college as an admissions counselor included attending college fairs across the country. Part of my recruiting territory was Illinois. My first overnight assignment was to attend a college fair in Kankakee. I was going to drive by myself from Chicago and check into a hotel room alone. I sat on my parents' bed gripped by fear and covered in tears. Mom was nervous too. I called home regularly from my Motorola car phone to let her know I was safe. When I arrived at the fair and then returned the next day, we all paused to thank Jesus.

Fast-forward three decades. I laugh at how that 60-mile drive to Kankakee seemed so far from Chicago. Seeing the sign reminded me of how far I've come in trusting Jesus's protection and peace and the knowledge that Jesus accompanies me wherever I go.
—ERICKA LOYNES

FAITH STEP: *Identify a sign or slogan that reminds you of Jesus's ever-present protection. Write it down and hang it in a spot where you'll see it often so you can thank Him for all He does for you.*

MONDAY, APRIL 22

If we acknowledge our sins, then, since he is trustworthy and just, he will forgive them and purify us from all wrongdoing. 1 John 1:9 (CJB)

WHILE LOADING THE WASHER, I spotted a grease stain on my jeans that I remembered seeing the last time I pulled them out of the dryer. The odds were against getting the stain out now. Still, I rubbed in my pink stain remover paste and gave it plenty of time to work. I figured it was worth a shot.

When I took them out of the washer, I saw it failed. The stain was set in. My pants were demoted to stay-at-home clothes.

In certain instances, when the Israelites were unclean, they had to wash their bodies and clothing, then wait to be declared clean. The leaves of the hyssop plant were used for purging and purification. Hyssop caused sweating in baths, cleansing the pores. It is an antioxidant, antimicrobial, and disinfectant. After sinning with Bathsheba, David said, "Purge me with hyssop, and I shall be clean: wash me, and I shall be whiter than snow" (Psalm 51:7, KJV). Before Passover, the Israelites bathed, then painted the blood of an unblemished lamb with hyssop branches onto the doorposts and lintels of their homes.

Ceremonial bathing and washing of clothes were never works of righteousness but rather the acknowledgment of sin, helplessness, and need. I sin daily, but Jesus shed His blood to wash me. When He thirsted on the cross, it was a hyssop branch that held up the vinegar-soaked sponge so Jesus could wet His lips.

I can't scrub away a grease stain, but I'm grateful Jesus cleansed me—all of us—from sin's stain. —SUZANNE DAVENPORT TIETJEN

FAITH STEP: *Confess your sins out loud while washing dishes or bathing this morning. Then watch the suds go down the drain.*

TUESDAY, APRIL 23

When Jesus saw him lying there and learned that he had been in this condition for a long time, he asked him, "Do you want to get well?" John 5:6 (NIV)

THE STORY OF JESUS'S HEALING of the lame man at the pool of Bethesda (John 5:2–9) intrigues me. The man sat poolside for days, weeks, months, and finally thirty-eight years, never reaching the water, which, superstitious legend at that time stated, would give healing to the first person in the pool when the water stirred. I wonder if he grew weary of the hopelessness of losing the race. And yet, he doggedly continued.

I get that. I've spent years waiting for a miracle. Like the man, sometimes just showing up is all I have left. I've raced to the waters only to find I've been beaten to the blessing once again. I've waited until my backside was sore from doing nothing and perfected excuses for my lack of success. Could I, or the man at the pool, have allowed this problem to become so familiar that it became part of my identity?

I forgot Jesus stood beside me all along, asking that one simple question. If I want and need Jesus to heal that broken something inside me, I just need to answer Him. My life isn't a race, and Jesus doesn't help just a lucky few—the fastest or the most worthy. He is here to help me overcome the obstacles holding me back.

It's time I pick up my mat and walk (John 5:9). —HEIDI GAUL

FAITH STEP: *Research ways to overcome or adapt to a physical or emotional infirmity. Apply at least one step daily, as you take up your mat and walk.*

WEDNESDAY, APRIL 24

One day Jesus was praying in a certain place. When he finished,
one of his disciples said to him, "Lord, teach us to pray, just as
John taught his disciples." Luke 11:1 (NIV)

ONE AFTERNOON, I WALKED AND talked with Jesus about a friend who seemed super-stuck in a spiritual rut. I'd prayed for her for years, but my prayers seemed to miss the mark, and her outlook only grew more negative. That day, I felt desperate on her behalf. "Teach me to pray," I said to Jesus. "Show me the root problem."

Jesus answered by placing this thought in my mind: *This is a spiritual battle. Pray against jealousy and unforgiveness in her heart.* I knew my friend's painful history with a couple of individuals, so this insight made complete sense. It changed the way I prayed for her from that point on.

Rather than offering generic requests such as "change her" and "work in her heart," I began doing strategic battle on her behalf by asking Jesus to transform her by renewing her mind (Romans 12:2). I asked Him to shine His light into her thoughts and to dispel the darkness by revealing those that weren't aligned with His truth. I prayed that she would begin to live by the Holy Spirit so that He could produce His good fruit in her life (Galatians 5:22–25).

I didn't see instant answers, but I gained confidence to believe my prayers now hit the mark. I trusted that Jesus would bring about a good outcome in His time and in His way. —GRACE FOX

FAITH STEP: *Go for a leisurely walk and talk with Jesus as you would a good friend. Ask Him to teach you how to pray for a loved one who's hurting.*

THURSDAY, APRIL 25

You do not have because you do not ask. James 4:2 (NKJV)

"WHICH HAND IS IT IN?" My husband held out clenched fists, urging our toddler granddaughter to guess where a treat was hiding. A toy? Fruit snack? Small box of raisins? She chose his left hand. An empty palm. She then tapped on his right hand, joy lighting her eyes.

Our granddaughter kept tapping, knowing a surprise or treat was in his grasp. But Grandpa didn't open his hand. So her little fingers tried to pry them open. But Grandpa was strong and thick-fingered. Our granddaughter was not likely to win that contest. Grandpa freely unfurled his fist and revealed the cookie she'd been waiting for. What kind of cruel man would he be if he demanded her small fingers force his hand open or withheld the treat?

I'm grateful I don't need to pry blessing or provision from Jesus's hands. His palms are always open and generous with us. He longs to give and demonstrates it daily. Consider His overt and outrageous generosity with the thief on the cross (Luke 23:39–43). The man had led a miserable life of crime and deceit, yet Jesus offered the penitent thief paradise with Him.

When I feel as though my prayers turn to begging or are no more effective than a tiny girl trying to pry open a strong man's grip, I'm reminded that I'm petitioning a generous Jesus who wants to give me gifts in line with His will. All I have to do is ask. —CYNTHIA RUCHTI

FAITH STEP: *As you pray today, sit with your palms opened and facing upward. Consider concluding your prayers with: "Thank You for hearing me. Thank You for Your generosity. Thank You for Your openhandedness toward me."*

Friday, April 26

Who can say, "I have cleansed my heart; I am pure and free from sin"?
Proverbs 20:9 (NLT)

My hubby and I love do-it-yourself projects and watching shows about people fixing and remodeling their homes. We're idealists who believe we can accomplish anything with a little time and effort. But after many projects that morphed into new challenges, we've begun to admit we can't do everything ourselves. We were recently planning to repair the sidewalk leading up to our front door. As we discussed the jackhammering required, we decided it might be time to hire a professional.

Likewise, there is a spiritual project I'm unable to do for myself. I can't reconcile myself to God through my own efforts. I can't cleanse my own heart. In my own power, I have no hope of freedom from sin and its effects. They are caked in like stubborn concrete.

Sometimes I dive into attempts to grow spiritually as if it's a do-it-yourself project that I can accomplish through my own aspiration and willpower. When I fail to see the progress I want, this effort can lead me to despair. Even worse, occasionally I notice improvements in my faith walk and give myself all the credit. If I think I'm doing great on my own, those small successes can stir misplaced pride.

Just as I need an experienced professional with the right tools to chip away our old sidewalk, I need Jesus to break through the hard places of my heart and restore me. Only He is the skilled contractor who can remodel my heart and mind. —Sharon Hinck

Faith Step: *Spiritual growth isn't a do-it-yourself project. Write down areas where you need renovation and growth and pray for renewal from the Master Carpenter.*

SATURDAY, APRIL 27

Your throne, O God, will last for ever and ever; a scepter of justice will be the scepter of your kingdom. Psalm 45:6 (NIV)

RECENTLY, I HAD THE PRIVILEGE of speaking at the funeral of my friend Thomas Graumann. I first heard of Thomas on a mission trip to the Czech Republic over a decade ago. At age eight, Thomas— a Jew—was placed on a train by his mother to prevent him from being taken to a concentration camp during World War II. Thomas survived and was raised by a single woman in Scotland while his family perished.

I had the opportunity to work with Thomas and write his life story. Amazingly, he became a Christian missionary and a nurse. Then, after he retired from nursing, he returned to the Czech Republic to share his story of being twice rescued, first on a train and second by believing in Jesus Christ.

While Thomas could have been bitter about all that had happened, he instead decided to trust in God's justice. Thomas knew everyone would someday stand before Jesus and receive eternal life or God's wrath (2 Corinthians 5:10), a message that made his job as a missionary so important. Until his last breath, Thomas did all he could to make sure others could know the hope he'd found in Christ.

Trusting that Jesus is on the throne changed everything for Thomas, me, and all believers. —TRICIA GOYER

FAITH STEP: *Is there bitterness in your heart against someone who hurt you? Journal about what happened, then write that person's name on a sheet of paper. Pray for that person, knowing Jesus's judgment is the only one that matters.*

SUNDAY, APRIL 28

---

*In a loud voice they were saying: "Worthy is the Lamb, who was slain,
to receive power and wealth and wisdom and strength and honor
and glory and praise!" Revelation 5:12 (NIV)*

THE FIRST TIME I ATTENDED a praise and worship service, I was intrigued. A band played upbeat songs. I looked around and saw many people with their hands raised and eyes closed. Some were even swaying and crying. I was new to this kind of worship. In the traditional church where I grew up, we sang a song or two from our thick hymnal, then listened stoically. We were devout, but we didn't show the exuberance these folks had when they worshipped. Newly saved and fresh out of college, I was excited to try it out.

At the next gathering, I joined in, raising my hand (only one) and singing along joyfully. I was hooked! This kind of worshipping took me to another level of intimacy in my relationship with Jesus. I didn't have enough words to thank Him for His goodness.

Then my life took a downward turn. During that dark period, I couldn't—or wouldn't—worship Him, and I couldn't think of anything to be thankful for. At the time, I thought I was just being honest, but in retrospect, I was being self-centered and irreverent to the King of kings. I now understand that praising Jesus and being thankful is not about me—it's about Him. It's not something to do when everything is going my way. Instead, praise and thanksgiving is due to Jesus always because He is worthy. —PAMELA TOUSSAINT HOWARD

FAITH STEP: *If you've been more of a stoic worshipper, try letting go and praising Jesus out loud. Start when you're alone—at home, in the shower, or in the car. He is always worthy of praise!*

MONDAY, APRIL 29

Be alert and of sober mind. Your enemy the devil prowls around like a roaring lion looking for someone to devour. 1 Peter 5:8 (NIV)

IT WAS A BEAUTIFUL DAY for a bike ride. The sun was warm, clouds skimmed the sky, and a breeze toyed with the leaves outside the garage.

After a morning at the computer, my brain felt foggy, so I pulled my bike from the rack and backed it onto the driveway. But when I lifted my foot to the pedal, searing pain shot through my shin.

Gasping, I managed to hold on to the wobbling bike while I looked down and realized what happened. The previous autumn, the kickstand had broken off, and the jagged edge had poked through the duct-tape temporary fix. Exposed metal had caught my leg.

It didn't take long to clean and bandage the cut, but I'd have to have a more permanent fix for my bike. I'd grown accustomed to not using the kickstand and had become numb to the need to steer clear of the broken part. My lack of alertness had caught me unaware.

Managing life can be like that broken kickstand. My attention to areas of concern can be numbed by busyness, creature comforts, keeping up with culture, ambitions, fears and anxieties, relationship discord, and everyday responsibilities. Daily life can divert my attention from Jesus too. Even when distractions are not bad, if I forget to attend to what's important, I might get hurt.

With a sober mind and alertness to Jesus, I carefully mounted my bike and thanked Him for the reminder that He is most important.
—ERIN KEELEY MARSHALL

FAITH STEP: *Ask Jesus to show you any area where you may be numb to His warnings and need to pay attention.*

TUESDAY, APRIL 30

Therefore everyone who hears these words of mine and puts them into practice is like a wise man who built his house on the rock. Matthew 7:24 (NIV)

DURING A TORNADO WARNING IN my city a few years ago, I was overcome with worry. The atmosphere of the sunny spring day changed drastically in just minutes. The skies darkened, the wind picked up speed, and sirens roared in the distance. I hurried to the basement, grabbing my Kindle and mobile phone so I could stay weather aware.

The Memphis home we live in is almost 100 years old and has withstood many storms, so I'm usually calm in extreme weather conditions. That day, however, I realized something about the house for the first time. Every room had windows and, unless I squeezed into one of our closets, I was likely to be in harm's way. I found comfort in heading to our basement, where the foundation is solid and less likely to be destroyed.

Within a few hours, the sirens stopped, the winds died down, and the skies cleared. The tornado did not hit our neighborhood, and I felt free to roam around the house again. And I realized that my true Foundation—Jesus—is solid and comforting and will keep me safe from harm. Next time there's a storm, wherever and however I decide to respond to it, I know my ultimate protection from danger lies in Jesus. —ERICKA LOYNES

FAITH STEP: *Don't wait until a spiritual storm comes to prepare for it. Draft a plan now. Will you call a prayer partner? Recite scripture? Something else? Write down what you want to do and display the list where you can view it regularly.*

WEDNESDAY, MAY 1

But the seed falling on good soil refers to someone who hears the word and understands it. This is the one who produces a crop, yielding a hundred, sixty or thirty times what was sown. Matthew 13:23 (NIV)

LIVING IN WISCONSIN, I MOURN that our garden's growing season is so short. I'm often scraping snow aside, wondering if my trowel will hit frost when digging in our first plantings. I watch others in warmer climates harvesting their crop of veggies while I'm still trying to keep the cold at bay from the varieties I planted that are designed for short growing seasons.

The hindrance means it's even more important to amend the soil well, giving my garden the best possible opportunity to produce a healthy, robust crop before the snow flies again. I don't even bother trying warm-climate crops, but I appreciate what does spring up—beans, peas, onions, cucumbers, tomatoes, potatoes, squash.

Good soil is important for my garden so my seeds and starter plants have the very best chance of producing an abundant yield. Like my garden, rich, fertile soil is also important in my life if I want Jesus's teachings to take root and grow.

I pondered the condition of my soil. Has it been properly prepared and tended by reading Jesus's Word and by prayer? Have I done what I need to so I can yield a life of abundance with His forgiveness, grace, and hope? With good soil—Jesus—I can bless others with the hope, faith, and love that grows in my spiritual garden. —CYNTHIA RUCHTI

FAITH STEP: *Consider planting a few seeds in prepared soil and watch them sprout. Think about how quickly you see changes in them each day. Thank Jesus that He can do the same in your life.*

THURSDAY, MAY 2

My command is this: Love each other as I have loved you. Greater love has no one than this: to lay down one's life for one's friends.
John 15:12–13 (NIV)

MY FRIEND LESLIE HAS ALWAYS been able to make me laugh. We spent ninety minutes on the phone yesterday, sharing the ins and outs of our lives, talking about our families, and rehashing who liked whom decades ago. In the real world, she is a high-powered lawyer. But to me, she is my college roommate, kindred spirit, forever friend. She texted me after we talked and said, "Those ninety minutes were good for my soul." Ditto. The thing is, I trust Leslie. I can tell her anything, sharing my biggest hopes, my deepest fears, and my silliest thoughts. She is a true friend. She makes me feel valued and loved. I know that she would do anything for me. I would do the same for her. That is the kind of friendship we have. Love upon love.

But the truth is, Jesus is the truest friend of all. Being in His presence is good for my soul. I trust Him and can tell Him anything. In Him, I am valued and loved. And He would do anything for me. In fact, Jesus showed His great love for me by laying down His life (John 3:16). He forgave all my sins and gave me a new way to live (1 John 1:9). In gratitude, I gave Him my life. That is the kind of friendship we have. Love upon love. —SUSANNA FOTH AUGHTMON

FAITH STEP: *Ponder your relationship with Jesus. As you thank Him for His great love, look through a photo album or pictures on your phone and remember specific ways Jesus has loved you.*

FRIDAY, MAY 3

Then some children were brought to Him so that He might lay His hands on them and pray. Matthew 19:13 (NASB 1995)

YESTERDAY, OUR TWENTY-YEAR-OLD SON, GABRIEL, a college junior, texted my husband and me in our three-way chat: "Dad and Mom, I've witnessed to three people! Please pray I'll have more opportunities like this."

Misty-eyed at the man he'd become, my mind traveled back to when Gabriel was a toddler. Our pastor had preached a sermon about blessing our children. He explained it's important to embrace them or hold their hands when blessing them.

Placing our hopes for Gabriel's future in Jesus's hands, my husband and I began blessing him aloud every night while putting him to bed. From the time he was three until he graduated from high school, our prayers often ran like this: "Lord, thank You for Gabriel's life, for the joy he brings our family. Fill him with Your love, Your Holy Spirit, and Your Word. Thank You for Your special calling on Gabriel's life. Bless him at school. May he grow up to be a man of godly leadership in his generation."

Even as Gabriel occasionally struggled, as all children do, we continued to bless him. Today, he's a committed Christian who loves sharing his faith. Seeing our hopes for Gabriel fulfilled taught me that I can trust Jesus wholeheartedly with all my hopes and dreams. Just as we blessed our son, Jesus desires to bless all of His children, and that includes me! —JENNIFER ANNE F. MESSING

FAITH STEP: *Pray a blessing aloud over your child, grandchild, niece, or nephew—in person or on a video call.*

SATURDAY, MAY 4

Then they were willing to take him into the boat, and immediately the boat reached the shore where they were heading. John 6:21 (NIV)

I WOULDN'T CALL MYSELF A seamstress, but I've sewn enough to know that having the right tools to work with is important. Sadly, I forget this from time to time.

One Saturday afternoon, I brought down the sewing supplies from my second-floor closet to make throw pillows for my daughter's bed and forgot the sewing scissors. Being too lazy to retrace my steps, I used our household scissors instead. They cut jagged lines and frayed the edges of the fabric. They also kept jamming, making a simple task take forever. A logical person would have gone to retrieve her sewing scissors. Not me. I forged ahead, wasting fabric and time as I cut and recut, my frustration increasing with every passing minute. My daughter finally had enough of my complaining. She marched upstairs and was back in no time with the right scissors. It was smooth cutting from there.

When I used to read John 6:16–21, about Jesus walking on water, my focus was on the strong wind and the rough waves. Both must have made it difficult for the disciples as they rowed. After my scissor debacle, I recognize that it was *after* inviting Jesus into their boat that they had everything they needed for the job. That's how they "immediately reached the shore."

Like the disciples, when I invite Jesus into everything I do, I'm fully equipped with the Right One for whatever task I tackle—including sewing. —CLAIRE MCGARRY

FAITH STEP: *Is there an area of your life that you are avoiding asking Jesus into? Identify what stops you and pray that Jesus will help you to invite Him in.*

SUNDAY, MAY 5

Each of you should give what you have decided in your heart to give, not reluctantly or under compulsion, for God loves a cheerful giver. 2 Corinthians 9:7 (NIV)

WHEN MY CHILDREN WERE LITTLE, my father-in-law would empty the change from his pockets and divide the coins among the four of them when we ate together after church on Sundays. Sometimes he had only a few coins, but other times, he'd dump whole pockets full of change onto the table and laugh as their eyes lit up and their tiny hands struggled to contain their windfall.

After one particularly generous distribution, I was frustrated to find my eight-year-old son, Canaan, dropping his coins in the restaurant parking lot as we walked to our car. I offered to keep his money safe for him, but he ignored me and continued tossing coins on the ground like a farmer scattering feed for chickens. "What are you doing?" I scolded. "Granddad just gave you that money, and now you're throwing it away!"

Canaan scrunched his nose and shook his head. "No, Mom. I'm leaving it here on purpose so someone else will find it and have a really great day!" His insight stopped me in my tracks. I marveled at the childlike simplicity of how he was becoming a cheerful giver. He knew Jesus's promise that it was more blessed to give than to receive, and he had faith to act on that promise in whatever way he could. I put my arm around his shoulder knowing that even the smallest gift can point others to Jesus. —EMILY E. RYAN

FAITH STEP: *Leave some spare change behind the next time you're out. Pray that those who find it will turn their thanks toward Jesus.*

MONDAY, MAY 6

I will meet with you there, above the lid between the two winged creatures on the Ark of the Agreement. Exodus 25:22 (NCV)

WANTING TO BLESS PASSENGERS WAITING to catch the bus in front of our house, my husband, John, and our friend Cyrus bolted a stout, rustic, hand-built wooden bench onto a concrete slab. My son, a professional illustrator, artistically painted it in multiple colors. Inevitably, summer sun and winter snow gradually wear off the paint, requiring periodic repainting. Once an anonymous volunteer secretly painted the then-naked bench white, primed and ready for a new coat of color. Another time, an anonymous hit-and-run driver left the bench in a collapsed heap, requiring rebuilding and reinstallation.

Nevertheless, despite wear and tear and mishaps, our bench is more than a seat useful for bus riders. It's also a handy meet-up place for exchanging gifts and ideas. Wanting to give me handmade gifts and handwritten encouraging words, my friend Brooke suggested, "Meet me at the bench!"

Although it's nice having a convenient, agreed-upon bench for meeting the bus or a friend, it's far better to have a regular meeting time and place for getting together with Jesus. Whether indoors or outdoors, on a bench or chair, Jesus invites me daily to meet with Him so He can bless me with His encouraging words. Every morning, I look forward to reading edifying stories from my favorite old book, the Holy Bible, and my favorite new book, *Mornings with Jesus*, as I hear Him calling, "Meet Me at the bench."
—CASSANDRA TIERSMA

FAITH STEP: *Designate a seat in your home, whether a chair or bench, as your prayer place. Prayerfully invite Jesus to meet you there.*

TUESDAY, MAY 7

Be devoted to one another in love. Honor one another above yourselves.
Romans 12:10 (NIV)

YEARS AGO, PHOTOGRAPHS OF A similar theme popped up in my Facebook feed. Each picture displayed flat, palm-sized rocks painted white then decorated with a cute angel dressed in blue with a yellow halo. Some anonymous artist had been sneaking around our community depositing angels at different homes.

As people posted pictures of an angel that had appeared on a stump near their back porch or in the corner of a windowsill, they often shared how much they needed a blessing that very day. Even those of us who had not received an angel were encouraged by the random act of kindness and had fun trying to figure out who the mysterious gift giver could be.

One day, my husband and I pulled into our drive and there, propped against the garage door, was an angel for us! We had returned from a routine oncology appointment where Russ had received his first "normal" lab report since his leukemia battle began two years earlier. What a perfect celebration!

Unexpectedly, I discovered the angel artist is a friend of mine. Of course! She always does kind things for others, quietly, expecting nothing in return. Not only does she place her painted rocks locally, but she also takes some with her when she travels. She places an angel in a public place and then returns a few hours later to see if it has been taken. The angel is always gone.

Her simple gift spreads so much joy in a community and across cultures, yet she wants no recognition. What an angel! —KAREN SARGENT

FAITH STEP: *Who can you be an angel to? Buy a stranger's coffee. Leave flowers on a neighbor's doorstep. Surprise someone with kindness today.*

WEDNESDAY, MAY 8

Fix your thoughts on what is true, and honorable, and right, and pure, and lovely, and admirable. Think about things that are excellent and worthy of praise. Philippians 4:8 (NLT)

OUR OLD HOUSE WAS LESS than 2 miles away from chemical plants and an oil refinery. After tasting the tap water, I started buying bottled water and then splurged on a water purifier that claimed to remove 99.9 percent of contaminants from any water source. The water tasted great, but since the canister was stainless steel, I didn't always know when it needed to be refilled. Sometimes I found it empty when I wanted to cook, make a pitcher of tea, or fill the water bottle I sipped from all day. Then it dawned on me: first thing every morning, I could empty the lower chamber and completely refill the top chamber. That would ensure I had purified water ready when I needed it.

One morning as I poured the water in, something else dawned on me: first thing every morning, I could apply a filter to my thoughts. Every day my mind can be polluted by outside influences such as images or conversations, or from the inside through negative emotions like anger, jealousy, or resentment. If I fix my thoughts on Jesus and His Word early in the day, I will be more likely to recognize any attitude that is not worthy of a Christ follower.

Each day, when I set a filter to purify my thoughts, I'll be ready to share the One Who Provides Living Water with anyone I meet.
—DIANNE NEAL MATTHEWS

FAITH STEP: *Honor Jesus by giving Him the first few minutes of your day. Ask Him to help you guard your thought life and filter out anything unpleasing to Him.*

THURSDAY, MAY 9

Now faith is the substance of things hoped for, the evidence of things not seen. Hebrews 11:1 (NKJV)

ON THE WALL ABOVE THE doorway to my home office, there's a decal that reads, "Where God guides, He provides." I've seen these words hundreds of times, but their truth was put to the test during my son, DJ's, senior year of high school. He had been accepted to several colleges, but our family had no college fund and not enough savings to send him. DJ wanted to get a degree, but I didn't know how we were going to pay for tuition and all of the other expenses. However, remembering how Jesus had interceded for my family over the years, I stood in faith, hoping that we'd find a way.

When defining *faith* in Hebrews 11, the writer explained it is hoping for something that can't be seen. I imagine that definition was not an easy one to relay to the Jewish Christians who had started losing energy and confidence in their beliefs. To encourage endurance, the writer reminded them of how they suffered early on in their faith (Hebrews 10:32–34) but also recounted how the words and actions of their godly ancestors were deeply rooted in that same faith (Hebrews 11:4–39).

That May, DJ received an email stating that he had been awarded a scholarship that would enable him to attend his first choice for college. We celebrated and gave thanks to Jesus. As I hugged DJ, I glanced up at the wall. Where God guides, He provides. —ERICKA LOYNES

FAITH STEP: *Read Hebrews 11 and boost your faith.*

FRIDAY, MAY 10

But store up for yourselves treasures in heaven, where moths and vermin do not destroy, and where thieves do not break in and steal. For where your treasure is, there your heart will be also. Matthew 6:20–21 (NIV)

YEARS AGO, I HAD A sound engineer boyfriend who toured with big-name stars. I was fortunate enough to join him on the road and saw a very famous singer in concert some twenty times all over the world. It sounded glamorous, I know, but it soon became evident that her success wasn't all it seemed to be.

I met the superstar once and saw her as fragile and self-conscious, even at the height of her fame. On stage, though, she was unfailingly dazzling, her famous voice flawless, night after night. Her entourage swarmed around her, following closely. We'd often dodge paparazzi waiting at the venue or hotel. At those times, her smile beamed—she was always dressed for the cameras.

A decade later, she was dead.

Surrounded by people and adoring fans, this performer was nonetheless very alone. Despite having fame and fortune, she was deeply unhappy. Celebrities sometimes epitomize the reality that things of this world, no matter how shiny, don't offer deep or lasting satisfaction. The empty promise of earthly success can be a distraction that not only diverts people from this truth but also can actually destroy them.

For true peace, I must anchor my hope in something more enduring and true. Jesus is that something. He is the only superstar I care to follow now. —ISABELLA CAMPOLATTARO

FAITH STEP: *Take a few moments to reflect on what is disappointing you today. Where are you hanging your hope—on worldly things or Jesus?*

SATURDAY, MAY 11

Be careful for nothing; but in every thing by prayer and supplication with thanksgiving let your requests be made known unto God. And the peace of God, which passeth all understanding, shall keep your hearts and minds through Christ Jesus. Philippians 4:6–7 (KJV)

ONCE OR TWICE A WEEK, my daughter and I head to a horse farm where she volunteers mucking stalls, tacking and untacking lesson horses, and exercising the older horses.

I don't share her affinity for barn scents, and I don't have her natural comfort with horses. But I've spent enough time around them to appreciate their personalities and strength.

My daughter especially loves riding bareback. She told me she feels like worshipping when she is on the back of a horse, and I've seen her throw out her arms and ride across a pasture with her hair flowing behind her. Recalling her words is a beautiful reminder of the carefree, trusting position believers have in Jesus.

The King James Version of today's verses is fresh to me. I love the nuances of "be careful for nothing" and "let your requests be made known." These phrases take a gentle, assured approach. They almost sing with ease. Instead of vigilantly self-protecting, I can revel and rest in faith. I can simply let Jesus know my requests. I don't need to fling them at Him in a panic, as if He didn't hear me the first dozen times. I don't have to convince Him or beg. Once I let Jesus know my burdens, I, too, can throw out my arms in worship, knowing He hears me and I am securely held by Him.
—ERIN KEELEY MARSHALL

FAITH STEP: *As you bring your requests to Jesus today, throw out your arms in worship, knowing He hears you.*

Mother's Day, Sunday, May 12

*Do not let any unwholesome talk come out of your mouths, but only
what is helpful for building others up. Ephesians 4:29 (NIV)*

I OPENED THE MOTHER'S DAY issue of a women's magazine and
read reader responses to the question, "What's a positive phrase you
remember your mother saying often?" The answers varied from
"those hardest to love are the ones who need it most" to "cleanliness
is next to godliness...so go clean your room."

My mother used to say, "If you can't say anything nice, don't say anything at all." Or the equally powerful, "If you can't be kind, be quiet."

Mother's Day seems like a good day to revisit motherly wisdom.
Did they know they were quoting scripture in some cases or at least
spouting thoughts with origins in God's Word and the teachings
and life of Jesus? For example, 1 Peter 3:10 (NKJV) states: "He who
would love life and see good days, let him refrain his tongue from
evil, and his lips from speaking deceit."

Today, I'm asking what my children might recall as an oft-quoted
phrase they heard from me. I remember telling them to "be good,
be wise, be careful," as I sent them off to school or work and "pick
up your socks" (not my most memorable words of wisdom). And of
course there was "Jesus loves you and so do I."

Yes! That's the one I hope my precious children not only remember but also pass down to their children for generations to come.
—CYNTHIA RUCHTI

FAITH STEP: *Did your mother remind you that Jesus loves you? If so, thank her.
If she's gone to Glory, thank Jesus for her influence and pass down her legacy of
love to the next generation.*

MONDAY, MAY 13

Therefore we do not lose heart. Though outwardly we are wasting away, yet inwardly we are being renewed day by day. For our light and momentary troubles are achieving for us an eternal glory that far outweighs them all. So we fix our eyes not on what is seen, but on what is unseen, since what is seen is temporary, but what is unseen is eternal. 2 Corinthians 4:16–18 (NIV)

I TURN FIFTY THIS YEAR, and as I grow older, I expect even greater things for my life. However, I didn't expect to experience drastic changes to my body so quickly. Unruly gray hairs have invaded the top and front of my head, replacing my curly black strands. Ruby-red frames with prescription lenses are settled on my nose to assist my failing brown eyes, and the skin I have lived in is now a bit loose and stretched out. I love growing older and being wiser, but it's tough seeing my youthfulness fade.

Paul reminded the Corinthians that their physical bodies were prone to the natural process of declining health and aging, but those same bodies also possess the miraculous life and power of Jesus. Though they couldn't see it, the diseases and tragedies wearing them down on the outside were no match for the hope they had in Jesus, who was making them stronger on the inside.

As much as I'd like to slow down the aging and going-gray processes, I know my body is a temporary vessel. Its true purpose and value are tied to housing the Spirit of Jesus and guarding my soul until it reaches eternity. —ERICKA LOYNES

FAITH STEP: *Instead of thinking about the effects of aging on your body, list a few ways your spirit is being renewed day by day.*

TUESDAY, MAY 14

For all have sinned and fall short of the glory of God. Romans 3:23 (NIV)

MY YORKIE PUPS MADE A game of batting back and forth the cords of our picture-window blinds, creating a tangled mess of the strings. Then, my robot vacuum sweeper finished off the job when it swirled the cords around its beater bar. I managed to free the jumbled ball from the vacuum, but it would take more than a little patience and effort to untangle the mass.

I spent a good deal of time on this little project, working a few minutes here and there until my frustration level soared too high. I'd walk away and try to calm my frazzled nerves, returning hours, or sometimes days, later to attempt it once again. Often, I was convinced I'd never be able to undo the cord chaos, untangle the knots, and restore things to their rightful order. It took some doing and determination to straighten things out so I could use the blinds again.

Like those mangled cords, I sometimes make a tangled mess of my life. My attempts to follow Jesus's laws and be holy fail. My sin separates me from Him. No matter what I do on my own, I can never make myself right with God—I will always fall short.

That's where Jesus comes in. Because He sacrificed His life to atone for my sin, I'm restored. Jesus straightens out any messes I make. He redeems me, restores me, and loves me.

Now to do something about those pups! —SUSAN DOWNS

FAITH STEP: *Through Jesus's death on the cross, He poured out His life to make you whole again. Today, consider and gratefully accept Jesus's supreme sacrifice.*

Wednesday, May 15

You know that under pressure, your faith-life is forced into the open and shows its true colors. So don't try to get out of anything prematurely. Let it do its work so you become mature and well-developed, not deficient in any way. James 1:3–4 (MSG)

Of all the fruit of the Spirit listed in Galatians 5:22, patience is the one I need to work on the most. I can spend two hours watching a movie, four years earning a college degree, and decades learning how to be a good wife, but when I need a prayer answered, I want it N.O.W.

Jesus doesn't panic as my calendar pages flip forward. Rather, in my experience, He seems to take His time to give me answers.

Looking back over my life, I see a common pattern. Whenever I've had to wait for an answer to prayer, I grow closer to Jesus in the process. When, in desperation, I dig into His Word to find promises applicable to my need, I repeatedly see His goodness, His mercy toward me, and His willingness to help.

Could it be that Jesus is more interested in what He can do *in* me than what He can do *for* me?

I know Jesus is not purposely trying my patience, but maybe He is providing trying opportunities so I will learn how to be more patient. Perhaps He knows that the growth of my faith—as I wait, and search the Scripture, and eventually surrender my will to His— is far more important than the culmination of my wishes. That's something worth waiting for. —Jeanette Levellie

Faith Step: *Find a scripture that applies to what you've been asking Jesus to do in your life. Write it down, commit it to memory, and rest in His love.*

THURSDAY, MAY 16

But he said to me, "My grace is sufficient for you, for my power is made perfect in weakness." 2 Corinthians 12:9 (NIV)

THE TRAIL BISECTED A COOL, dark section of forest. The scent of loamy soil and spicy cedar mingled with the fragrance of the evergreens to create a lovely perfume. Just ahead, the trees opened to a small meadow, a natural cathedral of sorts. At the base of one of the stately trees, I spotted a solitary wildflower, its leaves spread wide, its white petals open to the sun.

That evening as I settled into bed, my mind replayed all the beauty I'd encountered on the hike. My thoughts returned again and again to that petite flower. How could something so small have such an impact? Shouldn't the deep woods have dominated my attention instead? Yet, the very vulnerability of that blossom somehow multiplied the forest's magnificence.

I sensed my resemblance to that tiny bloom resting safe at the foot of the giant fir. Living my life in the shadow of Jesus's protection and love, I can lift others' spirits. In a world that can sometimes seem dark, I will spread joy and hope. Even those times when I feel afraid, or small, or weak.

Jesus is always with me. I feel His strength. As I stretch myself to fit His will, I remember that with Him, anything is possible (Matthew 19:26), no matter how small I am. —HEIDI GAUL

FAITH STEP: *Find a single flower or other small object and keep it near the place you spend your mornings with Jesus. Let it remind you that no matter how small you feel, Jesus is always with you. Spend a few minutes reflecting on the impact something so tiny can make in this world.*

FRIDAY, MAY 17

Though you have not seen him, you love him; and even though you do not see him now, you believe in him and are filled with an inexpressible and glorious joy. 1 Peter 1:8 (NIV)

I OFTEN SEE HERONS STANDING in ankle-deep water when I walk along the Fraser River near our marina. On one occasion, several stood in a cluster, enjoying the sun's warmth. Suddenly, a single bird took flight. It circled above its buddies and then landed in a tree about 30 feet from where I watched. Even though I couldn't see it, I knew it was there because I had proof: I'd seen it glide into the foliage.

Likewise, I can't see Jesus, but I can know He's real and present. I have proof. Creation, for instance, declares His wisdom, power, and glory (Psalm 8). He was with God the Father and played a role in designing our mind-boggling universe (John 1:1–3).

Fulfilled Old Testament prophecies also prove that Jesus is real. His birth, life, death, and resurrection fulfilled every Messianic prophecy made several hundred years prior (Luke 4:21).

Historical accounts outside the Bible, specifically those written by a first-century Jewish historian named Josephus, testify to Jesus being seen after His resurrection. And the Bible itself tells of several eyewitness accounts where Jesus appeared to individuals and groups after He rose from the dead (Luke 24:13–51).

Faith isn't based on random guesses or wishful thinking. Jesus is real. And I have all the proof I need. —GRACE FOX

FAITH STEP: *Write a prayer to Jesus. Begin with, "Jesus, I believe You are real because . . . " and then complete the sentence.*

SATURDAY, MAY 18

Even youths grow tired and weary, and young men stumble and fall; but those who hope in the LORD will renew their strength. They will soar on wings like eagles; they will run and not grow weary, they will walk and not be faint. Isaiah 40:30–31 (NIV)

I LOVE TO WALK WITH my friends. Grabbing a cup of coffee and heading down to the green belt, the path by the Boise River, rejuvenates me. We catch up on our kids. We discuss the wildness of life, how just when we think we have it all figured out, something else comes up. We chat about our struggles and our triumphs. Sometimes we talk about our dreams and what we are trying to accomplish. The rhythm of being in step with each other opens our hearts. It is soul-refreshing.

As much as I love walking with friends, I've recently started taking walks around my neighborhood by myself. I even leave my dog, Flash, at home. Walking by myself leaves room for conversation with Jesus. As I loop my neighborhood, I catch Him up on all that is going on in my life—my hopes and fears, my struggles and triumphs. I get a moment to breathe and recognize how He is already at work in my life. I focus on thanking Him for His grace and forgiveness. I praise Him for His awesomeness. He brings to mind all the ways He is changing my heart and ushering in healing and hope.

The rhythm of being in step with Jesus opens my heart to Him. It is soul-strengthening. —SUSANNA FOTH AUGHTMON

FAITH STEP: *Take a walk around your neighborhood and talk to Jesus. Share your heart with Him. Invite His hope and healing to come in.*

SUNDAY, MAY 19

Utterly amazed, they asked: "Aren't all these who are speaking Galileans?
Then how is it that each of us hears them in our native language?"
Acts 2:7–8 *(NIV)*

I RECENTLY ENJOYED A CONVERSATION with one of my college writing students about her manuscript. We discussed metaphors and symbols, dialogue and flashbacks, scene structure and word choices. We were speaking the same language.

Because her story included faith questions, we shifted into a more personal discussion about Christian beliefs. She had been deeply wounded by someone claiming to be a follower of Jesus. The abuse drove her away from Him, though she still grappled with spiritual longings.

I was able to gently share my belief that she was wholly loved and accepted by Jesus and that she could always find hope in Him. I recounted a few of my zigzags in the life of faith. We listened to each other's hearts.

That fruitful and meaningful talk came about naturally because we had a foundation of shared interest. A shared language about the world of writing.

In my zeal to tell others about Jesus, I may forget to find a common language first. I have babbled theological truth and seen reactions of shutting down or pulling back. But when Jesus poured out His Holy Spirit on Pentecost, His disciples reached people in their own language.

I'm learning to be alert to ways I can connect with neighbors and acquaintances—through gardening, writing, parenting, or caring for aging parents. When I get to know another's common experience, I can hear their heart and speak their language. —SHARON HINCK

FAITH STEP: *Have a conversation with a friend about common interests. Build a foundation to discuss deeper truths about Jesus.*

MONDAY, MAY 20

For the Son of Man came to seek and save those who are lost. Luke 19:10 (NLT)

WHILE WATCHING THE NEWS ONE night, I heard a story about the shortage of blood across the country. A plea was issued for donors. It had been a while since I had donated, so I promptly made an appointment.

Upon entering the donor center, I found every chair filled with people hooked up to machines that were pumping the life-giving fluid into bags. When it was my turn, I took a seat. After about thirty minutes, I was done. On my way out, one of the center's employees thanked me and pointed to a table. Navy-blue T-shirts were free to donors. I grabbed one.

Back home, I looked at the shirt. Bold white letters proclaimed: Just Here to Save. While I knew the slogan was meant to let people know I was a blood donor and aimed to inspire others to give, I felt uneasy about wearing those words. Yes, I'd given blood with the hope of helping someone, but I didn't feel comfortable taking credit for saving a life. Instead, I thought about Jesus. He truly came to save me—and others who are lost, trying to find their way in this dark world.

I still haven't worn that T-shirt. But every time I see it in my drawer, I'm reminded that Jesus is the One who has the real power to change and save lives with the donation of His blood.

—BARBRANDA LUMPKINS WALLS

FAITH STEP: *Think about how Jesus's sacrifice on the cross has saved your life.*

TUESDAY, MAY 21

Trust in the LORD with all your heart and lean not on your own understanding; in all your ways submit to him, and he will make your paths straight. Proverbs 3:5–6 (NIV)

MY SON ISAAC WAS STARTING middle school in the fall. *Oh, boy!* Middle school is scary under the best of circumstances, and the prospect of Isaac, who has Down syndrome, being victimized by bullies was more than I could bear. I wanted him in a safe school with good programs for special needs kids, so I talked to other parents of special needs kids about their plans. Several, including Isaac's best friend's family, considered applying for a program that enabled students to attend schools outside their designated area. I wanted Isaac to stay with his peers, and I prayed for direction. I emailed the agency in charge of this program for requirements and deadlines but discovered the deadline had passed.

My mind raced to awful scenarios, all magnified by the thought that Isaac would be separated from his familiar friends. I prayed fervently and emailed Isaac's current teacher for help. She promised to check into the situation with our zoned school. I begged Jesus to help. *I know You love Isaac, Lord, so I'm trusting You.*

The next morning, Isaac's best friend's mom texted me to say she'd decided to send her son to the zoned school. Later, I discovered that all of Isaac's classmates were going there too. The students would have their own mini-wing that would keep them safe while enjoying the middle school experience surrounded by familiar friends.

I whispered a prayer of thanks to Isaac's *very* Best Friend.
—ISABELLA CAMPOLATTARO

FAITH STEP: *Have carefully laid plans failed despite your best efforts? Reaffirm your trust in Jesus aloud and let go of the outcome.*

WEDNESDAY, MAY 22

But when all goes well with you, remember me and show me kindness; mention me to Pharaoh and get me out of this prison. Genesis 40:14 *(NIV)*

MY HUSBAND AND I ADOPTED children from foster care, and recently our twin girls turned eighteen. They decided to reach out to their biological mother, whom they hadn't seen in a decade. Our daughters had high hopes of a good relationship with her but soon realized that wouldn't be the case. I reminded them that while hope is important, sometimes people disappoint us.

The life of Joseph (Genesis 37–50) is an example of someone who never gave up hope in God, despite what life threw at him. Joseph was sold into slavery, which took him to Egypt. Then, being falsely accused landed him in jail. Later, after interpreting a dream for the king's cupbearer, Joseph had hope that he'd finally receive help from someone close to Pharaoh. Though Joseph offered support to others, years passed, and no help came in return.

Locked away in prison, Joseph had every right to lose hope and become bitter. Instead, he lived with integrity. Eventually, a dream given to Pharaoh reminded the royal cupbearer of how Joseph had helped him. The Lord proved Himself faithful to Joseph even after men had failed.

People may disappoint, but Jesus never does. When putting my hope in others doesn't work, putting my hope in Jesus strengthens my heart. I pray that someday my daughters can have a good relationship with their biological mom, but more than that, I hope they'll always put their faith in Jesus. —TRICIA GOYER

FAITH STEP: *Think about a time when hope in others has brought disappointment. Take that pain and give it to Jesus, asking Him to fill you with hope in Him instead.*

THURSDAY, MAY 23

Therefore I tell you, whatever you ask for in prayer, believe that you have received it, and it will be yours. Mark 11:24 (NIV)

JEWELRY HAS NEVER BEEN MY thing. I wear two rings—my Texas A&M college ring and my mother's wedding band. My three-year-old granddaughter, Blake, likes to play with my rings, and because I'm a pushover, I let her. But I keep a close eye on Mom's ring.

I was distracted that day as Blake and I sat at the piano. She'd placed my rings on the keys and was enjoying watching them bounce around as she banged. I looked down and saw my Aggie ring, but Mom's ring was gone.

I hopped up and scoured the floor, lifted the piano's lid, and shook Blake's clothing, but no ring. *It couldn't be gone!* Seventy-eight years ago, my dad had given my mother that slender band of gold. It was the only ring Mom had ever worn. *Jesus, please help me find it!*

Upset as I was, a feeling of calm slowly came over me. I felt Jesus whisper. *It's not lost.*

Weeks passed and I was at the piano again, this time with my one-year-old granddaughter, Sloane. As she pressed the keys with her tiny fingers, I saw a gleam between two white keys. *Mom's ring!* I yelled for my daughter, who thrives on challenges. It took her an hour, using a hair clip, tweezers, a Christmas ornament hanger, needle-nosed pliers, and a nail file, but she retrieved Mom's ring.

Finding it was like sweet music to my ears, but I wasn't surprised. Nothing is too hard for Jesus. —PAT BUTLER DYSON

FAITH STEP: *What do you need help with? Ask Jesus to assure you that if you believe, anything you pray for will be granted.*

FRIDAY, MAY 24

There are different kinds of working, but in all of them and in everyone it is the same God at work. 1 Corinthians 12:6 (NIV)

I DECIDED TO SEW A quilt—nothing elaborate, maybe a simple patchwork design. During a little Internet research, I discovered the quilt capital of the world is located only hours away in Hamilton, Missouri. A perfect excuse for a road trip!

A friendly young woman greeted me at the quilt shop. I asked for an easy pattern for a beginner like me. She pointed to a quilt on display and called it the Carpenter's Star. She'd surely misunderstood me. The star looked too complex. Then she pointed out the details, explaining how to stitch a line here and another there and cut between them to make a block, and then rearrange the blocks just so. Amazing! The simplicity of the design became visible. I left the quilt capital with a pattern and fabric for my first quilt.

Sometimes life looks too complex, and I think there's no way I can do it. When my husband was diagnosed with cancer one day and lightning struck our house with a direct hit the next, nothing was simple. When medical bills stacked up and my daughter's car died on her way home from college, things were complicated. When I was stuck mediating between family members who wanted peace only on their terms, I waved the white flag.

But complex and impossible are simple for Jesus. He mends, cuts, and pieces broken things together. I look back at complications, amazed by the Carpenter's handiwork in the fabric of my life.
—KAREN SARGENT

FAITH STEP: *Do you sew, crochet, or create in some other way? As you work on a project, thank the star Carpenter for His good work in you.*

SATURDAY, MAY 25

That is why I tell you not to worry about everyday life—whether you have enough food and drink, or enough clothes to wear. Isn't life more than food, and your body more than clothing? Look at the birds. They don't plant or harvest or store food in barns, for your heavenly Father feeds them. And aren't you far more valuable to him than they are?
Matthew 6:25–26 *(NLT)*

WHILE IN COLLEGE, A FRIEND and I attended a weekend leadership retreat. Before the first session began, our mentor led us in an exercise about worry. He told us to make a list of everything that was distracting us. My list was long and included things like finances, exams, papers, and roommates. Then he had us put our list in an envelope and return it to him sealed. He collected our envelopes and put them into his briefcase. "I have a lot planned for you this weekend, and I don't want you distracted by worry," he said. "While you are here, I'm going to hold your worries for you."

I can still recall the relief I felt with his offer. My entire body relaxed with peace, and it felt as if my mind had been set free from invisible shackles.

Now, over twenty years later, I continue to use what I learned from that experience any time worry begins to suffocate my soul. I remember that Jesus offers me even better freedom from worry than my mentor did. Not only can I trust Him to hold my worries for me indefinitely (no briefcase needed), but I can also trust Jesus, my Ultimate Mentor, to resolve them as well. —EMILY E. RYAN

FAITH STEP: *Make a list of your worries, then put the list aside, trusting Jesus to hold them for you.*

SUNDAY, MAY 26

Then Jesus placed his hands on the man's eyes again, and he saw clearly. His sight was restored, and he saw everything perfectly, even from a distance. Mark 8:25 (ISV)

A CAR SLOWED DOWN IN front of the stone chapel where I stood, without my glasses, after a Sunday morning service. The driver, a fellow church member, called to me, "Did you get contacts? Or laser eye surgery?" The answer was neither contacts nor laser surgery. It had happened during church.

Sitting in my usual place in the pew, the pastor looked a bit blurry to me. When I removed my glasses, I could see him clearly. I experimented with this strange new development multiple times during the remainder of the service, each time putting my glasses back on, only to find that the pastor again looked blurry but was in clear focus when I removed my glasses. Later, the eye doctor confirmed that my distance vision had so greatly improved that my old prescription was now way too strong for my new vision. Jesus had performed an unexpected Sunday morning miracle!

As I wondered at this, Jesus reminded me I'd been praying for spiritual insight, for vision, to be able to see the world as He wants me to see it. I'd prayed, "Give me eyes to see, Lord. Open my eyes that I may see." *Clarity* was the word He'd given me during a prayer meeting, and miraculously "clarity" was the gift I received. The recent improvement in my *physical* eyesight was just an unexpected bonus! —CASSANDRA TIERSMA

FAITH STEP: *Keep an eye out for everyday unexpected miracles. Ask Jesus to help you see them clearly.*

MEMORIAL DAY, MONDAY, MAY 27

I thank my God every time I remember you. Philippians 1:3 (NIV)

ONE OF THE HIGHLIGHTS OF my life was accompanying my Korean War veteran father on an Honor Flight trip to Washington, D.C. At eighty-eight, Dad suffered from pulmonary fibrosis and was very weak. We'd have a jam-packed itinerary and he'd have to use a wheelchair to get around, but Dad was adamant. He wanted to see those historic memorials.

Being with a group of other veterans and visiting the monuments dedicated to military service and sacrifice was a sacred experience for us both. Ever since that trip, I have thanked veterans or military personnel for their service to our country when I see them. However, one evening, when a young serviceman pulled beside me at a filling station, I was compelled to do something more than say thanks. I offered to pay for his gas, and a conversation ensued when I mentioned Dad's Honor Flight trip.

I described proud memories of passersby thanking my dad for his service and listening to veterans exchange military stories. As we finished filling our cars, the young serviceman said he was eager to get home from drills to see his family. He and his wife had lost a child in premature death, and she was pregnant again. His eyes glistened when I said I would pray for his family. We shook hands and said goodbye.

Like the Honor Flight experience, my meeting at the gas pump was a holy moment. My small act of thankfulness to a soldier was like a living memorial to Dad and those who have served our country.
—BRENDA L. YODER

FAITH STEP: *Consider talking to, thanking, or paying it forward for the next veteran or serviceman or –woman you see.*

TUESDAY, MAY 28

And I pray that you, being rooted and established in love, may have power, together with all the Lord's holy people, to grasp how wide and long and high and deep is the love of Christ. Ephesians 3:17–18 (NIV)

THE HERB COMFREY GREW LIKE a weed for me in Michigan, so I brought one when we moved to Wyoming, sure that it would multiply. I watered my comfrey morning and evening, only to find the plant distressed—leaves dry and papery, veins bulging. My comfrey plant didn't like it here. Sandy soil, hot winds, burning sun, and low humidity were killing it.

A gardening friend suggested I not water it from above to minimize evaporative loss. Watering from below was the only way to encourage the comfrey's taproot to go deep in the high desert. But how could I do that when my plant was already in the soil?

Enter ollas. These unglazed pots used for cooking can also be buried in the garden to act as an irrigation system. Dry soil pulls water through the walls of the olla, moistening the soil below and alongside thirsty plants. Nothing lost to evaporation, the roots can continue to grow.

Those buried clay pots got me thinking about my spiritual roots. My olla is daily time with Jesus. As I drink in His love on a consistent basis, I can become more deeply rooted in Him and grow more into the person He designed me to be. —SUZANNE DAVENPORT TIETJEN

FAITH STEP: *Poke a hole in the bottom of a clear plastic cup. Fill it with soil and plant a seed or seedling. Set the cup in a water-filled saucer. Observe how the roots grow each day as you pray for Jesus to grow your roots more deeply in Him.*

WEDNESDAY, MAY 29

My heart overflows with a pleasing theme; I address my verses to the king.
Psalm 45:1 (ESV)

YEARS AGO, I FREELANCED FOR the weekly newspaper of the tiny village where we lived. My favorite assignments were interviewing community members and writing profile pieces. I soon discovered that each person's life had an overarching theme that emerged during our conversation—one that made their story interesting and unique, no matter how ordinary their life may have appeared at first glance.

I remember our grocery store's manager, who valued his opportunity to mentor teens by providing them with their first work experience; a young business owner, who wanted nothing more than to build a career and family in the place where he had grown up; a fellow church member's passion for helping farmers with the business side of their vocation in his role as president of a farm credit agency.

Writers are often advised to distill their book idea into one paragraph, then one sentence or phrase, and sometimes into a single word. That's a good practice to use in evaluating our life. What sentence sums up where we invest our time, resources, skills, and natural abilities? What gives our life meaning and purpose?

When we reach the point where the word *Jesus* best describes our daily thoughts and activities, we are indeed living with a pleasing theme. And our hearts will overflow with joy and praise to our King. —DIANNE NEAL MATTHEWS

FAITH STEP: *Evaluate what the theme of your life currently seems to be. If you don't know or don't like the answer, ask Jesus to help you identify ways you can center your life on His plan for you.*

THURSDAY, MAY 30

Yes, my soul, find rest in God; my hope comes from him. Truly he is my rock and my salvation; he is my fortress, I will not be shaken.
Psalm 62:5–6 (NIV)

I SAT ON THE FLOOR, arranging plastic farm animals with my toddler granddaughter. Though Chloe rubbed her eyes and yawned a few times, I worked to engage her until lunch, ensuring a long afternoon nap. She smiled at my animated conversation between a cow and a donkey. She imitated me when I flew a chicken around her head. Then she crawled in my lap and lay on her belly. She wiggled back and forth, as if burrowing into a cozy position, and all went quiet.

"Chloe? Chloe?" I whispered.

No response. Peaceful sleep had overtaken her—even while she was still gripping a lamb in her left hand.

Truly resting in Jesus must feel like that. Jesus bids me to come to Him when I am weary and burdened and He will give me rest (Matthew 11:28–29). But I often lack the ability to lay it all down and relax. My brain swirls, especially at bedtime. I review the past day and plan for tomorrow. I worry about each family member, one by one. I cringe at things I've done and fume about things done to me. And if that's not enough, I throw in the problems of the world. Yet Jesus said I can find rest for my soul. So, picturing my sweet, snoozing Chloe, I'm going to ask Jesus to settle my troubled mind and bless me with peaceful sleep too. —BECKY ALEXANDER

FAITH STEP: *What keeps you awake? Write Psalm 62:5–6 on a note card and recite it when you can't sleep.*

FRIDAY, MAY 31

Surely he has borne our griefs and carried our sorrows; yet we esteemed him stricken, smitten by God, and afflicted. Isaiah 53:4 (ESV)

ONE OF MY FAVORITE RIDES at a theme park is actually more of a virtual-reality experience. The seats move slightly, creating sensations of flying up and down and banking around the scenery projected on the screen. Scents waft up from orange groves, and water mists riders as we seem to fly through the clouds. I love the exhilarating sensation of gliding over mountains and ocean waves, dipping and weaving.

But in a few minutes, the ride is over. I never actually touched the green hillsides or splashed in the rolling waves. I viewed beautiful settings from a distance on a screen.

Many people believe God created the universe and now sits back and views it from a distance. Like the drone photography that helped me see the world in the ride, some think God never actually touches their lives.

Isaiah's prophecy about Jesus corrects that misunderstanding. We are reminded that in Christ, God does not remain at a distance. Jesus not only walked on the earth, but He also intimately interacted with hurting people. And He still does. He shoulders our pain. He walks beside us through every struggle. He comforts us, intercedes for us, and interacts with us. He brings tangible change into our lives.

I'm grateful that Jesus doesn't hover at a distance. I have hope because He understands my circumstances up close. More exhilarating than any ride, His love is tangible and real. —SHARON HINCK

FAITH STEP: *Touch your shoulders. Ask Jesus to lift the weight from them and thank Him for being right beside you and carrying your burdens.*

SATURDAY, JUNE 1

You are the salt of the earth. Matthew 5:13 (NIV)

I'M A SALT FANATIC. I've been known to even salt tortilla chips at restaurants after dipping them in the salsa. (I've checked with my doctor and my sodium levels are fine.) As most people know, salt brings out the flavors of food and acts as a preservative. I love when God uses an everyday, ordinary item, such as salt, to make an essential spiritual point.

I've been reading Leviticus and recently studied the sacrificial systems introduced in this book of the Bible. The grain offerings in Leviticus 2 were an act of worship. The Israelites gave their finest flour as a sacrifice of thanksgiving to God for His love for them and His provision. They were told not to add leaven, as this is symbolic of corruption, but to add salt. Salt was a symbol of the people's covenant and acted as a preservative. Adding salt was an expression of their thankfulness for the relationship God made with them through His covenant. And salt symbolized that this relationship would never end.

In Matthew, Jesus calls believers "the salt of the earth." As salt, we are to show the world God's covenant and preservation. We can add spice to others' lives when we share our joy, peace, kindness, and love. In our speech, we can introduce others to Jesus and share how everyone can enter into this enduring relationship. If we act as salt in this world, we can change the flavor of each other's lives forever.

Knowing this, I love salt even more. —JEANNIE BLACKMER

FAITH STEP: *Think of one way you can be salt to someone else. How can you bring flavor through speech or an act of kindness to someone today?*

SUNDAY, JUNE 2

For God did not send his Son into the world to condemn the world, but to save the world through him. John 3:17 (NIV)

OVER THE YEARS AS I'VE taken part in outreach efforts to share Jesus with people, I've offered them little pocket-sized booklets about salvation. These little books vividly illustrate how people are separated from God due to their sin, complete with sad-face line drawings to emphasize their unfortunate spiritual situation. I admit, I had trouble sharing what seemed like bad news (that without Jesus they would face God's wrath [John 3:36]) to people who might not want to hear it. The few takers I had went away troubled. I felt there must be a better way to share the news about Jesus.

As I learned more about how much Jesus loves me, I decided to share my faith differently. During a family hotel stay, I tried it out when we encountered a friendly waitress at breakfast. Throughout the meal, she served us cheerfully and patiently. When we tipped her, I said, "Just wanted to remind you that Jesus loves you very much. He cares about you."

Immediately, she teared up. "You have no idea how much I needed to hear that today," she said.

What a different response from the other ones! At that moment, I realized that people might be more open to hearing about Jesus when they know how much He cares. After all, sharing the good news of Jesus is good news—and we all can use a little more of that!
—PAMELA TOUSSAINT HOWARD

FAITH STEP: *Think of a caring action or simple kindness you can do to let someone know the good news about Jesus.*

Monday, June 3

But everyone who hears these words of mine and does not put
them into practice is like a foolish man who built his house on sand.
Matthew 7:26 (NIV)

LAST NIGHT, JESUS GOT MY attention through a crime drama on TV. I learned that forensic investigators can tell where a crime happened by examining sand in the soles of a suspect's or victim's shoes. That means, each beach around the world is different enough to be recognizable and useful as an investigative tool.

Coarse or fine sand. Tan, white, pink, orange, black, even purple sand. Four beaches in the world have green sand. The minerals that make up the world's beaches can come from volcanic eruptions, ground-up seashells, or erosion of local landscape.

Another sand lesson came while visiting a wet soft-sand beach. If I stood still, the incoming and outgoing waves washed the sand out from under me, making it difficult to stand. The only way I could stay upright was if I kept moving. Standing still, I'd sink.

What a "moving" picture of my faith walk with Jesus! It's so easy to sink when I'm not progressing forward. Miss reading the devotional a day or two. Stop memorizing Scripture. Skip church. Let the world suck me into its vortex of noise and chaotic conversations rather than take time to listen to Jesus.

The sinking sand image sticks with me like…well, like beach sand on a hot day. May it always serve its purpose of reminding me to keep putting one foot in front of the other as Jesus and I walk together. —CYNTHIA RUCHTI

FAITH STEP: *Find a rock or seashell or small jar of sand you can label with the words of Matthew 7:26 as a heartening reminder of Jesus's faithfulness.*

TUESDAY, JUNE 4

May your unfailing love be my comfort, according to your promise to your servant. Psalm 119:76 (NIV)

WHEN MY HUSBAND, KEVIN, NOTICED what looked like a rash on my back, I wasn't concerned. But after I nearly fainted while getting dressed a couple days later, both of us were extremely worried.

The emergency room doctor diagnosed shingles. Having heard horror stories about this virus, I knew I was in for some pain. But I didn't have a clue about the severity of my suffering.

This nasty infection attacks the nerves by sending agonizing shock waves to the affected area throughout the day and night. I took all the meds the doctor prescribed. They helped only a little, so I also tried every over-the-counter remedy I could find. Nothing worked 100 percent.

Every time a jolt assaulted me, I'd cry out. Kevin always said, "Bless you." He never sighed or acted annoyed when I asked him for help getting dressed or applying a pain patch. His empathy and compassion spurred him to try to make me as comfortable as possible. I repeatedly thanked Kev for showing me the heart of Jesus.

I still have pain at times, but five months later the shingles are almost gone. Thankfully, I know I don't suffer alone. Like Kevin, Jesus, my Savior, listens to my cries, blesses me when I hurt, and comforts me with His loving Spirit of grace. —JEANETTE LEVELLIE

FAITH STEP: *How are you hurting? Close your eyes and boldly ask Jesus to bless you physically, mentally, spiritually, emotionally, financially, or in any painful area of your life.*

Wednesday, June 5

*First take the plank out of your eye, and then you will see clearly
to remove the speck from your brother's eye. Luke 6:42 (NIV)*

THIS WEEK, I FINALLY GOT around to cleaning all the grunge from
the bottom of my silverware drawer. I shake my head in shame
whenever I take on this chore because it reminds me of a time in my
life when I held a less-than-Christlike attitude toward my mother-
in-law.

It all began in my newlywed days, when Evelyn came to visit. As
we worked together to clean up after a meal, she stopped me from
putting the clean silverware back in the drawer. Instead, she emp-
tied the drawer's contents, removed the individual trays, dumped
out the dirt that had collected in the bottom of each one, then
scrubbed them until they were like new. She never said a word of
criticism, but I felt judged. Unworthy. I didn't think I'd ever be
able to live up to her exemplary standards. She kept an immaculate
household. Stately, refined, and highly intelligent, Evelyn seemed
to be the perfect wife and mother.

But as the years went by and I got to know my mother-in-law
better and understand her motives and intentions, the Lord taught
me a few lessons about myself. Actions I'd deemed as criticisms on
her part, I came to realize, were intended as genuine offers to help.
It was my own insecurities that negatively colored how I saw her.
Essentially, I'd criticized her for thinking she criticized me.

I now cherish my mother-in-law as a gift from God and welcome
her offers to help without hesitation. —SUSAN DOWNS

FAITH STEP: *Examine your heart and ask Jesus to expose those personal flaws
that might unjustly color your negative opinions of others.*

THURSDAY, JUNE 6

Therefore, my dear brothers and sisters, stand firm. Let nothing move you. Always give yourselves fully to the work of the Lord, because you know that your labor in the Lord is not in vain. 1 Corinthians 15:58 (NIV)

AFTER MY FOURTH BOOK—*Moving from Fear to Freedom: A Woman's Guide to Peace in Every Situation*—was published, every subsequent idea I pitched to editors for a fifth book was rejected over the course of several years. I began feeling as though my efforts were useless. I lost hope that my work could make a difference in someone's life and entertained thoughts of setting my writing aside to pursue other interests. After all, why invest time and energy into something that didn't bear fruit?

One morning, feeling completely deflated, I asked Jesus to show me *that day* whether He wanted me to continue writing. My phone rang about five hours later. The caller was a stranger who told me that she'd never phoned an author before, but she felt compelled to contact me. She said my book changed her life. She urged me to keep writing.

My friend, everyone has seasons of feeling overworked and underappreciated. We might feel as though our labor offers little value to anyone, but I implore you to hold on to hope knowing this truth: our work matters to Jesus. He encouraged me through a stranger to stand firm. So let me encourage you to do the same. Carry on and labor from a heart filled with love for Him. —GRACE FOX

FAITH STEP: *Think of someone you know who does work that often goes unacknowledged. Call, send a text, or mail a card to encourage them.*

Friday, June 7

Teach us to number our days, that we may gain a heart of wisdom.
Psalm 90:12 (NIV)

I SAT IN THE STYLIST's chair, energized for the jam-packed weekend. First, a hair appointment, then helping my daughter-in-law clean the house she and my son were moving into the next day. From there, I'd drive several hours to speak at a retreat. My tightly organized schedule included allotted time for each event. I liked my life to be full and busy.

My day was going smoothly when I received a phone call. My husband, Ron, was in a logging accident. He was being airlifted to the regional trauma center. My no-time-to-spare schedule collapsed under the weight of a life-and-death situation.

I pushed down my fear about Ron and tried to be calm as I called my kids, called the retreat event planner to cancel my speaking appearance, and cleared my upcoming week's schedule while driving to the hospital. Ron's injuries were non-life-threatening but significant. There were many uncertainties, and in the weeks ahead, we took life one day at a time, which was new to me. After months of recovery, he and I both adjusted to a slower pace of life.

A too-full schedule no longer feels right. I like a slower pace but didn't know that until I was forced to slow down. —BRENDA L. YODER

FAITH STEP: *Examine the way you schedule your days. Are they jam-packed as planned or slower paced? Ask Jesus how you can best spend your time and make adjustments, if necessary.*

SATURDAY, JUNE 8

Immediately Jesus reached out his hand and caught him. "You of little faith," he said, "why did you doubt?" Matthew 14:31 (NIV)

I DIDN'T REALIZE HOW AFRAID of heights I was until my family talked me into zip-lining in an underground cavern beneath the city of Louisville. Geared up and strapped up, I stood on a platform waiting my turn, my pulse elevated. I preferred my feet on the ground, not dangling above it, but I was determined to embrace the adventure.

After surviving a few zips, I relaxed a little. Speeding through the air on a cable wasn't so bad. Then we reached the rope bridge, suspended ten stories aboveground. One foot after another, I balanced on wood planks and ropes, panic expanding in my chest. *This bridge supports 400,000 visitors a year. It can support you too,* I reminded myself. My legs wanted to freeze. My eyes wanted to cry. But I focused on the guide waiting at the end and trembled my way across.

Walking on ropes a hundred feet aboveground felt as unnatural to me as walking on water must have felt to Jesus's disciple Peter. Stepping out on faith doesn't feel natural either. I look down and see how hard I could fall, or I look ahead and see an uncertain journey. I hear doubt thunder in my ears and feel fear pouring down. *What if I fail?*

I may flounder, but Jesus won't. Like Peter, I could sink, but the Savior won't let me drown. Though I feel afraid, I'll keep my eyes focused on Jesus and put one shaky foot in front of the other.
—KAREN SARGENT

FAITH STEP: *Recall a time you acted on faith. Thank Jesus for catching you. Share that experience with a friend.*

SUNDAY, JUNE 9

When Jesus heard what had happened, he withdrew by boat privately to a solitary place. Hearing of this, the crowds followed him on foot from the towns. Matthew 14:13 (NIV)

As I write this, I'm approaching three months since my mom's death. Caring for her, supporting her in her final weeks, organizing the funeral, dealing with paperwork—all of it was exhausting but somehow gave me the focus or distraction I needed. I felt sorrow but also a level of numbness.

In recent weeks, grief has come in waves that wallop me. I see her photo, I remember one of her sayings, I reach for the phone to tell her something—and the loss slams into the forefront of my heart. I know I'll see her again in heaven, but this time of separation hurts.

Jesus understands. In Matthew 14, He had just heard about the murder of His cousin John the Baptist. Even though Jesus experienced the wonders of heaven before His incarnation and knows He'll see John again one day, He feels the weight of grief over his death. He withdraws. He finds a solitary place. Jesus's example reassures me that He truly knows the many facets of grief.

When I'm tempted to scold myself and tell myself to be strong, to muscle through, to stay busy, I take comfort in knowing that when Jesus grieved, He withdrew. Of course, people continued to need Him, and before long He graciously ministered again. I know I'll gradually find my footing, but in the moments in which grief exhausts me, I'll back away for a time, find a solitary place, and let Jesus heal my heart. —SHARON HINCK

FAITH STEP: *Give yourself permission to withdraw today. Spend more time than usual with only Jesus, who understands whatever hurts your heart is facing.*

MONDAY, JUNE 10

For the eyes of the Lord are on the righteous and his ears are attentive to their prayer. 1 Peter 3:12 *(NIV)*

PRAYER IS MY WEAKEST SPIRITUAL discipline. I have daily rhythms of reading the Bible and journaling my thoughts, but I'm often distracted by formal prayer. Most often, I write prayers in my journal, but I consider them second-rate because they are more conversational than spiritual.

That was until Jesus answered a prayer I'd been journaling for several days. Recently, my husband began working for an Amish logging company after retiring from teaching math. Raised on a farm, Ron was excited about his new job working outdoors. I started worrying about Ron's safety, though, soon after he started. He worked long hours, often in dangerous situations. I routinely journaled prayers for Jesus to keep him safe.

Then, a tree fell the wrong way and hit Ron from behind. The emergency room surgeon said it was a miracle he was alive. He experienced several broken bones, a punctured lung, and a head wound that required several staples.

"That tree could have fallen 360 different degrees, but it fell on me," Ron said, shaking his head.

The next day, I flipped back in my journal to my prayer on the day of the accident: *Keep Ron safe.* I wouldn't have considered those three words to be powerful when I wrote them, and I still don't consider myself a prayer warrior. While Ron wondered why the tree fell upon him, I know Jesus answered my prayer and saved his life.
—BRENDA L. YODER

FAITH STEP: *Try journaling your prayers this week and take inventory as Jesus answers them.*

TUESDAY, JUNE 11

I consider that our present sufferings are not worth comparing with the glory that will be revealed in us. Romans 8:18 (NIV)

I WENT TO A BRIDAL shower this past weekend at a venue right on the ocean. The oceanside wall of the room was made up entirely of plate-glass windows. Nothing obstructed our view of the cobalt-blue sky, puffy white clouds, and dancing waves. As I raved about the vista to the father of the soon-to-be bride, he said that when he signed the contract for the space, he tried to write in, "Windows must be perfectly clean the day of." The manager explained he couldn't allow that. They clean the windows weekly but aren't in control of the weather. If a storm blows in between cleaning day and an event, there's always the possibility of streaks.

Sure enough, when I looked closer, there were streaks on the windows. I'd overlooked them in order to see that stunning view beyond. Newly aware of the smudges, I began to fixate on them, until I realized doing so was stealing my joy. So, I made a conscious decision to overlook them again and focus solely on the beauty beyond.

So goes my life. Nothing is perfect. There's no guarantee that Jesus will make my path clear or wipe away my hardships. But He always gives me the choice: fixate on what's wrong and miss the joy in life, or acknowledge and accept imperfections and consciously choose to look beyond. By doing that, I can clearly see all the ways He blesses my life with beauty and good. —CLAIRE MCGARRY

FAITH STEP: *When you look out your window today, work to overlook any imperfections, streaks, or smudges in order to give thanks for the beauty beyond.*

WEDNESDAY, JUNE 12

For the Spirit God gave us does not make us timid, but gives us power, love and self-discipline. 2 Timothy 1:7 (NIV)

A FEW WEEKS AGO, I was talking to my friend Tina about how I have changed over the years—and not in the best way. As a young adult, I was fearless, tackling new situations with gusto. As I've gotten older, I am more afraid. How did I shift from being an excited world traveler in my college years to a middle-aged mom who shoots anxious texts to her college-age children in the middle of the night? How did I go from believing that Jesus could fling open new and exciting doors of possibility in my career to just hoping I can land a writing gig that will cover the bills? There are moments when I find my hope faltering instead of flourishing. I grow anxious about family, work, and the world in general.

Then I remember who Jesus is. He is the Savior and Deliverer (Acts 4:12). The All-Powerful One (Hebrews 1:1–4). The Alpha and Omega (Revelation 1:8). The Storm Whisperer (Mark 4:37–39). The Light Bringer (John 8:12).

The fears that crowd my mind don't come from Him. They flood in when I forget that His power and love are working in my life and in the world. Jesus is my peace, no matter how old I am.

—SUSANNA FOTH AUGHTMON

FAITH STEP: *Write down all the names of Jesus on sticky notes and place them around your house. When fear starts to move in, call on His name. Rest in His love and power.*

THURSDAY, JUNE 13

I pray that your hearts will be flooded with light so that you can understand the confident hope he has given to those he called—his holy people who are his rich and glorious inheritance. Ephesians 1:18 *(NLT)*

A FEW MONTHS AGO, I went to a conference, and I took my two preteen daughters. While I attended the sessions, my daughters explored the beautiful conference center. They also learned the phrase, "Charge it to the room." They'd been standing in line, waiting to buy a snack, when they overheard a woman in front of them say, "Charge it to the room." When they asked me about this novel concept, I explained that the hotel had my credit card on file. I set a limit and gave them access to my account so they would enjoy more than the paltry sum of cash in their wallets allowed them to buy.

While I ensured my daughters knew I did not have endless resources, I'm grateful Jesus does. Through Him, I have unlimited means, more than I've ever dreamed possible. Yet I often forget and instead limit myself to the little I possess, ignoring my rich and glorious inheritance in Him.

This inheritance is not always physical riches. When I turn to Jesus, I can be rich in mercy, patience, faith, love, and hope. He has paid the price for my inheritance of heaven. Just as I took care of the charges my daughters owed, my sins were charged to the cross, a costly bill Jesus paid for me. —TRICIA GOYER

FAITH STEP: *Make a list of the emotional resources you lack. Mercy or patience? Faith, love, or hope? Ask Jesus to provide all that He has available for you.*

FRIDAY, JUNE 14

Help each other in troubles and problems. This is the kind of law Christ asks us to obey. Galatians 6:2 (NLV)

SOMETHING WAS WRONG WITH EARL, the lovable stray cat I'd adopted. He wouldn't eat, and instead of snoozing on his chair, he stayed outside. I made a vet appointment for the following day, but Earl didn't come in that night. The next morning, he was nowhere to be found.

Earl enjoyed hunting lizards in our next-door neighbor's wooded backyard. I thought he might be there, but an automatic gate prevented my access, and I didn't want to ring their doorbell. We'd been friendly with the Kays when our daughters were in school together, but now we had nothing in common. We rarely spoke.

Dusk had fallen, along with a cold drizzle, when I spotted Earl in the Kays' backyard, wet, limping, clearly sick. I ran to the door and asked Mrs. Kay to open the gate, but by the time I got back, Earl had disappeared. She turned on her outside lights to help my search, but after several hours, drenched and heartbroken, I gave up.

Early the next morning, a sad Mrs. Kay was on our front porch. "We found Earl. I'm so sorry."

For most of that morning, I cried. That afternoon, Jesus prompted me to write a note of thanks to the Kays and to take them cookies. When my neighbor greeted me at the door, it felt like old times. I'd lost my beloved Earl, but I'd revived a relationship.

—PAT BUTLER DYSON

FAITH STEP: *Do you have a relationship that has dissolved or someone you have little in common with? Ask Jesus to show you how you can reach out to someone you normally wouldn't.*

SATURDAY, JUNE 15

This is the day the LORD has made; We will rejoice and be glad in it.
Psalm 118:24 (NKJV)

MY HUSBAND AND I ARE avid gardeners, so it wasn't a surprise that for our special anniversary, we traveled to Kauai. On Kauai, known as the Garden Island, tropical flowers carpet the countryside, and blooming vines entwine the treetops. The prized orchids I nurture with painstaking care are so common in Kauai they are almost taken for granted. As are the chickens.

Hens, chicks, and roosters are everywhere. A bachelor struts past my car as I fill the tank, and a brood of six circle the table as I enjoy a meal at an open-air café. A couple of chickens even graced the lawns of the posh beachfront resort where we stayed.

Their proliferation is the result of two hurricanes usurping backyard chicken coops decades ago, setting the birds free. Because most have intermixed with the native red junglefowl, they are protected by law. That fact doesn't make their unexpected presence any less absurd. I found myself smiling at the random places the wild chickens appeared throughout the day.

Jesus enjoys adding surprise moments of joy to our lives. From sublime sunsets to rainbow-tailed cocks, He gifts us with reasons to smile. During times of trial, He offers delight and comfort, sometimes through a loving friend's touch or scripture, and sometimes with the kooky creatures Jesus sets in our path, including wild chickens. —HEIDI GAUL

FAITH STEP: *Search out the absurdities and joyful moments Jesus sends your way. Journal them as a reminder to keep you smiling.*

FATHER'S DAY, SUNDAY, JUNE 16

Jesus gave them this answer: "Very truly I tell you, the Son can do nothing by himself; he can do only what he sees his Father doing, because whatever the Father does the Son also does." John 5:19 (NIV)

I WAS PRIVILEGED TO HAVE a father worth emulating. I'm not uncomfortable with his reputation or the memories he created. I wasn't traumatized by his words or actions, although I must admit I didn't care for his choice of socks, and sometimes his ties sported a remnant of what he'd had for lunch. But I have not had to bear unpleasant or destructive dad memories, as some unfortunately have.

If, like Jesus, I were told I could only do what I saw my father doing, what kind of life would that be? I would be generous to a fault, making sure others didn't go without, even at great personal cost. Because I witnessed my father doing so, I would pore over God's Word, then flip through commentaries, fascinated by the discoveries. If I could only do what my father did, I would be caught in acts of incredible patience. I would sacrifice for the comforts of others. I would love Jesus and my family deeply. I'd use music as an expression of worship. If I could do nothing other than what I saw my father doing, I would leave a legacy in the community that would still be talked about nearly thirty years after my passing.

I would live—am living—a full and satisfying life. Thank you, Dad. And thank You, Jesus, for listening to Your Father and helping my father emulate You. —CYNTHIA RUCHTI

FAITH STEP: *Craft a card or write in your journal a note thanking Jesus for listening to and mimicking His Father, God.*

MONDAY, JUNE 17

So you have not received a spirit that makes you fearful slaves. Instead,
you received God's Spirit when he adopted you as his own children.
Now we call him, "Abba, Father." Romans 8:15 (NLT)

MY EARTHLY DAD WAS A great guy, and I enjoyed a nice childhood with him and my mom. He was a strict disciplinarian, though, and my years of young womanhood became a tug-of-war. In the process of growing up, I seemed to lose the closeness—the Daddy-ness—I'd had with him when I was a girl.

Not surprisingly, when I received Christ as my Savior during college, my relationship with Jesus was based on His *lord*ship, not His *friend*ship. He talked, I obeyed. I was so grateful to be forgiven of my sins that I was happy to do so. It took me a while to realize Jesus really wanted to be my heavenly Dad. I heard people call Him "Daddy" or "Papa" when they talked about Him or prayed out loud. And Jesus called His own Father "Abba," an expression of deep intimacy.

I didn't fully relate. I'd been under my biological father's "strong arm of the law" for so long that I saw fathers as authority figures. But Jesus wanted me to allow Him to be Daddy too. He lovingly talked to me like a dad talks to his child, telling me how precious I was as a daughter, how proud He was of the woman I'd become, thanking me for doing things I thought went unnoticed. Slowly, Jesus taught me to trust Him with my heart, and I'm never turning back. Thanks, Daddy! —PAMELA TOUSSAINT HOWARD

FAITH STEP: *Think about how your earthly father impacts the way you see Jesus. As you sit with Jesus this week, begin your prayers with "Dear Daddy."*

TUESDAY, JUNE 18

You were taught, with regard to your former way of life, to put off your old self . . . and to put on the new self. Ephesians 4:22–24 (NIV)

SOON AFTER RETIREMENT, I DECIDED to clean my closet. My unworn teacher's clothes took up too much space. I thought the process would be easy. But as I sorted through my skinny pants and fat pants and fatter pants, as I pulled blouses off hangers and sweaters off shelves, I removed more than clothes. I was removing twenty-five years of me. The identity that I valued, that gave my life so much purpose, lay in piles ready to be donated. Leaving the former me behind was difficult but necessary.

Like my closet, my schedule gained a lot of free space when I retired. I began filling my time with activities I hadn't prioritized in the past. A morning routine with Jesus is easier to keep when I'm not up late the night before grading papers. I write thoughtful prayers in my journal instead of writing lesson plans. I accept invitations to Bible studies because I'm not exhausted after teaching all day. Oh, how much I had missed!

I wish I could have convinced my former self that giving Jesus even fifteen minutes a day is better than zero. I wish she understood that letting others tell her what the Bible says is no substitute for reading scripture for herself. If she only knew how much she would enjoy studying the Bible with her friends! My former self didn't get it, but thankfully, my new self does. —KAREN SARGENT

FAITH STEP: *Does your identity as an employee, parent, or volunteer take time away from Jesus? Think about doing a little "cleaning out" to make more room for Him.*

JUNETEENTH, WEDNESDAY, JUNE 19

Then Jesus turned to the Jews who had claimed to believe in him. "If you stick with this, living out what I tell you, you are my disciples for sure. Then you will experience for yourselves the truth, and the truth will free you." John 8:31–32 (MSG)

LIKE MANY AMERICANS, I DIDN'T know about Juneteenth until it was signed into law as a federal holiday a few years ago. The origins of Juneteenth fascinate me. Even though President Lincoln issued the Emancipation Proclamation on January 1, 1863, it took a while for the word to spread that enslaved people in America were now free. Slaves in Galveston, Texas, for example, remained in bondage until military troops arrived with the news of their freedom—on June 19, 1865.

In contrast to the slaves in Galveston, who were free and yet believed they were enslaved, the Jewish leaders in John 8 were enslaved and thought they were free. Jesus was not speaking about their bondage to an oppressive government but their bondage to sin. Spiritually, they were slaves to sin, and Jesus was challenging them to walk in the divine freedom that only He could provide.

Jesus provided for my freedom more than 2,000 years ago by His death on the cross, but I, too, needed to hear about His sacrifice before I could accept the free gift He had for me. And once I chose to accept the salvation He offered, I was truly free. —ERICKA LOYNES

FAITH STEP: *In which area of your life are you acting as if you're in bondage when you are actually free? Resist the lies from the enemy who says you're enslaved and remind him that the Truth has set you free.*

THURSDAY, JUNE 20

Is anyone crying for help? GOD is listening, ready to rescue you.
Psalm 34:17 (MSG)

I HAVE ALWAYS BEEN A caregiver. My most important role in this vein may have been as a transport nurse. I careened across hundreds of miles of two-lane roads in the Upper Peninsula of Michigan in ambulances with lights blazing and sirens blaring. I even did this once in a state trooper's car (the speedometer hit 99!). I flew in helicopters over Central Illinois to stabilize and safely provide intensive care to very sick and tiny babies for many years. The helicopters and ambulances had radios to communicate with the neonatologists. The team stayed ready. Speed and readiness were truly a matter of life and death.

I carried a dedicated phone, with my own as a backup. When I was on transports, I checked our equipment and supplies immediately after hearing report, which is the status notes from the preceding care team. With no patient assignment, I became an extra set of hands in the NICU, helping change linens, comforting an agitated baby, or starting an IV—anything that wouldn't tie me down. I had to be ready whenever I was called for help.

God sent Jesus to rescue us from sin. And Jesus stands at the ready. All we have to do is call to Him, cry out to Him, and ask Him for His protection and healing. He is the only One who can truly save us. —SUZANNE DAVENPORT TIETJEN

FAITH STEP: *Are you struggling? Trying to manage your problems on your own? Imagine yourself as a helpless infant as you pour out your heart to Jesus. Cry out and pray to Him for help today.*

FRIDAY, JUNE 21

I am the Light of the world. So if you follow me, you won't be stumbling through the darkness, for living light will flood your path. John 8:12 (TLB)

I WENT TO AN OUTDOOR concert with some friends to hear one of my all-time favorite R&B groups. Before we even made it to the entrance gate, we discovered we had to return a small cooler to the car because we couldn't take it into the venue. Two of us told the others to go ahead and grab spots on the lawn for our blankets and chairs. We'd catch up with them later.

By the time we returned to the concert site, the sun had set, and it was hard to find our friends in the throng of people. Luckily, our group spotted us wandering around in the darkness. They turned on their phones' flashlights and waved wildly so we could see them.

Later during the show, one of the singers asked everyone in the audience to turn on their phone flashlights in a show of peace and solidarity. Suddenly, there was great light in the darkness. It was like a megawatt switch had been turned on.

Those two encounters with darkness and light on a summer night made me think about Jesus. While on earth, Jesus declared that He was the Light of the World and those who chose to follow Him would see and live differently. Indeed, walking with Jesus is like having an ever-ready light at my disposal to guide me down the right path. That beats stumbling around in darkness every time.
—BARBRANDA LUMPKINS WALLS

FAITH STEP: *Turn on a flashlight or your phone's flashlight and find a darkened place to pray. Ask Jesus to light your way as you face difficult times.*

SATURDAY, JUNE 22

Now to him who is able to do immeasurably more than all we ask or imagine, according to his power that is at work within us, to him be glory in the church and in Christ Jesus throughout all generations, for ever and ever! Amen.
Ephesians 3:20–21 (NIV)

MOST MORNINGS, MY HUSBAND, TED, and I take a walk around our neighborhood. We chat, talk about the coming day, and enjoy the sunshine, fresh air, and each other's company. There are mornings when it's hard to drag myself out of bed, but I'm always glad afterward.

Yesterday as we walked, admiring neighbors' flower beds and blooming trees, I turned my head and noticed something unusual coming from a side street. I stopped short, my eyes widening. "Look!" I could barely get the word out.

A man on a unicycle rode toward us. Ted and I applauded as he zoomed past. It felt as if we had an impromptu circus act entertain us.

That happening flooded me with gratitude. It symbolized the unexpected ways Jesus surprises and delights me—often when I'm not watching for His amazing gifts. I'd hoped for birdsong and flowers when we set out on our daily walk, but I never expected a unicyclist.

Sometimes I treat Jesus as if He begrudges the provisions I pray for. But the opposite is true. He loves to give not only what I need but more than I can even hope for, including an improbable unicyclist.

One never knows what surprises and delights await when walking with Jesus. —SHARON HINCK

FAITH STEP: *Watch for Jesus to delight and surprise you today with something you haven't asked for or imagined. Thank Him for the amazing reflection of His love.*

SUNDAY, JUNE 23

For this reason I remind you to kindle afresh the gift of God which is in you through the laying on of my hands. 2 Timothy 1:6 (NASB 1995)

SOON AFTER ARRIVING AT THE Youth with a Mission (YWAM) base in Manila, Philippines, I attended a short worship service. I'd come to live at the center to attend its six-month Discipleship Training School as I searched for God's will and purpose for my life. I'd just graduated with an associate's degree but had no idea what I wanted to do. Twenty years old, I felt lonely and insecure since I did not know any of my classmates.

At the morning service, a winsome young man, carrying only his guitar, walked up to the front and began to lead us in praise and worship. Various family problems weighed heavy on my mind, and as we sang, tears streamed down my cheeks. My anxieties melted and I felt enveloped in Jesus's arms of comfort and love. The Holy Spirit ministered deeply to my hurting heart.

How I appreciate that man who answered Jesus's call on his life to become a worship leader! I never formally met him, but Jesus used him to help me find my calling. Today I serve as a worship leader. Through Jesus, I minister to others who are needy and hurting. I have learned that when we answer God's call on our own life, a domino effect takes place, and we enable others, through our obedience and example, to answer God's call on *their* lives.
—JENNIFER ANNE F. MESSING

FAITH STEP: *Thank Jesus for the special talents He has given you. Seek His will to specifically use one of the gifts He has bestowed on you to help someone find their purpose.*

MONDAY, JUNE 24

From this one man . . . came descendants as numerous as the stars in the sky and as countless as the sand on the seashore. Hebrews 11:12 (NIV)

THE MORNING AIR WAS PLEASANT on the beach when our family set out with our metal detector to navigate miles of white sand near Destin, Florida. I watched the detector head swing left and right. Every now and then, it beeped, prompting one of us to dig for the object.

We collected can tabs, coins, an earring, part of a necklace, and even a stone-studded ring that we wiped off with the hope that the stones were diamonds. (They weren't.)

I love the beach in the morning. It smells fresh, the air feels cooler, and the quiet calm is mesmerizing as we greet other early risers. People on a beach hold great fascination for me, and not only the ones I see. The ones whose treasures we find with the detector capture my imagination too. Each item we find buried in the sand connects to someone's story, and I wonder about each person and where they are now.

I, too, am leaving a legacy and not just by the possessions I leave behind. I want my life to portray gems of truth and grace. I try to exhibit Jesus's love to touch people I meet and, hopefully, those I will never meet. I'm reminded to be deliberate and intentional in following Jesus each day. After all, I never know who is going to pick up what I accidentally leave behind. —ERIN KEELEY MARSHALL

FAITH STEP: *Think of a time when you discovered something of value. Ask Jesus to show you what your life means for others.*

TUESDAY, JUNE 25

He who did not spare his own Son, but gave him up for us all—how will he not also, along with him, graciously give us all things? Romans 8:32 (NIV)

I'D BEEN BROWSING THE ZILLOW site for a couple of years as my husband and I planned our move back to our home state. Then suddenly my search results dropped from the usual twenty properties to three or four. It didn't help much when I reset the filters to include older homes and smaller lots. Clearly, this was a terrible time to buy a house. A seller's market with a shortage of homes—most of which were overpriced. A Realtor told me that many houses sold even before being listed.

I became obsessed with searching online. Then I found an old tote bag in my closet that soothed my anxiety. Sounds crazy, but I can explain. Years ago, I bought a leather tote that was absolutely perfect for work use. I didn't exactly pray, but I wished I could find the item in brown. Since it was discontinued, I doubted there was any chance. But three months later at a new outlet mall, I found the brown version. It wasn't perfect; it had a black mark along one edge. *Marked and saved for me*, I thought.

Jesus gave His life to pay for our sins. He is the proof that all our needs will be met in this earthly life and in the one to come. But beyond that, He delights in giving gifts and extra blessings. How can I doubt that He has already marked out a house for us?
—DIANNE NEAL MATTHEWS

FAITH STEP: *Make a list of all the blessings Jesus has given you that go beyond the basic necessities. Thank Him for being a gracious giver.*

WEDNESDAY, JUNE 26

Therefore, with minds that are alert and fully sober, set your hope on the grace to be brought to you when Jesus Christ is revealed at his coming.
1 Peter 1:13 (NIV)

IN THE PAST SEVERAL YEARS, circumstances beyond my control have dashed one hope after another. For instance, my husband and I intended to invite our marina neighbors into our boat-home for Saturday morning coffee and conversation at least once every three months, but pandemic restrictions canceled our plans.

We'd hoped to take a road trip to Alberta to see family and friends, but our intentions fell by the wayside when cancer struck a loved one there. Her medical treatments postponed our visit.

We'd hoped to attend our mission's staff conference in Poland recently, but two family emergencies hit us within days of our scheduled departure. We sensed God leading us to cancel our airline tickets and stay home to address the urgent needs.

Life is unpredictable, and basing my hopes on circumstances over which I have no control guarantees disappointment. But here's a truth that will never let me down: Jesus will descend from heaven someday as the conquering King. Those who have placed their hope in Him for salvation, though they are dead, will rise to meet Jesus and spend eternity in His presence (1 Thessalonians 4:16–17). Biblical promises made about the glories of our salvation will be completely fulfilled at that time. This is one hope that guarantees no disappointment. —GRACE FOX

FAITH STEP: *Identify a dashed hope and acknowledge the disappointment you felt. Thank Jesus for understanding your feelings and ask Him to help you focus your thoughts on the hope He brings.*

THURSDAY, JUNE 27

Jesus, Master, have pity on us! Luke 17:13 *(NIV)*

A FEW WEEKS INTO MY shingles nightmare, I started to feel a bit better. I could wear real pants instead of loose-fitting yoga pants. My appetite had returned, and I could go several hours without pain medication.

I told my husband, Kevin, I believed I was going to live through this ordeal, and added, "Just because I'm feeling better doesn't mean I don't still need your pity."

Where did that come from? I've always contended that pity never helped anyone. If I was hurt, I didn't need pity, thank you very much, just prayers. Now I was admitting that I would take all the pity I could get.

In Luke 17, ten lepers noticed Jesus approaching. They must have heard of His reputation as a man full of mercy. They didn't say, "Jesus is God; He'll figure out what we need and give it to us." No. They asked for Jesus's help. They called out to Him to have pity on them.

As long as I've walked with Jesus, I sometimes forget to ask Him for His help, or His pity. My self-sufficiency sends me to the nearest toolbox, trusted friend, or favorite search engine for answers. I forget that Jesus knows everything, has all the solutions I'll ever need, and longs to help me. I also forget that because of His great compassion, He is willing, able, and ready to show me pity.

The real pity is that I don't call on Him more often.
—JEANETTE LEVELLIE

FAITH STEP: *Put aside your self-sufficiency and believe that Jesus's heart is full of pity for you. Make a list of ways Jesus can show you His great compassion.*

FRIDAY, JUNE 28

And we know that in all things God works for the good of those who love him, who have been called according to his purpose. Romans 8:28 (NIV)

MY FRIEND JESS RECENTLY TOOK a trip overseas with her kids. Upon their return, her kids presented my kids with the barf bag from the plane (clean and unused, of course). In it were small mementos from their trip, including silly things that were given out free at their hotel: mini-shampoos, hand sanitizer, and the like. My kids thought it was the greatest thing ever and vowed to do it for them on our next trip.

I think what made it so special was that Jess and her family took what was intended for terrible circumstances (if you've ever been sick on a plane, you'd understand) and repurposed it by filling it with little blessings intended for joy.

Wouldn't it be amazing if I could do the same in every difficult circumstance of life? When a young mother is struggling with a crying child at the store, I can offer to carry her bags to her car. If someone I know loses his job, I can cook a meal or make a care package to leave on his doorstep. As my neighbor ages, I can offer to do her errands or shovel her driveway.

Life will never be smooth and easy on this side of heaven. But when Jesus helps me change how I view difficult circumstances, I'm able to fill them with blessings and repurpose them for joy. —CLAIRE MCGARRY

FAITH STEP: *Find something in your home you no longer use. Repurpose it, gifting it to someone who could use it or could use some joy.*

SATURDAY, JUNE 29

Jesus said to her, "I am the resurrection and the life. The one who believes in me will live, even though they die." John 11:25 (NIV)

A FEW MONTHS AGO, I traveled to Kansas with a friend. When I looked at a map, I realized where we'd be staying was only an hour away from where my grandfather had grown up. One of eleven children, Grandpa Fred lived on a farm until the Dust Bowl, when his whole family moved to California in 1936. With the information provided by a relative, my friend and I traveled to that farm. I was amazed by the beautiful rolling hills, expansive fields, and endless sky. Even though the old farmhouse was no longer there, I was delighted to see the one-room schoolhouse Grandpa attended still stood.

My grandfather passed away in 1999 and I miss him. I'm thankful for the stories he left behind and the new, sweet connection I had with him decades later when I visited his homesite.

I'm also grateful that because of Jesus, I'll be reunited with Grandpa again. My hope in heaven grew stronger when I walked with my grandpa through the shadow of death. In the days before he passed away, he spoke of the beauty of heaven he had glimpsed and the sweet aroma like wildflowers. Grandpa Fred even said he saw Jesus with His arms outstretched, welcoming him.

The beauty of Grandpa's death experience is even more remarkable now that I've seen the beauty of his Kansas farm. A rich heritage, indeed. —TRICIA GOYER

FAITH STEP: *Consider the heritage you are leaving behind. Write one thing you can do to share your love of Jesus with a family member or friend. Follow through sometime this week.*

SUNDAY, JUNE 30

Then the LORD came down in the cloud and stood there with him
and proclaimed his name, the LORD. Exodus 34:5 (NIV)

I COULD FEEL THE EXCITEMENT as we arrived at the huge parking
lot of FedExField, home of the Washington Commanders football
team. A friend and I were there for an outdoor Sunday morning
worship service with fellow believers. Greeters lined the roadway,
waving enthusiastically as we drove past, and pointed us in the direction we needed to go. Thousands were gathering on the grounds,
anticipating good music, wonderful fellowship, and great preaching
on a warm summer day.

We set up our lawn chairs and welcomed those around us. We had
prayed for good weather. As we settled in, I looked up. Clouds were
gathering in the sky. *Could rain be on the way?* The choir started
to sing, and we began to clap and joyfully praise Jesus. But after a
while, I looked upward again. The clouds were hanging so low that
I felt as if I could touch them. Surely, the Lord was there, just as
He had been with Moses when He appeared in a cloud on Mount
Sinai. Tears came to my eyes as I prayed that the Lord would be
a pillar of cloud for us too. Throughout the service, the billowy
clouds hovered over the stadium and the surrounding parking lots-
turned-sanctuary, providing cover from the blistering sun.

I knew without a doubt that Jesus was with us. I was so captivated
by the scene that I snapped several pictures of those clouds. Whenever I look at them, I'm reminded that Jesus covers me wherever I
go, rain or shine. —BARBRANDA LUMPKINS WALLS

FAITH STEP: *Imagine Jesus covering you as you take some time and look at the*
clouds today.

MONDAY, JULY 1

I myself will see him with my own eyes—I, and not another.
How my heart yearns within me! Job 19:27 (NIV)

MY EYESIGHT HAS ALWAYS BEEN poor. I got my first pair of corrective eyeglasses at age six, then needed stronger and thicker prescription lenses every couple of months over the next few years. By nine, I exchanged my glasses for rigid contact lenses. Without them, I was legally blind. Since both of my parents lost their sight from glaucoma, my eye doctor keeps a close watch on my pressure readings.

One July, I suffered my first detached retina in my right eye and underwent emergency surgery. For the next two weeks, I had to keep my head parallel to the floor 24/7 to facilitate healing. Soon after, I underwent another surgery on that eye to repair lingering damage, which meant another two weeks facedown. While traveling across Morocco on the trip of a lifetime two years ago, those familiar dark shadows began to descend over my left eye, necessitating an emergency trip home, another surgery, and another two weeks facedown. The day I hoped to get clearance from the surgeon to lift my head, I got word of another macular hole in that same eye. Days later, I underwent my fourth retina surgery in as many years. And—you guessed it—another two weeks facedown.

All those days spent facedown established a new pattern of prayer. After all, I could do little else but talk to Jesus. While my vision challenges continue to this day, the eyes of my heart are open, knowing every hardship is an opportunity for prayer. —SUSAN DOWNS

FAITH STEP: *Want to see Jesus more clearly? Set a timer for ten minutes. Close your eyes and pray, then listen for His answer.*

TUESDAY, JULY 2

Fools think their own way is right, but the wise listen to others.
Proverbs 12:15 (NLT)

WHEN I GOT MY FIRST mountain bike years ago, I refused to wear a helmet. I liked the feeling of the wind in my hair. My husband, Jeff, said, "Even as hardheaded as you are, Pat, if you fell and hit your head, it could break." I tried to ignore him, but he'd taken some of the joy out of my freedom. Finally, his constant nagging about how sad it would be for our kids to grow up without a mother guilted me into wearing a helmet.

Jeff's most recent focus was trying to convince me not to listen to music with earbuds while I rode. "You can't hear oncoming traffic. You could get distracted and have an accident," he warned.

But wasn't Christian music a good thing? How could something bad happen while songs about Jesus filled my head? So I continued to listen to music as I flew along. As the land whisked by, a sense of unease surrounded me. I had an awareness that I wasn't in sync with my husband or Jesus, despite the positive music playing through my earbuds. It bothered me but not enough to give up doing what I enjoyed.

Then one day, after a rain, I swerved to avoid a puddle and a UPS truck almost clipped me. *OK, Jesus, I get it!* I rode home and hung up my earbuds, knowing it was safer to listen to Jesus (and my husband) than praise music. —PAT BUTLER DYSON

FAITH STEP: *Sit quietly and concentrate on hearing Jesus. What is He trying to tell you? Listen and obey Him.*

WEDNESDAY, JULY 3

Come to me, all you who are weary and burdened, and I will give you rest.
Take my yoke upon you and learn from me, for I am gentle and humble in
heart, and you will find rest for your souls. Matthew 11:28–29 (NIV)

WHO WOULD HAVE IMAGINED THAT a simple spelling mistake could become a spiritual aha moment? It happened upon discovering that I'd written "reset" where I'd intended to write "rest." As I paused to consider the connectedness between these two words, I thought about how incredibly busy my life feels at times. Perhaps you can relate.

Family and household responsibilities combined with work and church-related activities leave me tired. Add personal concerns, worries about loved ones, and fear about the future, and I feel bone-weary.

Jesus promises rest for my soul when I spend time in His presence. Reading the Word and conversing with Him in prayer give me clarity to see where I've picked up burdens He never meant for me to carry. Jesus helps me understand where I've tried to control circumstances rather than giving Him control. He helps me discern where I've said yes to commitments because I felt obligated, not called. Responding to the insights He gives means resetting my priorities and perspective to align with His.

A simple spelling mistake has caused me to examine my life for thoughts and behaviors that need a reset. It's a rewarding exercise because it identifies and helps me work on those things that hinder me from experiencing the rest Jesus offers. —GRACE FOX

FAITH STEP: *Identify one thought, attitude, or behavior that needs a reset in order for you to experience soul rest.*

INDEPENDENCE DAY, THURSDAY, JULY 4

Blessed is the nation whose God is the LORD, the people He has chosen as His own inheritance. Psalm 33:12 (NKJV)

TODAY, A PARADE WILL MARCH down the streets of my town. My family will gather at my house to grill burgers, churn homemade ice cream, and play cornhole. Then we'll join our community at the park to enjoy live music until it's time for the fireworks display.

Interestingly, the way Americans celebrate this historical holiday hasn't changed much since 1777, when Philadelphia celebrated the first Independence Day. While those fireworks were not the elaborate displays we witness, the evening began and concluded with the firing of thirteen rockets—breathtaking to those colonists no doubt. However, while the early Americans celebrated freedom from tyranny, today we celebrate patriotism.

The birth of this nation represents more than politics and patriotism, though. We have a rich Christian heritage. Many early colonists and immigrants viewed America as the "promised land." In the wake of religious conflicts in Europe in the 1600s, America represented a safe haven for the religiously oppressed and exiled. Thus, the biblical story of the exodus and the search for a promised land resonated with many early colonists. Some who suffered oppression under British rule believed God orchestrated the independence of America and the creation of a new nation—their promised land.

This year as I admire the fireworks, I will thank Jesus for His blessings, the sacrifice of those early colonists, and the Christian heritage America is built upon. —KAREN SARGENT

FAITH STEP: *As you celebrate America's freedom on this Independence Day, pray for our leaders to honor our rich heritage.*

FRIDAY, JULY 5

Let us hold unswervingly to the hope we profess, for he who promised is faithful. Hebrews 10:23 (NIV)

RED, WHITE, AND BLUE FIREWORKS lit the sky above the dark country road. Our family Fourth of July picnic had ended, and I was driving home alone. I gripped the wheel from curve to curve. Just as I started down a hill, my headlights caught movement up ahead.

Boom! The road in front of my car exploded with streams of sparkling color and deafening blasts. I swerved left and then right, before driving straight into the smoke. I screeched to a terrifying stop, while a group of teenagers hee-hawed nearby.

Like those wayward teens, the enemies of my faith would like to wreck me. They laugh and claim my biblical beliefs are closed-minded and outdated. When they whisper these insinuations in my ear, I can't swerve to the left. When they stand near and proclaim untruths, I won't swerve to the right. And when their voices grow angry and frighten me, I must never hit the brakes on the hope I have in Jesus.

Jesus experienced relentless persecution during His thirty-three years on earth, even to the point of crucifixion. But His hope didn't waver. He stayed the course and "endured the cross, scorning its shame, and sat down at the right hand of the throne of God" (Hebrews 12:2, NIV).

Though worldly voices and circumstances sometimes scare me, I know that Jesus is with me. He gives me courage to hold the wheel, unswervingly, as I travel on my road of faith. —BECKY ALEXANDER

FAITH STEP: *Identify the voices in your life that cause your hope to swerve—television, toxic people, social media, inappropriate music and books, etc. Remove what you can, and ask Jesus to help you stay the course.*

SATURDAY, JULY 6

Then I will ask the Father to send you the Holy Spirit who will help you and always be with you. John 14:16 (CEV)

MY FRIEND ANGELA AND HER husband have lovingly restored a historic waterfront home in Virginia. Angela graciously offered the house to me and four other friends for a weekend stay. We jumped at the chance for a girls' getaway.

The couple greeted us after we arrived, showed us around the beautiful house, and then left. We had a great time relaxing, laughing, taking walks along the water, and exploring area restaurants. We also enjoyed some impromptu late-night chats around the large dining room table. It was a joyful time of restoration.

Right before we departed, we five sister-friends gathered in a circle in the foyer to thank God for a wonderful weekend. As we held hands and bowed our heads, the back door slowly creaked open. I opened my eyes to see who it was, but no one was there. As we continued praying, the door opened wider and wider. I decided Jesus and the Holy Spirit had joined us.

I texted Angela the next day to thank her and tell her we'd prayed over her and the house before we left. "I did feel that prayed-up, peaceful spirit when I walked in," Angela admitted. "I kept asking myself, *Why am I tearing up?* Now I know why."

Yes, Jesus had been there and His Spirit had lingered.
—BARBRANDA LUMPKINS WALLS

FAITH STEP: *How or when have you experienced the presence and peace of Jesus?*

SUNDAY, JULY 7

I assure you and most solemnly say to you, unless you repent [that is, change your inner self—your old way of thinking, live changed lives] and become like children [trusting, humble, and forgiving], you will never enter the kingdom of heaven. Matthew 18:3 (AMP)

I'VE HEARD MANY GOOD SERMONS over many years, and when I take notes, I think I learn more. Lately, the children's sermon has been my greatest blessing. The little ones walk (or are carried) to the front of the church, where Pastor sits on the steps and tells them about Jesus. The children listen all a-wiggle, guessing at and shouting out answers to Pastor's questions.

He tells a Bible story, teaches some simple truth, and recites a Bible verse, which the little ones might repeat after him. Jesus is central. The children are assured and reminded of His love. Sometimes there's a song. They finish with prayer, then they head back to their seats.

The children of our congregation demonstrate how to accept and receive simply. Where I might overthink and analyze, they look and see. They hear and believe. If some small gift is offered, they reach freely to receive it.

Their backs to the congregation and faces lifted to Pastor, the children of our church lack self-consciousness. They aren't taking notes. They enter the story.

I want a heart like that. I want to express myself freely and honestly as I seek Him earnestly. Just like a child. —SUZANNE DAVENPORT TIETJEN

FAITH STEP: *If you have a children's Bible or Bible storybook, read it and revel in the simple presentation of the Gospel. Consider volunteering to be a helper in Sunday school or the nursery, and observe both the experienced teachers and the children. Practice applying what you learn to your faith.*

MONDAY, JULY 8

And my God will meet all your needs according to the riches of his glory in Christ Jesus. Philippians 4:19 (NIV)

I WAS WITHIN A MILE from our house after picking up my husband, Ron, from the hospital after his life-threatening accident. I stepped on the car's accelerator to get us home quicker. It decelerated instead. *Oh no!* The car barely coasted into our driveway.

A major car repair was not something we needed in addition to everything else. Ron had left his teaching career a few months earlier to work outdoors for a local business. Now our financial future was uncertain because of his injuries and his inability to work during an undetermined time of recovery. *What now, Jesus?*

That evening, I remembered a conversation I had with a friend after Ron's accident. She offered to set up financial assistance to help with our medical needs and expenses while Ron was unable to work. I'd planned on declining the offer, though she asked me to let the body of Christ care for us. Receiving such help felt vulnerable and risky. My pride overshadowed her caring gesture.

I tried to dismiss the idea but couldn't. I mentioned it to Ron. After we prayed, we agreed to accept her offer. Doing so was humbling.

Over several weeks, we experienced the outpouring of Jesus's grace as He met our every need through others. I'm so glad I didn't let pride stand in the way of receiving care, generosity, and blessings from people and Jesus. —BRENDA L. YODER

FAITH STEP: *Do you find it difficult to receive assistance from others, even when you need it? The next time someone offers, set aside pride and be willing to accept Jesus's provision through the care of others, even if it feels uncomfortable.*

TUESDAY, JULY 9

*And I pray that you . . . may have power . . . to grasp how wide and long
and high and deep is the love of Christ. Ephesians 3:17–18 (NIV)*

A YOUNG MOM STOOD A few feet from me. The toddler in her arms sported long, dark curls. The little one's shoulders shuddered as if she had just experienced a hard crying spell. Watching that tiny body spasm with the involuntary remainders of her sobs, I had no doubt she was only slowly recovering.

Then the little girl tightened her grip on her mama's neck and laid her head on the safe shoulders.

That's like me. The immediate crisis may be over, but I occasionally shudder. The tears may stop, but the convulsive sniffs aren't finished. Nothing changed for the toddler, but she threw herself deeper into her mother's embrace, her mother's safety.

My one safe place is the embrace of Jesus. My ultimate comfort lies in diving deeper into the limitless love of my Savior, burying my tear-stained face into His more-than-wide-enough shoulder.

A few minutes later, the child I'd observed was whining, acting out. Again, her mother took her into her loving arms and held her close. And the lesson struck even closer to home. It would not have mattered if that little girl had been injured by someone else, frightened by the world around her, or behaving badly. Her place of comfort and hope lay in the same spot—diving deeper into the loving arms and the unconditional love of a caring parent. I'm so grateful that's true for me too. —CYNTHIA RUCHTI

FAITH STEP: *Close your eyes for a few moments and picture yourself—with your current cares—nestling into that spot over the heart and heartbeat of your Savior. Stay as long as you need as you feel comforted and loved.*

WEDNESDAY, JULY 10

Godly sorrow brings repentance that leads to salvation and leaves no regret. 2 Corinthians 7:10 (NIV)

THE HVAC SYSTEM IN OUR attic had a small leak that soaked through the ceiling in our master bathroom. We quickly called in a professional who fixed the problem, but the stain on the ceiling remained. Painting the whole ceiling seemed like overkill. I took a shortcut and purchased a can of spray paint that sprays straight up, kills any accumulated mold, and, of course, covers the stain. Unfortunately, the shade of white covering the spot was too bright for the age of the ceiling. The new paint stuck out like a sore thumb. So, I kept spraying, trying to blend and fade the edges to match the old paint.

I ended up spraying half the ceiling, and residual spray hit the walls, floor, and tub. It looks terrible! I guess I'm going to have to pay someone to paint the entire ceiling after all.

Like that small stain, the little mistakes in my life bother me. But rather than addressing them correctly the first time, I sometimes take shortcuts, looking for a quick fix or easy way out. That only turns my molehill mistakes into mountains, made worse by my laziness and denial.

Jesus calls me to true repentance, not a fudging over of my sins to hide them away. As uncomfortable as it is to admit my mistakes to Him, His forgiveness and mercy wash me clean. Wisdom has taught me that avoiding the process widens the chasm separating me from Him. I'd much rather use my sin as a bridge to find true forgiveness in Him. —CLAIRE MCGARRY

FAITH STEP: *If there's a mistake or sin you've been avoiding, come clean with Jesus. Make amends and repent.*

THURSDAY, JULY 11

When he had finished speaking, he said to Simon, "Put out into deep water, and let down the nets for a catch." Luke 5:4 (NIV)

SIX MONTHS AFTER OUR FAMILY moved, we felt Jesus leading us to move again, this time across several hundred miles. We closed on our fifth home in less than five years. To some people, that much moving may not make sense. In some ways, even to us, it felt like too much. We were weary.

Despite those feelings, however, the move has felt purposeful every day since we heard Jesus's voice urging us to go. We continue to see Him show up in fresh ways we would not have experienced if we had not obeyed.

What makes sense to Jesus is often absurd by human logic.

But I'm human. I'm more comfortable with logic. Jesus had a pattern of audacious action. The fishermen disciples had made careers of catching fish. After they had a long, fruitless day on the water, imagine their response when this career Carpenter instructed them to try something different—to defy logic and put their nets down in the empty sea.

But that's what Jesus did. If the fishermen had not listened to His instruction and taken the obedient step, they would have missed the blessing of an abundant eleventh-hour catch. Even more than that, they would have missed seeing Jesus for who He is and His willing power to transform their everyday lives.

I remember the double rainbow stretched over our home on moving day. I set aside my need to follow human logic and, like those fishermen, gladly followed Jesus where He wanted me to go.
—ERIN KEELEY MARSHALL

FAITH STEP: *In what area do you rely on human logic instead of Jesus's direction? Trust Jesus no matter what.*

FRIDAY, JULY 12

And after you have suffered a little while, the God of all grace, who has called you to his eternal glory in Christ, will himself restore, confirm, strengthen, and establish you. 1 Peter 5:10 (ESV)

THE LAST FEW YEARS HAVE been personally challenging for me. My husband had been laid off, and it became apparent that my struggling marriage would not survive. On a global scale, we were dealing with COVID-19, civil unrest, political upheaval, natural disasters, economic instability, and global conflicts. At this writing, there is scant evidence of lasting relief or a return to anything like normalcy.

Yet I've been able to move through challenge after challenge by claiming and reclaiming the spiritual promise of 1 Peter 5:10. I remind myself of the times I have suffered, the trials I have endured, and I turn to this verse in 1 Peter. Jesus restores my faith, confirms my commitment to Christ, strengthens my resolve, and establishes my footing.

Restoration and regrowth come after wildfires in large part from sunlight and growth of the trees underground, where we can't see it. In a similar way, Jesus provides Sonlight to feed the growth of my soul and heart as He works in my life, even when I struggle to see it. Even through suffering and temptation, my eternal Jesus will deliver the grace I need to be strong and endure. —ISABELLA CAMPOLATTARO

FAITH STEP: *Think of a trial you've endured. List at least one way Jesus has restored, confirmed, strengthened, and established you through that crisis.*

SATURDAY, JULY 13

You keep track of all my sorrows. You have collected all my tears in your bottle. You have recorded each one in your book. Psalm 56:8 (NLT)

"DON'T SHAKE THAT BOTTLE, JEANETTE. It will make tons of bubbles, and we'll get a glass full of those instead of the grape juice."

I blinked in confusion at my husband, Kevin, who's rarely bossy. Especially this early in the morning. "But that's what Daddy always did when we had grape juice. My brother and I would argue over the glass with the most bubbles."

I had less than a dozen distinct memories of my father, who left when I was six and died when I was ten. Grape juice bubbles was one of the happiest.

"Aha," he said, as an understanding smile lightened Kevin's face.

Jesus sees every wound of my soul, even the broken places I've hidden from myself. He understands why I need that silly reminder of Daddy and the purple bubbles. Jesus sees the tears that slip down my cheeks in secret for all the disappointments and lost opportunities. Better yet, He fills every hole in my heart with His love and compassion.

When I was young, I often asked Jesus why I was fatherless. Now that I'm not so young, I realize He's given me the best Father ever. My heavenly Father, who will never leave me.

My bottle of tears may be huge. But Jesus's fondness for me is immeasurable. —JEANETTE LEVELLIE

FAITH STEP: *If you have a hole of disappointment or pain in your heart, ask Jesus to fill it up with the love and kindness that only He can supply.*

SUNDAY, JULY 14

The LORD who rescued me from the paw of the lion and the paw of the bear will rescue me from the hand of this Philistine. 1 Samuel 17:37 (NIV)

WHILE IN BEIRUT, I MET a young man named "A." Born and raised in Syria as a Muslim, A was tortured by ISIS for refusing to withdraw from his studies in social justice. One day, while in prison, he cried, "God, rescue me if You're real." A bomb destroyed the prison soon afterward, and A escaped to Lebanon. That's where he learned about Jesus.

After training to become a career missionary, A founded a school for Syrian children. He trusted the Lord to provide a facility, food for hot lunches, and educational supplies. North American donors contributed to the cause, a team of six national coworkers joined the work, and the ministry grew to include Bible studies for the students' parents. However, A lived in constant danger because he could neither safely return to Syria nor gain Lebanese citizenship.

Canada recently granted A refugee status. My husband and I will soon welcome him and help him settle. Quite honestly, I feel anxious about finding suitable and affordable housing. I fear the negative effect of North American affluence. I worry about his finding work and a wife, whether his school will flourish without his presence, and what ministry he'll find to do here.

When fear for A's future hits me, I remember his past. Jesus has delivered him from dangers and difficulties too many to count. My fear subsides when I choose to trust that He'll be faithful to A in the future. —GRACE FOX

FAITH STEP: *Pray that A will adjust well to Canadian life and that his relationship with Jesus will remain passionate.*

MONDAY, JULY 15

*If we confess our sins, he is faithful and just and will forgive us
our sins and purify us from all unrighteousness. 1 John 1:9 (NIV)*

MY LAPTOP WAS DYING, AND it was time for a replacement. When
the new one arrived, I was excited to transfer my files and take
advantage of the chance to clean out old data. Skimming through
folders, I was horrified at my terrible "cyber hygiene." Duplicate
documents. Folders that were tucked inside of other folders. Files
with vague labels. No wonder I'd struggled to find things.

I've committed to deleting items that take up valuable space on my
new computer's hard drive. Without a diligent eye each day, emails
pile up, folders get filled, and my former friend, chaos, creeps in.

Like a computer that's cluttered with old or useless data, my life
can become cluttered with sins. Perhaps I'm rehearsing grievances
and need to instead take my concerns to Jesus. Or maybe that television show I watch that is fascinating but leaves me feeling dark
and sad isn't contributing to the life to which Jesus calls me. Or
perhaps my desire to control everything comes at the expense of
offering hospitality and flexibility. One by one, those obsolete folders in my heart and mind can be removed. Not by my own strength,
but by the grace of our Savior.

As He points out problems, He is also faithful to forgive and set me
on a new course. Jesus can purify my inner "hard drive" and delete
that which keeps me from running smoothly. —SHARON HINCK

FAITH STEP: *Take a look at what you've saved on your computer or smart
device. Delete anything that isn't necessary as you pray for Jesus to do the same
in your heart.*

TUESDAY, JULY 16

But pray and ask God for everything you need, always giving thanks.
Philippians 4:6 (NCV)

MY FRIEND JUDY AND I were walking on a trail when a young man pushing his bike walked toward us. "The worst thing *ever* just happened," he said. "A part fell off my bike and now I can't ride it." He showed us where the missing piece used to be. As a bike rider, I knew exactly what it looked like. I told him we'd look for it and if we found it, we'd get it to him. His shoulders slumped, and I sensed his hopelessness as we walked off in opposite directions.

Judy and I thought it impossible to find the tiny part on the trail with knee-high grasses aligning both sides. But Jesus encourages believers to pray about everything, including lost things. He told three parables about loss. A lost sheep, a lost coin, and a lost son (Luke 15). Judy and I prayed that God would show us the lost bike part.

After walking a bit, I looked to my left and spotted it on the ground. "I can't believe it," Judy said. "It's a miracle!" A young woman was jogging toward us. We stopped her, handed her the bike part, and gave her the mission to deliver the piece to the man pushing his bike on the trail ahead. She sprinted off. We imagined his joy when she caught up to him.

Like this young man, I, too, feel hopeless at times. Thankfully, the Finder of lost things—and souls—walks with me, reminding me that hope is only a prayer away. —JEANNIE BLACKMER

FAITH STEP: *Are you feeling hopeless today? Turn your discouragement into a hope-filled prayer and ask Jesus to help you find joy.*

WEDNESDAY, JULY 17

But we ought always to thank God for you, brothers and sisters loved by the Lord, because God chose you as firstfruits to be saved through the sanctifying work of the Spirit and through belief in the truth.
2 Thessalonians 2:13 (NIV)

MY NIECE, LILY, IS ONE of my favorite people. She is six years old, loves unicorns, and adores all things sparkly. We live in different states, so we don't see each other that often. But when we do, she greets me with a giant hug and a shout of "Aunt Sue!" I sweep her up in my arms and kiss her all over her face.

This summer when we were on a family vacation together, Lily chose me to be her pal at the community pool. The pool had a lazy river with inner tubes for floating. Lily and I spent a good hour being pulled by the gentle current, drifting around the lazy river. I sat in the inner tube, and she sat on my lap. We trailed our fingers in the water, tried not to bump other river riders, and laughed a lot. I love her like crazy. I am so glad that she chose to be close to me.

It is a precious thing to be chosen. Jesus chose me to be His before the beginning of time. He knows who I am inside and out, the beautiful and the not-so-beautiful. He forgives and accepts me. He loves me like crazy. He wants to spend time with me now and for the rest of eternity. Choosing to be close to Jesus is the best choice I've ever made. —SUSANNA FOTH AUGHTMON

FAITH STEP: *Carve out time today, in prayer and worship, to talk to Jesus. Let Him know that you choose Him and love Him like crazy.*

THURSDAY, JULY 18

For the vision is yet for an appointed time; but at the end it will speak, and it will not lie. Though it tarries, wait for it; because it will surely come, it will not tarry. Habakkuk 2:3 (NKJV)

OUR SON AJ JUST OPENED his first bank account. I thought it was smart that he chose a bank that offered a substantial monetary gift for new customers, but months passed and the money never arrived. I figured he wasn't eligible somehow and shrugged it off. (Easier for me to do than it was for him.)

One evening, the manager at the supermarket where AJ worked after school told him they needed to cut his hours. AJ was dejected. He relied on the money for snacks and sneakers and other incidentals. As parents, we wanted him to share the responsibility for buying things he wanted as he prepared for adulthood. He needed to learn to problem-solve and budget for himself.

One day many weeks later, AJ brought in the mail and there was the gift check from the bank. He was so amazed he asked us to verify it was real—it was!

Isn't it just like Jesus to answer our needs in His time and His way? While I was trying to teach AJ about financial responsibility, Jesus was teaching us both about how to trust Him. Despite how circumstances may appear, I was reminded that Jesus always comes through—and you can bank on it! —PAMELA TOUSSAINT HOWARD

FAITH STEP: *Decide today to release anxiousness about something you're waiting for. Stop thinking Jesus has forgotten, trust Him, and rest in the fact that it will surely come.*

FRIDAY, JULY 19

Being confident of this, that he who began a good work in you will carry it on to completion until the day of Christ Jesus. Philippians 1:6 (NIV)

HOME RENOVATION PROJECTS CAN BE nerve-racking, and updating the bathroom in our century-old Memphis home was no exception. During the first few days the contractors were there, I crammed my home office into my laptop bag and went to work with my husband, who is a college professor. His tall, dark, and neatly lined bookshelves against the white cement-brick wall were a perfect backdrop for video calls, but I had difficulty getting much done while I was displaced from my home office.

After three months, the renovation was almost complete. The crew had to make only a few touch-ups, but part of the tiling was uneven and, honestly, sloppy. The lead contractor agreed to return in a few days to redo that section. Even though this inconvenienced him and he had to put off new projects in queue, he was committed to finish the work his crew started.

I'm thankful for the contractor's commitment. I'm also thankful that Jesus always finishes what He starts. When I don't feel like my optimistic self or when I'm feeling broken and barely able to hold things together, Jesus doesn't leave me to tend to someone else. His masterful hands restore me and remind me that He will help me carry out His work, no matter where I am. —ERICKA LOYNES

FAITH STEP: *What unfinished work do you need to complete to improve your faith walk? Begin now, trusting that Jesus will help you finish what you start.*

SATURDAY, JULY 20

Yea, though I walk through the valley of the shadow of death, I will fear no evil; For You are with me; Your rod and Your staff, they comfort me.
Psalm 23:4 (NKJV)

I SAT ACROSS THE TABLE from my dear friend and reached for her hand as she searched for words that wouldn't come. Her eyes revealed the sorrow trapped inside. When the waitress brought our meal, we prayed and made an effort to eat. But food was the last reason we'd met that day. A week earlier, my companion had lost her mother following a brief illness, and her pain burned deep and raw. She hungered to be comforted and understood.

At home, I'd prayed to Jesus to give me the words to soothe her, and He provided. Our time together spread from one hour to the next. Conversation moved from precious memories of a woman's life well-lived to tears and finally to laughter. Thoughts of the future braided through our talk like a golden thread of hope. When we parted that afternoon, a sense of calm filled both our hearts.

I was honored to walk beside my friend for even a few steps as she travels the valley of the shadow of death. Like so many of us, it's a place I'm familiar with. It can seem a lonely, soul-searching hike and difficult to find your footing. What a great relief it is to know Jesus walks with us, guiding and protecting us with His rod and staff. And what a blessing when we find friends willing to walk alongside. —HEIDI GAUL

FAITH STEP: *Bless a friend walking that lonesome valley with a card, a visit, or a phone call. Join Jesus as He walks alongside her.*

SUNDAY, JULY 21

*But as for you, be strong and do not give up, for your work
will be rewarded. 2 Chronicles 15:7 (NIV)*

I HAVE A CONFESSION TO make. For the last few months, almost a year in fact, I've felt anything but on fire for the Lord.

I pray every morning and throughout the day. I read my Bible regularly and write stories for Christian magazines and anthologies. But the zeal I'd like to feel is absent. That dancing-on-the-front-lawn, uninhibited excitement of a three-year-old. Fervent prayers. Enthusiastic worship. The kinds of intense feelings I experienced as a new Christian.

Back then I was relieved—no, thrilled—to discover that Jesus had already forgiven my sins. His love gave me a fresh start in life. I openly praised Jesus for every blessing—from a high grade on an essay to my friend Katie's decision to follow Him. I talked about Jesus all day long. I felt His presence every minute.

Decades later, I plod along, telling Jesus how much I love Him, promising I'll never leave or forsake Him (I stole that phrase from Him), and asking for His help.

If I'm hearing Jesus's voice correctly, He assures me that I don't need to have feelings of elation to follow Him. I just have to keep going and not give up.

That encourages me. Because when life gets hard and complicated, persevering with Jesus's help is just the right amount of excitement. —JEANETTE LEVELLIE

FAITH STEP: *If you don't feel all the exhilaration you felt as a new Christian, don't give up! Make a list of the ways you persevere in tough times and thank Jesus for His help.*

MONDAY, JULY 22

But whoever drinks the water I give them will never thirst. Indeed, the water I give them will become in them a spring of water welling up to eternal life. John 4:14 (NIV)

I HAVE A HUGE WATER jug that I fill up in the morning and keep on my desk to sip from throughout the day. It's marked with various encouraging words at two-hour intervals, starting with "Good morning!" at 7 a.m., "That's it!" at 3 p.m., and finally, "Well done!" at 9 p.m.

There are days when I drink steadily from the jug. Sometimes I guzzle the water to catch up and stay on task so that I can finish the container. Other days I hardly put a dent in it. When I fail to drink up as I should, I realize that hydration is not a priority in the story about Jesus and the Samaritan woman at the well, when Jesus says He is "living water" and those who drink this water will never be thirsty again. I wonder what my life would look like if I guzzled the living water that Jesus offers me like the filtered water I drink from my big jug. I imagine I would have more peace, less fear, and increased courage. I'd also be more obedient to His will and more focused on Him.

So instead of taking little sips of Jesus every day through short prayers and quick devotional readings, I am drinking more deeply with even more quiet time with Him. That's the real way to quench my undying thirst. —BARBRANDA LUMPKINS WALLS

FAITH STEP: *How will you drink in Jesus today? Instead of a sip in the morning, plan to drink in moments with Him all day long.*

TUESDAY, JULY 23

And we all, who with unveiled faces contemplate the Lord's glory, are being transformed into his image with ever-increasing glory, which comes from the Lord, who is the Spirit. 2 Corinthians 3:18 (NIV)

MY TWENTY-SOMETHING DAUGHTER AND HER husband have joined the "skoolie" movement. They purchased a seventy-two-passenger, flat-nose Blue Bird school bus from a district replacing its fleet. Why would they want to own a school bus? Good question. I wondered that too.

The enormous yellow vehicle is stripped of all lettering on the outside, the seats were removed, and the walls and floor have been reduced to a metal shell. On paper, my daughter has put her interior design degree to work. They will rebuild the interior of the bus into an RV, complete with a kitchen, bedroom, and bathroom. The exterior will be painted to match the inside, a striped 1970s pastel color scheme—powder blue, tangerine, salmon, and eggshell. Once the old bus has been transformed into a new motor home, they'll climb aboard and drive across the country.

Fully surrendering to the Master used to feel a bit like that bus redesign to me. I feared the outcome. What if He stripped away something I thought I needed or added something that didn't really suit me? What if He sent me in a new direction I didn't intend to travel? What if I no longer knew myself?

But you know what? My daughter's new layout and delightful color choices don't change the fact that a skoolie is still just a bus. Jesus can remove the brokenness I cling to, clean up my heart, and transform me into His image. He can change me inside and out, but I am still me—just a much better design. —KAREN SARGENT

FAITH STEP: *What is Jesus asking you to redesign? List the what-ifs interfering with His plan.*

WEDNESDAY, JULY 24

The boundary lines have fallen for me in pleasant places. Psalm 16:6 (NIV)

AN ACQUAINTANCE REMARKED ABOUT HOW busy I was when I declined an invitation for a social event. I felt irritated and judged because she didn't understand why I said no. It wasn't because I was too busy. I was setting boundaries around my priorities—rightsizing my life.

I'd been working with an organization that used the term "rightsizing" as it was aligning its workforce with a new mission and work strategy. The concept fit what I needed, both professionally and personally. My husband and I worked different jobs, were new empty nesters, expecting a grandbaby, and planning a child's wedding. I often felt depleted from doing everything I used to do in addition to new responsibilities.

In recent months, I'd heard Jesus say "no more" to activities I'd been doing for years. Although I let go of several commitments, it took me a while to realize they didn't fit the priorities in my current season of life. Jesus was drawing new boundary lines for me. At first, I felt guilty, but as I continued to rightsize my life, I listened to Him, prayed about opportunities and responsibilities, and considered my energy levels. Jesus's new boundaries for me fit just right. —BRENDA L. YODER

FAITH STEP: *Do you need rightsizing? Ask Jesus to reveal the best priorities for your current stage of life. Learn to be comfortable saying no and yes as you rightsize your life.*

THURSDAY, JULY 25

For the earth will be filled with the knowledge of the glory of the
LORD as the waters cover the sea. Habakkuk 2:14 *(NIV)*

ONE OF MY FAVORITE THINGS to do is to attend online tours of historical sites. Virtually, I've walked through royal tombs in Egypt. I've explored ancient ruins in Rome. And I've also seen carvings in the burial chambers of four kings in the Persian Empire. It's interesting to visit those primitive places from the comfort of my living room. Even more interesting to me is that some of the people from history who received great glory during their time on earth are barely known today. For example, I would imagine few of us in 2024 have heard of the pharaoh Horemheb.

Over time, great empires are overthrown. Those in power change, and their grand palaces are reduced to rubble. Honored leaders and their dynasties are forgotten, and the cities they built are eventually buried under rocks, dirt, and sand.

But the glory of Jesus never ends. Whenever I get discouraged about our current culture and how secular and sometimes ungodly aspects are glorified today, I close my eyes and picture the glory of Jesus flowing over every part of the earth. Like waters cover the sea, no spot will remain untouched by Him.

As history has taught me from my online visits, man's glory is for a season, but Jesus's glory is for eternity. While King Horemheb and what he stood for is all but forgotten, the name of the greatest king of all, King Jesus, endures forever. —TRICIA GOYER

FAITH STEP: *Find a map, either physical or virtual, and pray over it, envisioning the glory of Jesus touching each continent, country, city, town, and village.*

FRIDAY, JULY 26

But the eyes of the LORD are on those who fear him, on those whose hope is in his unfailing love. Psalm 33:18 (NIV)

A YOUNG PASTOR FROM MY church enjoyed a day at a water park with his family. His six-year-old daughter asked permission to go to an adjoining area where she could swim laps. Since Adam wanted to stay and help his wife with their younger daughter, he gave Hannah specific instructions: "Each time you come up out of the water, look over at me. As long as you can see me, I can see you. And I can save you if you get in trouble."

We have Someone who always keeps His eyes on us like a loving earthly father. But Jesus can see where we are physically, emotionally, and spiritually. As Philip the apostle approached Jesus to introduce his friend, Jesus pronounced Nathanael a man of integrity. Amazed, Nathanael asked Jesus how He knew anything about him. Jesus responded, "I could see you under the fig tree before Philip found you" (John 1:47–50, TLB).

Jesus sees all our character traits—good and bad. He also sees the illness and disabilities we live with, the sins we struggle with, the fears we're fighting, and the loneliness that threatens to engulf us. He knows exactly what we need in every circumstance. And He is ready and willing to meet our needs in the best way possible. That fills me with peace, hope, and a deep sense of security. What better reason to keep my eyes on my loving Savior, who always keeps me in His sight? —DIANNE NEAL MATTHEWS

FAITH STEP: *Think of something you try to hide from people. Talk to Jesus about it, thanking Him for always seeing the real you while loving you unconditionally.*

SATURDAY, JULY 27

If you remain in me and I in you, you will bear much fruit;
apart from me you can do nothing. John 15:5 (NIV)

I TEND TO CHARGE MY cell phone at night. Just as I wake up with physical energy after a good night's sleep, my phone is fully charged and ready to go. Unfortunately, that wasn't the case last week. For two mornings in a row, my phone didn't charge at all. The first time, I thought it was a fluke. The second time, I searched out why.

Upon close inspection, I found the cord had a loose connection at my cell phone's port. It was a bit baffling because I hadn't damaged the port in any way and the cord seemed perfectly fine to my eye. Yet, sure enough, when I changed to a new cord, all was well. I guess cords only last for so long. I'll just have to keep swapping them out when they stop working.

In addition to the Bible, I like to use different study guides and prayer prompts as springboards to Jesus in my time with Him. They help me connect more deeply to the Source so I can be recharged. Inevitably, over time, though, that connection weakens, and I find I'm not restored as strongly as I once was. Outwardly, I seem to be in reverent prayer. But inwardly, I'm daydreaming and writing my grocery list.

The first few times it happened, I thought it was a fluke and reprimanded myself to focus. After that, I realized the different methods I used for connecting to Jesus only worked for so long. Fortunately, there are many wonderful resources I can switch to when my current ones stop working. —CLAIRE MCGARRY

FAITH STEP: *Is your current method of connecting with Jesus working? If not, consider a new resource to restore your energy and fully connect with Him.*

SUNDAY, JULY 28

Worship the LORD in holy attire; Tremble before Him, all the earth. Psalm 96:9 (NASB)

SERVING AS A WORSHIP LEADER at our church for the past several years has been a joy and privilege. In preparing to take the stage, I often ask the Lord for wisdom and insight that I can share to enhance our congregational worship or deepen my own spiritual growth.

Once, while reading Psalm 96, verse 9 caught my attention: "Worship the LORD in holy attire." Intrigued, I asked Jesus what this meant.

For several moments I waited, trusting the Holy Spirit to illuminate this scripture. Then all at once, deep in my spirit, I understood. Worshipping in holy attire means coming before Him with a clean and pure heart. Feverishly, I flipped the pages of my Bible to Isaiah 61:10 (NASB) and read, "My soul will be joyful in my God; For He has clothed me with garments of salvation, He has wrapped me with a robe of righteousness."

I thanked Jesus for saving me—for His marvelous, free gift of grace by the Holy Spirit that I never could have earned by my own works. I realized the proper way to adorn myself for worshipping in Jesus's presence was not with any specific outward clothing but rather with a heart yearning for His perfect goodness and holiness—an outfit that never goes out of style. —JENNIFER ANNE F. MESSING

FAITH STEP: *What are you wearing these days? Peer into your spiritual closet and take a closer look. Ask Jesus to cleanse you of any sins and hidden faults that hinder you from worshipping Him in holiness.*

MONDAY, JULY 29

Keep your roots deep in him and have your lives built on him.
Be strong in the faith, just as you were taught, and always be thankful.
Colossians 2:7 (NCV)

AFTER SEVERAL RELOCATIONS OVER THE years, my husband and I will move to the state where we were raised. We haven't lived there since 1982, and our children and grandchildren now live in different parts of the country. I recently mentioned to a friend that I felt as though I had no roots. "Does an adult need roots?" he asked. I silently responded: *Yes, unless you want to be a tumbleweed.*

A *tumbleweed* is defined as the aboveground part of any of a number of plants that, once mature and dry, disengage from the root and tumble away in the wind. I first encountered tumbleweeds while living in Utah and something scratchy bumped into my leg. I got used to seeing these skeletal orbs blowing around or stuck in all sorts of places. One morning, I came across a giant tumbleweed blocking the sidewalk. Although it felt weightless, it was covered with sharp edges, which made it difficult to move.

In the biological world, roots anchor the plant in the soil, provide necessary nourishment, and help it produce leaves, blooms, and fruit. In the spiritual world, Jesus is the only One who can do those things for me. He's the only way to have a full, bountiful life. Whenever I start to feel empty, dry, or prickly like a tumbleweed, that's a signal to check how deeply rooted I am in Him, no matter where I'm living. —DIANNE NEAL MATTHEWS

FAITH STEP: *List steps you want to take to stay rooted in Jesus: prayer, Bible study, praise, obedience, service, or any other ways He shows you.*

TUESDAY, JULY 30

My soul, wait silently for God alone, for my expectation is from Him. Psalm 62:5 (NKJV)

WRITERS ARE, BY NATURE, OBSERVANT. Because I'm a noticer, I'm particularly vulnerable to distraction. As I write this, I'm sitting in my hairstylist's chair, waiting for my color to "cook." Another patron is engaged in lively conversation with his stylist. The air buzzes with dialogue about future appointments, new hairstyling gadgets, and the latest political buzz. I'm creating devotional thoughts. But the space is too crowded with noise for me to engage with the silence of hope in my heart.

Many people aren't accustomed to silence and try hard to avoid it. I fill my home and car and office and ears with noise, perhaps to avoid having conversations or hearing myself. Or Jesus.

And even when I crave silence and solitude, it isn't easy or natural to find. So much competes for my attention. If it isn't work, it's family or other responsibilities. And if not those, it's noise in the name of entertainment or "relaxation" that does anything but help me relax.

If I truly want to connect with Jesus, to hear Him, I have to have silence. If hope is what I seek, then solitude and silence are where I'll find it. It's where Jesus can have my full attention.

My to-do list has a voice, and it only knows how to scream. So today I will raise my hand to it to say, "Silence! I need to hear my Jesus!" —CYNTHIA RUCHTI

FAITH STEP: *What do you need to silence today so you can settle into sweet communion with Jesus?*

WEDNESDAY, JULY 31

All you need to remember is that God will never let you down; he'll never let you be pushed past your limit; he'll always be there to help you come through it. 1 Corinthians 10:13 (MSG)

ONE OF MY FRIDGE MAGNETS contains a quote by Mother Teresa that says: "I know God will not give me anything I can't handle. I just wish that He didn't trust me so much." Her words make me smile.

I've heard many people express gratitude for the opportunity to slow down during the pandemic. I experienced the opposite. My international travels stopped, but staying home made it possible for me to write three books. Then came their launches. This meant developing launch teams, writing relevant magazine articles, and doing media interviews.

My career as a devotional podcast host also began during the pandemic. This involved researching historical and biblical context before writing and recording nearly a dozen episodes per month. My workload increased exponentially, and then speaking events and overseas ministry returned.

I consider being involved in ministry a privilege, and there's nothing I would rather do. At the same time, I often feel woefully inadequate. Strength comes when I look to Jesus and His promises.

Do I lack wisdom? For this, I have Jesus (James 1:5). Do I lack fresh ideas for writing assignments? For this, I have Jesus (Hebrews 13:20–21). Is my enthusiasm or passion waning? For this, I have Jesus (Colossians 3:23).

I trust Jesus to help me serve Him now, and I also trust Him to show me when I'm through. In the meantime, for this I have Jesus.
—GRACE FOX

FAITH STEP: *Fill in the blank according to your circumstances: for _____, I have Jesus.*

THURSDAY, AUGUST 1

"For I know the plans I have for you," declares the LORD, "plans to prosper you and not to harm you, plans to give you hope and a future." Jeremiah 29:11 (NIV)

I'M A FAN OF TOMATOES. This spring, I planted four different kinds: heirloom, Early Girl, Sun Gold, and Roma. The starter plants I placed in my gardening beds weren't much bigger than my palm. I had no idea how they would do and tried to make growing conditions perfect. I added organic mulch to the soil and placed a shiny green tomato cage over each plant. Bright sun and regular watering caused an abundance of growth. The plants were so huge and heavy with fruit that they bent the tomato cages sideways. Each afternoon, I filled a mixing bowl with the day's bounty. But the plants were doing exactly what they were made to do: grow, grow, GROW.

Sometimes, I forget that Jesus wants me to prosper. I get sidetracked with worries about my family, friends, and work. My ability to navigate life with wisdom and clarity seems to be overrun by my struggles with anxiety and fear. But He has plans for me anyway.

Jesus is preparing the soil of my life with goodness and mercy. He is lifting me with His grace and truth. He wants the fruit of His Spirit to flourish in every area of my life. Jesus is the Spring of Living Water (John 7:38). He wants me to grow, grow, GROW.
—SUSANNA FOTH AUGHTMON

FAITH STEP: *Take a walk near a garden or park. Notice the growth in nature. With each step, praise Jesus for an area in your life that He is growing in you with His grace and truth.*

FRIDAY, AUGUST 2

*Let your conversation be always full of grace, seasoned with salt, so that
you may know how to answer everyone. Colossians 4:6 (NIV)*

I SAW A POST ON social media from a woman who said she offered
a cart to another shopper in a grocery store parking lot. The shopper kept walking, so the woman thought the person didn't hear her.
The woman spoke a little louder and repeated herself. The person
stopped and hurled some profanities at the woman, who was so
shocked that she didn't say another word.

Replies to the post told me a lot about the respondents. Some said
they would have had a few choice words for the shopper. Others
wondered why the woman couldn't have just been civil. Still others said they would have just let it go because that's the way people
are today. Only a few said they would have prayed for the unkind
shopper.

I thought about how I would have reacted. Would I have been
offended and said something mean-spirited under my breath—or
worse, out loud? Would I have allowed the incident to ruin my
day? Or would I have been Christlike and silently prayed for the
shopper? To be honest, I've had all those reactions when I've been
in similar situations.

Jesus says we are the salt of the earth (Matthew 5:13). He wants
me and my words to be an example of love, kindness, goodwill,
compassion, and grace. If I'm sprinkling around those things, then
I'm doing my job as a saltshaker. —BARBRANDA LUMPKINS WALLS

FAITH STEP: *When you encounter unpleasant or ungrateful people, sprinkle
them with grace as Jesus would.*

SATURDAY, AUGUST 3

Therefore you shall be perfect, just as your Father in heaven is perfect. Matthew 5:48 (NKJV)

I HAVE A PROBLEM WITH perfection. I want to be perfect!

Perfectionism holds me back from simple joys like having my friend Terri over for lunch. When I consider the chaos in my craft room, the tracked-in sand on the floor, or any of the other ways my house is not cleaned or organized, I put it off.

A friend in my newlywed days didn't worry about being perfect. Carolyn invited us often for dinner, sometimes before even checking to see what she had to serve. Her house was clean under the clutter, but she wasn't self-conscious and didn't apologize. She loved the Lord, loved company, and loved me well. Carolyn didn't try to be perfect, but she made friends feel perfectly at home.

Yet here is Jesus talking to His disciples (and to me), saying, "Be perfect." The word Jesus used that was translated in Matthew 5:48 as "perfect" was *teleios*, Greek for "having reached its end, completeness, or fulfillment and maturity." It's not the sinlessness of never doing anything wrong. Jesus's context of "perfect" means loving people and treating them well, just as He did.

Jesus wants me to grow in love for everyone with my eyes on them and my heart tuned to their needs. I won't get things perfect, but Jesus isn't asking me to. He wants me to mature and be complete in who He created me to be. And that sounds pretty perfect to me.

I believe I'll invite Terri over to lunch after all. —SUZANNE DAVENPORT TIETJEN

FAITH STEP: *Watch for an opportunity to be perfectly loving to someone today. Make this a practice, focusing on someone Jesus loves, knowing there's no one He doesn't love.*

SUNDAY, AUGUST 4

*If anyone has material possessions and sees a brother or sister in
need but has no pity on them, how can the love of God be in that
person? Dear children, let us not love with words or speech
but with actions and in truth. 1 John 3:17–18 (NIV)*

THROUGH A NEW MINISTRY AT church, Nelda was assigned to be
my mentor. At our first meeting, I shared that I was between jobs
as a teacher and nervous about transitioning from private to public
school. As a former educator herself, she reminded me to trust Jesus
with the details of my career.

I also mentioned my concern about the added expenses we were
facing now that our oldest son was entering high school. The aca-
demic year hadn't even started yet, and there were already talks of
school trips that would cost several hundred dollars. I had no idea
where that money would come from.

Nelda's eyes lit up, and she leaned forward in her chair. "I know!"
she said. "We'll sell pot pies!" She explained that her signature pot
pies were in such demand that she only needed to mention them
and she'd be flooded with orders. She often used the proceeds to
fund mission trips and nonprofit opportunities.

Several months later, my family gathered in Nelda's kitchen and
helped assemble more than seventy pot pies that Nelda sold on our
behalf. I was overcome with gratitude. Nelda had shown me a perfect picture of the love of Jesus through her words, actions, *and* her
delicious pot pies. —EMILY E. RYAN

FAITH STEP: *What act of kindness, big or small, can you do today to share the
love of Jesus?*

MONDAY, AUGUST 5

You have turned my mourning into joyful dancing. You have taken away my clothes of mourning and clothed me with joy. Psalm 30:11 (NLT)

I RECENTLY EXPERIENCED A TSUNAMI of sadness that spanned ten weeks. During this time, five friends passed away. The oldest was only fifty-three. In addition, my brother contracted COVID-19 and ended up on a ventilator for nine days. At the same time he was in the hospital, a ministry coworker landed in the ICU with a serious infection and a family member sent me an email teeming with criticism that arrived on the day I'd scheduled a Facebook live broadcast. His comments caused my confidence to waver. I don't believe the timing was a coincidence. I pushed down my nervousness and smiled.

Scripture promises that followers of Jesus will experience suffering (John 16:33). It's hard and it hurts, but we hold on to hope when we remember that it's only temporary. Our season of suffering on earth is but a blink in time compared to the eternal joys we'll experience in heaven.

I keep hope alive by remembering, too, that suffering refines my character and makes me more like Jesus, when I look to Him for strength to endure (1 Peter 5:10). The circumstances causing concern might not turn out the way I wish, but He heals my broken heart. By trusting Him with my deepest pain, He draws me into deeper, sweeter intimacy.

I gave thanks when that ten-week tsunami of sadness ended, but I also gave thanks for the opportunities it provided me to experience waves of Jesus's grace and the spiritual growth it accomplished in me. —GRACE FOX

FAITH STEP: *Write down three ways in which suffering has grown your relationship with Jesus.*

TUESDAY, AUGUST 6

*Therefore, we are Christ's representatives, and through us
God is calling you.* 2 Corinthians 5:20 (GW)

AFTER HURRICANE LAURA RAVAGED SOUTH Louisiana in August 2020, a massive cleanup began with volunteers pouring in from all directions. Some groups brought chainsaws and equipment to cut up thousands of trees that had fallen on houses, roads, and power lines. On my local Louisiana town's social media page, I saw a picture of a tree stump that had a big, chunky cross carved into its top. The ground below it was covered with branches and debris, but what grabbed my attention was the image of beauty amidst chaos.

I later talked with Keith, who has been carving crosses for many years during his cleanup work with the Shreveport Volunteer Network. Amazingly, this man can carve a cross in five minutes with a chainsaw. If there is no stump available, he often finds a big branch that lets him leave the symbol of hope after disaster, which Keith says mirrors what God has done for him personally—brought him out of disaster into a new life. To Keith, the cross represents the greatest love story ever told.

If we believe in Jesus as our Savior, then we serve as His representatives on earth. Each of us has different skills and resources that provide unique opportunities to show the hurting world His forgiveness, unconditional love, and eternal life. Whether with words or with acts of kindness, I can, like Keith, leave behind a reminder of Jesus's love everywhere I go. —DIANNE NEAL MATTHEWS

FAITH STEP: *Ask Jesus to show you ways to leave behind a reminder of His love in every interaction you have today.*

WEDNESDAY, AUGUST 7

And in him you too are being built together to become a dwelling in which God lives by his Spirit. Ephesians 2:22 (NIV)

I OFTEN WATCH VIDEOS OF home construction projects. It's not that I'm likely to ever work in construction. That would take a stronger back, arms, knees, shoulders—pretty much everything stronger than what I could offer to the task. But I do enjoy virtually peeking behind the scenes. *What makes a solid foundation? What steps are necessary before a foundation is even poured? What kinds of weather, climate, or terrain dictate the materials, timing, and details of construction?* Because I'm also an armchair archeologist, I'm curious about the remnants of long-ago civilizations, and ancient construction techniques fascinate me too. *How did that building remain intact for so many centuries? Is that one still inhabitable?*

Today, I took another look at the intentional building practices Jesus employed in creating God's kingdom. He built on a foundation laid by prophets and ancient words. He was named the very cornerstone of that kingdom (Ephesians 2:20). And wonder of wonders, He included all of us as we together become a dwelling for the Holy Spirit.

It's not often I take time to consider what had to happen "underground" to afford me the opportunity to become part of that structure, one that will outlive every building on earth. Today, though, I'm truly in awe. Aren't you? —CYNTHIA RUCHTI

FAITH STEP: *In Ephesians, Paul used a verb tense meaning "being built" together. Ongoing. Take a moment today to consider how you are living out the "in the process" of forming an unshakable kingdom.*

THURSDAY, AUGUST 8

Be alert and of sober mind. Your enemy the devil prowls around like a roaring lion looking for someone to devour. 1 Peter 5:8 (NIV)

THE VOICE IS HARSH, CRITICAL, and condemning. It picks at every problem, magnifies my mishaps, ridicules each wrinkle. It is persistent, sometimes whispers, but often nags with urgency. Merciless and mischievous, it tends to blindside me when I'm feeling really good about myself or about something I've done.

Whose accusatory voice is it? My own, encouraged by the enemy, who wants me to believe the worst about myself. Thank goodness I have a friend, Jesus, who also talks to me.

Unlike the enemy, my Advocate and Savior Jesus speaks softly, gently, kindly. Even in redirecting me, He speaks simply, without shaming. He does not condemn me but instead speaks the truth that I am chosen (1 Peter 2:9), loved (John 3:16), and made in His image (Genesis 1:27). When I go astray, which is often, Jesus waits patiently for me to feel the weight of my waywardness and return to Him. He sometimes looks me in the eye with compassion and concern and reminds me of His wise and loving ways. His peaceful presence is always available.

Whenever I hear that other inner voice, I acknowledge it and remind it that Jesus is bigger, stronger, and full of love. His voice is the only one I want to hear. —ISABELLA CAMPOLATTARO

FAITH STEP: *Whose voice are you listening to? List what your destructive voice says, then speak out loud to each comment: "Jesus is bigger, stronger, and full of love. I don't have to listen to you anymore!"*

FRIDAY, AUGUST 9

Therefore everyone who hears these words of mine and puts them into practice is like a wise man who built his house on the rock. Matthew 7:24 (NIV)

A STATE PARK A FEW hours from our home is popular with rock climbers. Jagged cliffs rise up from a river valley. Sharp contours and steep angles seem impossible to traverse. After exploring a few trails, my husband and I stopped to watch a man scale one of those cliffs. His climbing partner observed from the ground, directing him to good footholds or handholds. The climber tested each jutting stone before putting his weight on it. By choosing the solid rocks, he made it to the top.

I learned a lot watching that climber. Gripping an unsteady support could cause scraped skin, a collision with the rock face, or worse. Not to mention that dislodging stones could hurt the partner below.

When I'm struggling on Jesus's path for my life, I sometimes grab for anything that seems as though it could offer me support. I might focus on bolstering my bank account or build connections with people so I feel armed with the opinions of others. I might devour information so I can forestall any potential problems. But human answers to eternal questions are wobbly at best. Not only do they eventually give way, but also my floundering might cause damage to someone else.

Jesus is our Cornerstone, our solid Foundation, the Rock we can trust. Putting faith in my finances, my popularity, my intellect, or any other fleeting security is a poor substitute for trusting my Savior. —SHARON HINCK

FAITH STEP: *Find a video or picture of a rock climber. Ask Jesus to help you choose His strong, supportive path for you today.*

SATURDAY, AUGUST 10

As for me, I will always have hope; I will praise you more and more.
Psalm 71:14 (NIV)

I GREW UP ON THE land next to Grandpa Chip's homeplace. He had a hill for sledding in the winter, a garden of sweet corn in the summer, and a pond full of fish year-round. I often escaped the noise of my two younger siblings to sit by that peaceful pond. I hid my secret treasure there too, beneath an overturned canoe on the bank.

My treasure, a pink New Testament, stayed completely dry within a plastic zipper bag. I'd pull it from under the old wooden boat and read the most miraculous things: Jesus walked on water. He fed thousands of people with a few loaves of bread and two fish. A man's daughter died, and Jesus brought her back to life! The stories stirred my young heart and strengthened my hope in Jesus.

King David penned Psalm 71 (NIV) when he was old, looking back over a lifetime of hope. "From birth I have relied on you; you brought me forth from my mother's womb. I will ever praise you" (verse 6). He mentioned his childhood: "For you have been my hope, Sovereign LORD, my confidence since my youth" (verse 5). And ended with old age: "Even when I am old and gray, do not forsake me, my God, till I declare your power to the next generation" (verse 18).

If I wrote a hope review of my life, I'd have to start with those special days sitting by Grandpa Chip's pond. A little girl, a quiet place, and a pink Bible opened to the stories about Jesus. —BECKY ALEXANDER

FAITH STEP: *Find a quiet place and think about where and when your hope in Jesus began.*

SUNDAY, AUGUST 11

You have put off the old man with his deeds, and have put on the new man who is renewed in knowledge according to the image of Him who created him. Colossians 3:9–10 (NKJV)

WE'RE NOT BANANA EATERS, YET somehow the fruit appears in my kitchen, where it lingers until it's too ripe and draws pesky fruit flies. I'm inclined to toss a brown bunch into the trash, but my husband prefers to whip up a batch of banana muffins. I can't get him to stop buying bananas, but I'm grateful he will salvage the throwaways.

I'm also grateful Jesus salvages castoffs like my friend Jon, a former high school dropout and drug addict who owns a motorcycle shop. Or Craig, who still has the 1980s rocker look, even though he quit touring the heavy-metal circuit decades ago. If I'd met either of them years ago, I would have considered them too far gone. But both were renewed by Jesus.

Today, when Jon meets someone, he often asks, "Do you know Jesus?" Many Sundays he arrives at church with someone clad in a black leather vest and biker boots. Craig's powerful story began with a desperate, late-night Internet search. "Is God real?" he typed. Now he shares his renewed life with musicians who record in his studio.

Jon and Craig make a church-raised girl like me inspect my own fruit a little harder. Does my life draw people to Jesus, or is it wasting away, attracting flies like a bunch of old bananas? As I mature in Him, I yearn for Jesus to turn the rotten parts of me into something sweet. —KAREN SARGENT

FAITH STEP: *What parts of your past are you hiding? Pray for an opportunity to share your story with one person this week.*

Monday, August 12

Why do you notice the little piece of dust in your friend's eye, but you don't notice the big piece of wood in your own eye? How can you say to your friend, "Let me take that little piece of dust out of your eye"? Look at yourself! You still have that big piece of wood in your own eye. You hypocrite! First, take the wood out of your own eye. Then you will see clearly to take the dust out of your friend's eye. Matthew 7:3–5 (NCV)

Sometimes I journal my prayers, pouring out my heart on paper to Jesus. Writing my worries and cares somehow frees them. Afterward, I sit quietly—a huge challenge—and listen to Jesus. But yesterday He interrupted me.

I'd asked the Lord for deliverance from a spending addiction, to fill my soul with His Spirit of grace until I craved His fellowship more than I longed to make up for my empty places by buying more stuff.

From that point, I went on to request that Jesus help a friend overcome her penchant for collecting things. That's when He interrupted me. "Work on your own logs" was all He said. As I gazed at the purple ink on the page, I remembered the red-lettered verse and chuckled. *OK, Lord,* I thought, *I get it. I've gone from praying to prying.*

I smile when I recall that lightning-fast response from Jesus. In His kind yet straightforward way, He reminded me that I'm responsible for managing only my life and concerning myself only with the log in my own eye. Jesus will take care of the specks in everyone else's eyes without any help from me. —Jeanette Levellie

Faith Step: *Try writing out your prayers on paper. Remember to focus on your own "logs" or concerns as you write to Jesus.*

TUESDAY, AUGUST 13

Now faith is confidence in what we hope for and assurance about what we do not see. Hebrews 11:1 (NIV)

YEARS AGO, A DEAR FRIEND told me she prays for me daily. Learning she'd brought my needs before Jesus, I felt humbled and grateful. Her devotion in prayer reminded me of when my daughter was younger. She and I shared everything in prayer, pouring out all our hopes to Him. She often prayed for the man she'd marry, whom she hadn't yet encountered. They were simple requests, like asking for him to have a good night's sleep or that he might be looking at the moon at the same moment she was. The simple faith of those prayers touched me.

Lately, with her trusting petitions to Jesus in mind, I've begun reciting some of my own but with a twist. I'm praying for a friend I haven't met yet.

Somewhere, there is a woman Jesus wills for me to befriend. Not out of necessity but as an act of obedience. During my private prayer time, I ask Jesus to grant her health and happiness, to protect her heart, and to allow her dreams to come true. Though I can't see her, I know she exists. She's as real as Jesus to me. I don't know what she looks like or how she acts, but I have faith that I'll recognize her when I see her, and we'll grow a relationship grounded in Him. And then I'll pray for the next friend I haven't met. —HEIDI GAUL

FAITH STEP: *Make it a point to pray for someone you've not yet met—a future friend, a spouse for yourself or a loved one, or the new school year's teachers for a student you know.*

WEDNESDAY, AUGUST 14

You are no longer foreigners and outsiders but citizens together with God's people and members of God's family. Ephesians 2:19 (GW)

I USED TO CLAIM DUAL citizenship. Being American and a registered tribal member of the Chickasaw Nation, I'm both a citizen of the United States and of the Chickasaw Nation. I'm also a registered voter in two nations: the United States and the Chickasaw Nation. And I have two presidents: POTUS and the president of the Chickasaw Nation.

But then it dawned on me. I actually have *triple* citizenship. When I accepted Jesus as my Lord and Savior, I was adopted into the family of God. I became a citizen of His kingdom with a permanent standing that became a reality the moment I accepted Jesus as Lord and Master of my life. I'm an eternal citizen of heaven.

I became an American citizen automatically upon birth. But I didn't officially become a citizen of the Chickasaw Nation until it was confirmed that I'm a true bloodline descendant of an ancestor listed in the original rolls of the Chickasaw Indians. Similarly, my name is listed in the Book of Life (Revelation 3:5), confirming my permanent standing in the tribe of Jesus. Sure, I'll continue to interact with and participate in my two earthly nations, but ultimately, my true allegiance is and will always be to Christ and His kingdom—the everlasting family of God. —CASSANDRA TIERSMA

FAITH STEP: *Claim your eternal citizenship in the family of God. Tell Jesus you want to be on the roll in the Book of Life with those who are His. Celebrate your "dual citizenship" by singing (or listening to a recording of) the old hymn "When the Roll Is Called Up Yonder."*

THURSDAY, AUGUST 15

May God give you heaven's dew. Genesis 27:28 (NIV)

I HAVE LITTLE LEFT TO GIVE, I typed in a weekly text to two prayer partners. I pushed back my discomfort and was honest about my emptiness. It was a difficult month of caregiving for my widowed mom and adult kids, who called when life was hard.

As a counselor, I know about self-care. I set professional boundaries to avoid burnout. My job, however, was not the problem. Reciprocal, caring relationships were lacking in my life. I often am the encourager people seek out when they are down. My prayer partners are among the few people in my life who ask how *I'm* doing. It felt vulnerable to tell my family and friends how exhausted and emotionally depleted I was.

During my time with Jesus the next morning, I read Jacob's blessing about heaven's dew (Genesis 27:27–29). It intrigued me. God sends dew when there is no rain, saturating nature with moisture on dry, arid days. It's His perfect provision. Like His creation, I longed to be drenched in the care and nurture of heaven's dew.

Yet, Jesus had already supplied it. He showed me that my prayer partners were the dew He'd provided in this dry, empty season. They listened to, prayed for, and carried my burden without judgment, guilt, or shame. Jesus's goodness met me right where I was, saturating my soul in His care. —BRENDA L. YODER

FAITH STEP: *Share a need you have with someone you trust, even though it feels vulnerable.*

FRIDAY, AUGUST 16

Praise be to the God and Father of our Lord Jesus Christ! In his great mercy he has given us new birth into a living hope through the resurrection of Jesus Christ from the dead, and into an inheritance that can never perish, spoil or fade. This inheritance is kept in heaven for you. 1 Peter 1:3–4 (NIV)

OH, NO! NOT AGAIN. I bolted from my couch to my office. I had dismissed the phone alerts all week and now it was almost midnight, which meant my Kohl's Cash was about to expire. I had to decide if twenty minutes was enough time to make a quick online purchase or if I had to accept losing another valuable offer.

The worst kind of rewards programs for me are the ones that attach expiration dates to the points I've earned. I'm so glad Jesus's offer of an inheritance in heaven, an eternal reward, is not a vain hope, not based on earnings, and not in limited supply. Because His work and reach are not time-sensitive, His other offers, such as peace and protection here on earth, are always available. It's never too late for me to redeem what Jesus gives.

Fortunately, I wasn't too late redeeming my Kohl's Cash this time either. I purchased a pair of double silver hoop earrings and a dark-wash denim jacket. But I know the best reward I'll get isn't valid for just a specific period of time. Because of Jesus, my heavenly reward will never tarnish, expire, or be taken away. —ERICKA LOYNES

FAITH STEP: *Create a coupon book illustrating the number of benefits you've received from Jesus. Add to your book each time you discover a new offer from Him.*

SATURDAY, AUGUST 17

The thief comes only to steal and kill and destroy; I have come that they may have life, and have it to the full. John 10:10 (NIV)

MY HEART RACED AS I logged on to the service center website and saw the status of my computer repair: Repairs complete. Computer picked up.

Who picked up my computer? Certainly, no one in my household. Had some villain absconded with my newly repaired laptop and, along with it, all the information needed to assume my identity and empty my bank accounts? And why hadn't I received a call saying my repair had been finished, apparently weeks ago?

The local store hadn't opened yet that morning, so I called the computer company's twenty-four-hour helpline. After an hour of being shuffled from one representative to the next, I was no closer to finding out where my computer had gone. I'd need to speak with an employee at the store. With each passing minute, my stress level soared higher. Finally, the time came for the local franchise to open. I was the first customer through its doors.

Thankfully, my computer and my identity were safe. An employee had entered misinformation into the system. None of my personal information was stolen.

Back home, I logged on to my laptop and thought of the time I'd wasted in worry. My financial identity wasn't compromised, but what about my identity in Christ? Why had I allowed circumstances to steal my peace? I resolved that the next time I faced uncertainty, I'd trust Jesus and rest in the abundant life He gives instead of worrying.
—SUSAN DOWNS

FAITH STEP: *Today, write down a recent circumstance that stole your peace. Think about how you could have reacted by trusting Jesus. Pray that the next time you will turn to Him first.*

Sunday, August 18

A hand touched me and set me trembling on my hands and knees.
Daniel 10:10 (NIV)

It was just another Sunday. My husband, Jeff, and I drank our coffee, read our devotions, and got dressed for services. Early on, my attention strayed from the Sunday school lesson. *Had I unplugged the coffeepot?* Before I knew it, class was over, and Jeff and I moved to the sanctuary.

There my random thoughts turned to worries. *Would my daughter find a doctor for her son's headaches?* I rose automatically to sing the first song, projected on a large screen above the stage. When I did, it felt as if someone had placed hands on my shoulders and was pressing inward. I glanced at Jeff, but his hands were by his sides. After I sat down, I still perceived the steady, gentle pressure of hands holding my shoulders.

All my life, I've prayed to have Jesus touch me. In times of grief, I've cried out to Him, yearning for a physical reminder of His presence. It had never happened, but I knew as surely as I was sitting there, the hands holding my shoulders belonged to Jesus. *Why now?* I felt Him whisper, *Pay attention, Pat. This is the life I gave you. Don't miss an instant because of worry and distraction.*

As I sang the last song, I felt myself relax. My worries dissolved while Jesus held my shoulders. I have never felt so secure, so loved. I prayed the feeling would continue, but by the time we left church, it was gone.

That sensation has never returned, but I have no doubt Jesus still holds me. Just another Sunday? Absolutely not! —Pat Butler Dyson

Faith Step: *Pray and ask Jesus to touch you in a meaningful way today.*

MONDAY, AUGUST 19

For you know that when your faith is tested, your endurance has a chance to grow. So let it grow, for when your endurance is fully developed, you will be perfect and complete, needing nothing. James 1:3–4 (NLT)

I LOVE THE WORD *GRIT*, which means to me emotional and mental tenacity. Strength of character. The keep-on-keeping-on, bounce-back ability that helps a person endure difficulties. I first heard the buzzword years ago when a friend told me I have it. (I cherish that compliment.) Since then, the trendy word has been showing up everywhere, inviting me to pause and consider its impact. Even the sound of it boosts my courage.

But the other day, I had an aha moment. It was a relaxed Saturday morning, and I was enjoying some pampering time. Standing at the bathroom sink, I splashed cool water on my face, then rubbed exfoliator scrub in circular strokes, enjoying the gritty feel and the expectation of smoother skin. After that, I reached for my manicure set to fix chipping polish and an uneven nail. I thought of grit as the rough file reshaped each nail and the buffer smoothed and refined their surfaces.

I realized that grit is not only an enduring strength. It also includes the exterior circumstances and experiences that refine me, smoothing away my rough traits so my life glows with Jesus's character.

James 1:3–4 speaks of this power of grit to grow enduring faith and to beautifully shape believers. *Grit* used to sound strong but not lovely to me. Now I think it is among the most beautiful of words. —ERIN KEELEY MARSHALL

FAITH STEP: *Take time for yourself with a favorite exfoliator while you ask Jesus to create strong and beautiful faith from the grit in your life.*

TUESDAY, AUGUST 20

For the hope which is laid up for you in heaven, whereof ye heard before in the word of the truth of the gospel. Colossians 1:5 (KJV)

LAID ASIDE. LAID UP. PUT aside. Squirreled away. All those phrases collided in my mind as I watched videos of smart and simple means of storing produce, meat, beans, soup mix, and fruit for the future. A new generation of homestead-like households, even in suburbia, is taking more seriously the wisdom of having food set aside in case of power outages, supply chain shortages, storms, or even health issues that might prevent our traditional "go get it from the store" patterns.

Throughout our early marriage and child-raising years, our basement shelves bulged with glistening jars of peaches, pears, tomatoes, and applesauce. We learned how to dehydrate to supply our children's insatiable appetite for fruit leathers and jerky. The pantry and freezers were full with homemade pickles, jam, sweet corn, venison, and bulk purchases.

But these words, "hope which is laid up for you in heaven," make my stocking-up efforts pale in comparison. Oh, to be able to bottle hope for the pressure-cooker days ahead! What if I could dehydrate hope so it would "keep" in my pocket or purse, able to be pulled out when I'm hungry for it?

Modern food preservationists have perfected traditional techniques that my generation muddled through. But hope? Hope is already stored up for me in heaven. Jesus's sacrifice enabled me to have endless shelves of more than enough. —CYNTHIA RUCHTI

FAITH STEP: *Fill a canning jar to the brim with "hope" verses from the Bible. Let it remind you of the never-ending supply Jesus has preserved for you.*

WEDNESDAY, AUGUST 21

---

*Give your entire attention to what God is doing right now, and
don't get worked up about what may or may not happen tomorrow.
God will help you deal with whatever hard things come up when
the time comes. Matthew 6:34 (MSG)*

AFTER LEAVING THE DRUGSTORE, I sat in my car, preoccupied with
worry over a troubling situation. A tap on my window startled me.
A thin woman in a tattered gold sweater motioned for me to lower
the glass. She'd just gotten out of the hospital and didn't have food
or a place to stay. I gave her all the cash in my billfold and told her
I hoped things would get better.

Unexpectedly, she burst into song: "One day at a time, sweet Jesus;
that's all I'm asking of You..." Her voice was deep and mellow. The
message was one I needed to hear.

Curious about the origin of the song, I researched it. In 1973,
Nashville songwriter Marijohn Wilkin drove a Cadillac and wore a fur
coat, but she was miserable. Struggling with addiction, she drove to a
church. After confessing her problems to a pastor, she went home and
sat at her piano. The words of the song "One Day at a Time" flowed
out of her. Later, she reflected that the lyrics were a cry for help.
Who better to turn to than Jesus?

I considered how much the homeless woman and I had in common. She had almost nothing and I had nearly everything, but
we both needed to let Jesus take care of us one day at a time.
—PAT BUTLER DYSON

FAITH STEP: *Listen to the song "One Day at a Time" and let the lyrics soak away
any worry or cares as you rely on Him.*

THURSDAY, AUGUST 22

Therefore, since we have these promises, dear friends, let us purify ourselves from everything that contaminates body and spirit, perfecting holiness out of reverence for God. 2 Corinthians 7:1 (NIV)

YESTERDAY, I WENT TO THE dentist's office and learned a cavity had developed in one of my molars. I had visions of the dentist, brows furrowed in judgment, asking me, "How in the world could you have let this happen? Don't you floss?" (Clearly, not enough.) I let fear creep in. *Maybe the tooth needed to be pulled!*

My experience with the dentist was the opposite of what I imagined. She was kind, gentle, and understanding. She told me I needed a filling and that they would get me in as soon as possible. She wanted me on the road to good oral health.

There are places in my heart that are at risk of decaying too. Left unattended, they eat away at my soul. I often worry about approaching Jesus with my sin, bitterness, and pride. I don't want Him to know how broken I am. But as a follower of Jesus, I don't need to fear His shame. Just the opposite is true. Jesus doesn't judge me or anyone else (John 12:47). He came into the world to love and save it (John 3:16). And He loves me no matter what. By Him I am cleansed from all unrighteousness (1 John 1:9). Jesus sets all of me on the road to health. —SUSANNA FOTH AUGHTMON

FAITH STEP: *Use your morning and nightly toothbrushing as opportunities to connect with Jesus. Ask Him to do a deep cleaning of your soul and cleanse you from all unrighteousness.*

FRIDAY, AUGUST 23

Fix your thoughts on what is true, and honorable, and right, and pure, and lovely, and admirable. Think about things that are excellent and worthy of praise. Philippians 4:8 (NLT)

RECENTLY, ZANE AND I HAD dinner with Zane's college friend Mike. When we got married, Mike showed up at our wedding as a surprise. When Zane and I returned home from our honeymoon, we couldn't find our unity candle. Then on our one-year anniversary, our candle came in the mail with a note from Mike. I assumed he planned this surprise as a joke, and I didn't think it was funny.

Fast-forward to our dinner recently, thirty-five years later. I reminded him of that incident. At first, Mike didn't recall doing it, but as we talked about it, he remembered. Turns out, after Zane and I departed for our honeymoon, he noticed no one had collected the candle. He took it home with the intention of mailing it to us a year later because he valued the significance of it and our unity as a couple. Unfortunately, I had mistakenly labeled him as insensitive and a jokester.

That dinner, and conversation, reminded me how important my thought life is, especially what I think about others. If I believe something about someone that is not true, it impacts my feelings, thoughts, and actions toward that person.

Sadly, Zane and I hadn't pursued a consistent friendship with Mike, but I was thankful to have reconnected with him and learn the story behind the missing unity candle. I also learned a lesson on making false assumptions about a good, thoughtful friend.
—JEANNIE BLACKMER

FAITH STEP: *Is there someone in your life you might be making up a false story about? Consider calling that person and discovering the truth.*

SATURDAY, AUGUST 24

. . . to those loved by God the Father, called and kept safe by Jesus Christ. Relax, everything's going to be all right; rest, everything's coming together; open your hearts, love is on the way! Jude 1:1–2 (MSG)

MY SOAKING TUB ISN'T VERY big, but it's deep—deep enough to float in. Floating might be my favorite thing now, but that would surprise my mother, who thought I'd never master it when I was a child. I was fine if my parent's or swimming teacher's arms supported me, but I panicked whenever they tried to transition me to floating on my back solo. I immediately tensed up or flailed in order to grab anyone or anything nearby.

Finally, Mom convinced me to practice in the Gulf of Mexico, saying that I'd float higher in salt water. The difference was probably miniscule, but there at the beach, I relaxed enough to lie back, rock on the waves, and float. All I had needed to do was not to do anything—to yield and give the water my weight. To give it the chance to hold me at the surface.

It seems like a paradox, this doing something by relaxing into doing nothing. And, paradoxically, I struggle with this in my walk with Jesus. I want to *do*. Jesus wants me to *be*. To relax and roll with the waves of life. There is no need to be tense or on guard. I just need to lean back, let go, and trust Him that everything's going to be all right. —SUZANNE DAVENPORT TIETJEN

FAITH STEP: *Float in your bathtub or swimming pool, or lie on your bed. See how easy it is to yield to these things? Now lean back and relax into Jesus.*

SUNDAY, AUGUST 25

*Not that I have already obtained this or am already perfect,
but I press on to make it my own, because Christ Jesus has made me
his own. Philippians 3:12 (ESV)*

SEVERAL YEARS AGO, I WON a scholarship to a California Christian writers' conference. The contest was called the "First Timers Contest" and was only open to those who had never attended before. After I arrived and unpacked, I walked to the dining hall, eager to meet the other scholarship recipients for our first meal together. We found the table that had been set up especially for us and immediately laughed at the blatant typo on the centerpiece. A bold red-and-white sign read: "Winners of the First Timmers Contest." We discussed whether we should bring the mistake to the attention of the conference coordinators and request a reprint, but in the end, we decided that we liked it that way. Not only did the misspelling become fodder for inside jokes and sideways glances in crowded rooms, but it also helped foster a foundation of humility as a group of aspiring authors. We remembered that the goal of our writing was not to pen the perfect novel or inspire the greatest online review. The goal was to disappear behind the page so that others could meet Jesus.

Now whenever I struggle with doubt and begin to question my worth, I think back to that long weekend in California. Jesus uses me despite my imperfections. My value is not in my own abilities, but instead, I want Jesus to be seen in all that I do. —EMILY E. RYAN

FAITH STEP: *Think of an imperfection or an area where you fall short. Ask Jesus to help you see how you can disappear so He will shine through you.*

MONDAY, AUGUST 26

In fact, we felt sure we were going to die. But this made us stop trusting in ourselves and start trusting God, who raises the dead to life. 2 Corinthians 1:9 (CEV)

RECOUNTING HER LATEST ADVENTURES IN farm life, my daughter described how her shovel hit a rock when digging a hole for a tree she was planting. Certain she could just dig out the rock, she shoveled away. But the bigger she dug the hole, the bigger the rock became. Finally, she called in reinforcements to help excavate what was an enormous boulder. The task required a backhoe along with a massive steel pry bar and heavy chains to wrench the behemoth boulder free.

Visualizing the intense excavation process reminds me of the equally hard yet rewarding work of healing and recovery. Years of personal and ministerial experience in Celebrate Recovery, a Christian twelve-step program, taught me that digging deep to remove heavy, buried obstacles is not a solo job. It calls for reinforcements.

Whenever I'm in a hard place in life and bump into a deeply buried issue that I need help with, I call on Jesus for spiritual strength. He is the One who came to set me free. He's the only One who can help me pry out those heavy "boulders"—those buried issues—that would otherwise impede my growth. Jesus, the Son of the God who can raise the dead to life, can certainly raise and remove any obstruction from the soil of my life. I thank Jesus that He frees up space in me so my faith and hope in Him can grow.
—CASSANDRA TIERSMA

FAITH STEP: *What issue in your heart needs to be healed? Ask Jesus to free you from the weight of it. Trust Him to do the heavy lifting.*

TUESDAY, AUGUST 27

The LORD is my light and my salvation—whom shall I fear? The LORD is the stronghold of my life—of whom shall I be afraid? Psalm 27:1 (NIV)

MY HUSBAND AND I BOTH admit to having a fear of the dark, especially when we were young teenagers. Neither of us knew Jesus as our Savior at that time, and it didn't help that we both loved watching scary movies and TV shows at night. Little did we know, we were inviting fear to come live with us. Thankfully, my fears subsided by the time I went off to college, but my husband says his fear of darkness lingered well into adulthood. Growing up in the sparse Mississippi Delta might have added to his dread. But the fear seemed to follow him wherever he went, even when he summered "up north" with his family in the Connecticut suburbs. He describes it as being bullied in his sleep. He couldn't shake it and didn't know what else to try.

When we started dating, I shared with him that as a believer in Jesus Christ, he had the authority over fear and the demonic realm. I encouraged him to speak out loud to the darkness and tell anything ungodly lurking there, real or imagined, to be gone. He summoned up his courage and took my advice that very night (what a smart guy!). He rebuked fear, declaring his authority over that "bully" in Jesus's name. Afterward, he never again experienced fear of the dark. Invoking the strong name of Jesus in faith causes fear to flee! —PAMELA TOUSSAINT HOWARD

FAITH STEP: *Identify a fear that plagues you and command it to leave in Jesus's name.*

WEDNESDAY, AUGUST 28

Trust in the LORD with all your heart; do not depend on your own understanding. Seek his will in all you do, and he will show you which path to take. Proverbs 3:5–6 (NLT)

PEOPLE HAVE DIFFERENT AREAS OF expertise. Maybe they've earned a reputation as an expert through honing their natural gifts or dedicating themselves to perfecting a specific skill. Me? I'm an expert second-guesser. I have a talent for dwelling on past decisions and wondering if I made the best choice. You might be impressed if you knew how much anxiety I can wring out of a moment from my distant past, or if you could count how many of my thoughts begin with "if only I had" or "I should have." I'm also pretty good at analyzing other people's actions and how much better my life would be if *they* had chosen differently.

I have to admit, that's a miserable way to live, and it's not the lifestyle Jesus wants for me. He came to give us a life filled with meaning, joy, and peace. But how can I trade in my undesirable "expertise" for something that will help me be who Jesus wants me to be?

Psychologists in an area of research known as "expert performance" studied how people get really good at what they do. They identified the key as—no surprise—deliberate practice. So instead of honing my natural bent toward worry and regret, I plan to diligently practice trusting Jesus and seeking His will. I want to be an expert at that. —DIANNE NEAL MATTHEWS

FAITH STEP: *Is there a personal decision from your past that nags at you or even haunts you? Thank Jesus for His forgiveness and commit to living a lifestyle based on Proverbs 3:5–6 with His help.*

THURSDAY, AUGUST 29

---

*To them God has chosen to make known among the Gentiles
the glorious riches of this mystery, which is Christ in you,
the hope of glory. Colossians 1:27 (NIV)*

"SHE IS THE EPITOME OF GRACE." "He oozes kindness." "As a couple, they are the picture of generosity." "My grandfather embodied quiet strength." I do it all the time: I observe a trait so clearly demonstrated in another person that it's difficult to separate the human from the admirable trait.

I watched my hostess for the weekend, her eyes and ears always attentive to the needs of her guests, including me. Her thoughtfulness and ability to anticipate what might bless or encourage or—yes—feed us wrote these words on my heart: she is what hospitality was always meant to be.

As I considered how this hostess personified hospitality, I was reminded of the way Jesus personified everything God the Father is and everything we could ever need—Provider, Protector, Defender, Comfort, Rescuer, Love, even Mystery.

"Christ in you, the hope of glory." Jesus is both Clarity and Mystery. He does not merely *provide* hope. He *is* Hope in the flesh and now in the Spirit.

In times of struggle or hopelessness, I don't need a lesser hope that is based on a wish or longing. I need more Jesus—Hope with a capital *H*. In darkness, I can either scramble to find scraps of hope or I can lean in to the One who *is* Hope.

Today, I intend to rearrange the way I word things about what Jesus personifies and represents, including Him *as* my hope of glory.
—CYNTHIA RUCHTI

FAITH STEP: *If you've been accustomed to praying, "Thank You, Jesus, for providing hope," consider rewording your prayer today to, "Thank You, Jesus, that You ARE my hope."*

FRIDAY, AUGUST 30

Be alert and always keep on praying for all the Lord's people.
Ephesians 6:18 (NIV)

I HAVE A BAD HABIT of placing my cell phone on the arm of my comfy chair during my morning devotion time. I convince myself the phone won't be a distraction because the ringer is off and the screen is facedown. I also don't delete texts very often. If you texted me six months ago, chances are I can search for a minute or three and find your message. Recently, these two phone facts changed how I pray.

One morning while thinking about a friend facing a significant life transition, I felt led to text a prayer to her. As I scrolled through old messages to find our conversation thread, all those texts suddenly turned into a prayer list.

I scrolled past a text from the superintendent of the school district from which I had retired. I bet he could use some prayer. I saw the name of my hairdresser, the women's ministry leader at church, a former student, and even the town librarian. Had I ever thought to pray for them before? How easy it was to scroll from name to name, pausing to ask Jesus to meet their individual needs that day! I knew exactly how to pray for my hairdresser, who was caring for her disabled father-in-law. The librarian? I hadn't a clue what she needed, but Jesus did.

Who knew a backlog of texts could transform my morning prayer time? Not only am I more thoughtful of others' needs, but I also enjoy praying for people who might be surprised to know I'm talking to Jesus about them. —KAREN SARGENT

FAITH STEP: *Scroll through the texts on your phone. Pray for someone you might not think to pray for otherwise.*

SATURDAY, AUGUST 31

All Scripture is God-breathed . . . so that the servant of God may be thoroughly equipped for every good work. 2 Timothy 3:16–17 (NIV)

I LAUNCHED MY BOOK DURING the second year of the pandemic and did as many virtual interviews as I could to promote it. Not being very tech-savvy, I learned to navigate in cyberspace by trial and error. With each virtual call, I had to troubleshoot a new issue, things like improving the area where I recorded by increasing the lighting for better visibility and rearranging the items behind me for a more pleasing backdrop.

Now, when I look back on that first interview, I'm embarrassed by all my rookie mistakes. Not only was I nervous and tripped over my words, but also the space was so dark that the shadows made my slightly discolored incisor tooth look like Witchiepoo's blacked-out tooth in *H.R. Pufnstuf.* I was mortified! The worst part is it's out there in cyberworld for all to see until the end of time.

Like my first online interview, each of Jesus's disciples revealed their shortcomings and proverbial discolored teeth. James and John sought their own glory (Mark 10:37). Thomas had his doubts (John 20:25). Peter denied Christ three times (Luke 22:61). Worse yet, their faux pas are captured in the most-read book of all time, the Bible, which will remain throughout eternity.

If such fallible people were chosen by Christ to be the first church leaders, it gives me great hope. Jesus doesn't call me to perfection so the glory goes to me. He calls me to do the best I can and point the praise to Him, even with a discolored tooth. —CLAIRE MCGARRY

FAITH STEP: *Take one proactive step today toward something Jesus is calling you to do, even if you don't feel equipped.*

SUNDAY, SEPTEMBER 1

So Christ himself gave the apostles, the prophets, the evangelists, the pastors and teachers, to equip his people for works of service, so that the body of Christ may be built up. Ephesians 4:11–12 (NIV)

SITTING IN CHURCH, I BROWSED the bulletin. A list of opportunities called out for volunteers. Sing in choir? Usher? Decorate the church? Teach Sunday school? Lead a small group? My pulse quickened. I wanted to do it all. Then a wave of pain reminded me of physical limitations, and I sank back.

I'm easily enthused by opportunities and forget I'm not supposed to do it all. My husband directed traffic in the church parking lot for food distributions last year. He has also packaged meals, raised money for Christian ministry by running a marathon, and served in other ways that use his gift of service and his physical strength. I can't do those things. But he reminds me he doesn't want to write a book or teach a room full of writers or do a podcast interview.

When I was a young mom of four and serving as a church organist, I eventually felt overwhelmed with the workload. But I struggled with guilt at the thought of stepping back. My pastor gently suggested there might be someone who would love the opportunity to play, and they wouldn't have the chance until I released my role.

What freedom in realizing Christ equips His body with unique gifts and roles for specific times and places, as well as the freedom of understanding that every task that needs doing is not up to me.
—SHARON HINCK

FAITH STEP: *Pray about an opportunity to serve, acknowledging the priorities and callings that Jesus wants you to focus on. Listen for His will.*

LABOR DAY, MONDAY, SEPTEMBER 2

There are six days when you may work, but the seventh day is a day of sabbath rest, a day of sacred assembly. You are not to do any work; wherever you live, it is a sabbath to the LORD. Leviticus 23:3 (NIV)

WHEN I LOOKED UP THE origin of Labor Day, I found that there's a controversy over who first proposed the idea in 1882: either carpenter Peter McGuire or machinist Matthew Maguire. What are the odds that a single letter differentiates them—McGuire vs. Maguire? Regardless of who initiated the idea, the concept of this first-Monday-in-September federal holiday is to have a parade that shows the strength and spirit of the labor force, followed by a festival or picnic to provide recreation for families. It sounds an awful lot like the Sabbath, doesn't it?

Yet, there's no confusion whatsoever over who the Founder of the Sabbath is. God very clearly decreed that one day a week we needed to stop the busyness to gather as a sacred community of believers to rest in Him, pay attention to the spiritual aspects of life, and spend time with family.

Moreover, where Labor Day is just once a year, the Sabbath isn't restricted to just once a week. Sabbath moments can happen whenever I need them. During any minute of any day, Jesus is ready to rejuvenate my spirit. Regardless of where I am or how small the increment of time, when I rest in Him, I am restored.
—CLAIRE MCGARRY

FAITH STEP: *See how many Sabbath moments you can have today by turning to Jesus for restoration.*

TUESDAY, SEPTEMBER 3

And my God will supply every need of yours according to his riches in glory in Christ Jesus. Philippians 4:19 (ESV)

"ARE YOU SEEING ANYONE SPECIAL?" a well-meaning friend asked. The ink was barely dry on my divorce papers when people started inquiring about my dating status. I'd been with my husband for twenty years, fresh on the heels of becoming a Christian. I'd raced into marriage, ignoring all the warning signs that it was not God's will for me. Consequently, our marriage had been difficult from the outset and I was emotionally bruised. I wanted to be sure not to make the same mistakes again. Instead of jumping into a dating relationship, I resolved to get close to Jesus and depend on Him to supply all my needs.

I've been divorced for more than a year now, and I am finding an increasingly comfortable rhythm. This season has been precious and powerful. I'm enjoying getting reacquainted with myself as I rebuild a new kind of life. My boys are doing really well, and I have a very kind and cooperative rapport with their dad. Sometimes I feel stirrings of longing, but I have no intention of actively looking for love. My life is full with my kids, new and deepening friendships, a fresh sense of calling, and opportunities unfolding before me.

Jesus has filled my needs—and supplied some wants—for all things. I'm choosing to believe that when the time is right, Jesus will supply new love for me too. —ISABELLA CAMPOLATTARO

FAITH STEP: *Take a few moments to list all the needs and wants Jesus has supplied, taking special note of the ones you thought Jesus might never fulfill. Thank Him.*

WEDNESDAY, SEPTEMBER 4

Let all that I am wait quietly before God, for my hope is in him.
He alone is my rock and my salvation, my fortress where
I will not be shaken. Psalm 62:5–6 (NLT)

"I AM WEAK BUT THOU art strong," the first line of the old hymn "Just a Closer Walk with Thee," describes how I've often felt in the past three years. I've learned to make this admission to Jesus without shame or apology because it's absolutely true. Apart from His presence and power at work within me, I am weak and woefully inadequate when it comes to knowing how to pray, love and forgive others, and persevere under pressure.

Spending time in Jesus's presence knowing He knows everything about me and loves me still brings a sense of relief and freedom. I am, at times, inadequate, scared, frustrated, tired, empty, and feeling rejected. But when I admit my shortcomings, honesty lifts a weight from my shoulders. I don't have to fake it. I come just as I am and find my hope renewed in who He is.

Jesus is more than adequate to meet my needs today, tomorrow, and forever. He is my Rock, the unshakable One on whom I can depend even when global events rattle and shake me. He is my Savior who cleanses my sin stains and gives me a fresh start. He is my Fortress, my hiding place, my safe space when Satan launches attacks on me.

As I walk closer with Jesus, I rely on His strength. All that I am waits quietly on Him. He alone is my hope. —GRACE FOX

FAITH STEP: *Review the lyrics for "Just a Closer Walk with Thee," then fill in the blanks: I am _____ but Jesus is _____ for whatever circumstance I face today.*

THURSDAY, SEPTEMBER 5

For we are God's handiwork, created in Christ Jesus to do good works, which God prepared in advance for us to do. Ephesians 2:10 (NIV)

THIS FALL, OUR SECOND SON, Will, left home for college. He was ready to fly. We made the trek from Idaho to Southern California in two days. I was excited for Will, for his future, and for all that Jesus had for him. I kept reminding myself of that so I wouldn't weep uncontrollably when I said goodbye. But I could barely see through my tears as I drove onto campus to drop Will off at his dorm. He patted my shoulder lovingly and asked, "Mom, are you able to drive? You're crying a lot." I was, but I got us safely to his dorm.

Saying goodbye was difficult, but I hugged Will as hard as I could, knowing great things were in store for him. Even when life becomes difficult and Will doesn't understand what is going on, Jesus does. Jesus planned Will's life before he was born (Jeremiah 29:11). Jesus is going before Will, leading him every step of the way, surrounding him with mercy and grace (Psalm 139:5).

Jesus is going before me too. Part of His plan for me was to raise three boys and let them fly, knowing He will take care of them. He is leading me every step of the way. As I dried my tears for the drive home, I felt Jesus's mercy and grace surrounding me on every side. —SUSANNA FOTH AUGHTMON

FAITH STEP: *Take a walk on your favorite path with the One who surrounds you with mercy and grace. Ponder the plan and the future He's prepared for you.*

FRIDAY, SEPTEMBER 6

Rejoice always, pray continually, give thanks in all circumstances; for this is God's will for you in Christ Jesus. 1 Thessalonians 5:16–18 (NIV)

DURING MY LAST YEAR OF junior high, I took a career personality test. As I tallied the results, I discovered my talents and interests pointed toward a vocation in education. Seeing this, my home economics teacher allowed me to visit the third-grade classroom and read stories to the students once a week. Hope filled me as I sat reading to the children circled at my feet. *This is wonderful. I've found Jesus's will for my life,* I thought.

Yet, instead of getting a teaching degree, I married young and we started a family. When I began homeschooling, I'd joke that I'd followed my career path, only with a smaller classroom. But, recently, talking with my high-school-aged daughter about her future vocation, I saw Jesus's will for my life had been more about my daily choices than about achieving a specific career. I explained to my daughter that Jesus's will isn't about finding the right spouse or job and then being finished in the journey of following Him. Instead, it's more of a daily decision that includes choosing to rejoice, pray, and give thanks in all things.

Even when I found myself on a completely different path from what I once hoped for, I could still be in Jesus's will. While a career personality test provided insight, I've learned that turning to Jesus in prayer and thanksgiving every day fills me with hope and allows me to be in Jesus's will each day. And that's the best path I could imagine! —TRICIA GOYER

FAITH STEP: *Take three minutes to rejoice and then three minutes to pray, thanking Jesus that this is His will for you today.*

SATURDAY, SEPTEMBER 7

How can a young person stay on the path of purity? By living according to your word. Psalm 119:9 (NIV)

I USED TO PANIC WHEN my gas tank dropped below half full. My husband was battling leukemia, and we had to be vigilant about infections that could attack his weakened immune system and become fatal within hours. If he spiked a fever, we'd rush to the emergency room, where he'd receive antibiotics by IV before being transported to the cancer center two hours away. I never wanted to be caught with an empty gas tank.

I wish I were as diligent about keeping my spiritual tank full. As soon as I begin my quiet time, the cat begs to go outside. After obeying her orders, I settle in with my Bible and discover a scripture that will speak to a friend in her struggle. I pause to text the encouraging words to her. She texts back, and the next thing I know, we're planning a shopping trip.

Cats and cell phones are obvious distractions. Less obvious is the book I'm reading by my favorite Bible teacher. I've substituted her words for *the* Word several days in a row. The biggest disruptions that upset my morning routine are coffee dates, medical appointments, or sleepless nights. It seems my friends and doctors and insomnia always want to visit the same week. Yours too?

Then Saturday arrives. My tank is dangerously close to empty, which isn't healthy for me spiritually, emotionally, mentally, or relationally. I need to check my gauge often, eliminate distractions, and protect my morning schedule. Filling my spiritual tank isn't complicated. I just need to take the time to connect with Jesus—the fuel I need for a spiritually full life. —KAREN SARGENT

FAITH STEP: *How full is your spiritual tank today? What distractions do you need to eliminate in order to fill it?*

GRANDPARENTS' DAY, SUNDAY, SEPTEMBER 8

The heartfelt and persistent prayer of a righteous man (believer) can accomplish much [when put into action and made effective by God— it is dynamic and can have tremendous power]. James 5:16 (AMP)

I WAS INTRIGUED BY A public figure's testimony about his wayward life that changed radically when he came to faith in Christ. The person being interviewed said, "But I knew my grandmother loved me and was praying for me." Those prayers and that love served as a lodestar, or inspirational guide, for this man's eventual journey to or back to Jesus.

As one of those unconditional-love-praying grandmothers, I find those words resonating in me. How many hours have I invested in praying for my kids and grandchildren? Maybe I'll be blessed to add great-grandchildren to the list someday in the future. I wonder if any will include me in their faith story by saying, "And I knew my grandmother was praying for me."

My hope is that they'll be spared deep regrets and know they were loved by far more than me. But even in biblical times, children and grandchildren of godly parents and grandparents often found themselves caught up in the world's way of thinking and acting, seeking relief for their wounds, or wandering in dangerous places. I won't—can't—stop praying and loving unconditionally. It was modeled for me by Jesus, who we're told in Scripture, ever lives to intercede (Hebrews 7:25).

I don't pray for the purpose of being mentioned in my children's or grandchildren's testimonies. I pray because heartfelt, persistent prayer may be someone's lodestar to Jesus. —CYNTHIA RUCHTI

FAITH STEP: *Draw a heart on a sheet of paper. Inside the heart, write today's date and your grandchildren's names or the name of another person for whom you're offering long-standing prayers. Put it somewhere to remind you that Jesus intercedes with you.*

Monday, September 9

For since the creation of the world God's invisible qualities—his eternal power and divine nature—have been clearly seen, being understood from what has been made, so that people are without excuse. Romans 1:20 (NIV)

Oh, no! Not again. Another pesky chin hair. They've been showing up more frequently, much to my chagrin. I can easily see the wrinkles starting to surface on my neck and the loose skin on my arms. But what really gets me are the chin hairs. I can't readily see them, but I can feel them as I run my hand over my face, which I often do while I read or sit thinking about everything and nothing.

I recently purchased a magnifying mirror to make it easier to see the hairs so that I can promptly pluck them out before they get too long. They are nearly invisible to the naked eye, but I know they are there. No doubt about that.

I've never seen Jesus, but like the tiny hairs that keep showing up on my face, I know He's there. Jesus may be hidden from sight, but I still can feel and even see Him clearly through heart-lifting worship music, the beauty of nature, the loving kindnesses of friends and strangers, and the sincere prayers of fellow believers. Through those things and more, Jesus shows Himself to me—just like chin hairs, although He's a welcomed sight. —Barbranda Lumpkins Walls

---

Faith Step: *In what ways do you experience the invisible power and presence of Jesus? Look to see how He will make Himself known to you today.*

TUESDAY, SEPTEMBER 10

You prepare a table before me in the presence of my enemies. You anoint my head with oil; my cup overflows. Psalm 23:5 (NIV)

WHILE RAISING OUR THREE CHILDREN, I spent many hours of my days cooking and serving meals to my family. Often I'd hurry through these chores, considering them menial and thinking that I must get on to my "more important work."

One day, I meditated on the words in Psalm 23, one of the most memorized passages in the Bible, and I realized that preparing meals must be significant work since God, the King of the universe, lovingly does so for us in this psalm.

Jesus, too, prepared a meal for others. After His resurrection, Jesus Himself cooked breakfast over a campfire on the beach for a few of His disciples (John 21:9–14). Food and meals were often the way Jesus connected with others. He wasn't rushed or in a hurry. Meals with Him were opportunities to build relationships.

I can demonstrate Jesus's love by serving meals to my family and friends. The warmth and acceptance others experience as they are seated around my dinner table can give them strength to face physical, as well as emotional and mental, enemies they encounter in life—shame, defeat, loneliness, or discouragement. Through my caring hospitality, I can serve up a hearty helping of Jesus's presence in a very tangible and delicious way. —JENNIFER ANNE F. MESSING

FAITH STEP: *Think of a neighbor, coworker, or church acquaintance who is going through a tough time. Encourage her and spread the warmth of Jesus's love by taking her a meal or inviting her to your house for some home cooking.*

WEDNESDAY, SEPTEMBER 11

I will always thank the LORD; I will never stop praising him. Psalm 34:1 (GNT)

DOES ANYBODY REALLY COUNT SHEEP to fall asleep? Though I've never done that, the Lord has given me another way to shut down my busy, overactive mind so sleep can come—alphabetical acrostic poems. It's nothing new. Some authors of the Bible must have also had busy, overactive minds because multiple Bible passages—including Psalm 119 and Proverbs 31—are poetry created by the method I use for falling asleep.

Sometimes my poems are prayers of gratitude. Sometimes they're prayers of praise. Either way, the method's the same. I pray alphabetically. I silently talk to Jesus, addressing Him by His different names beginning with each subsequent letter of the alphabet, praising and thanking Him for His various attributes beginning with each subsequent letter of the alphabet.

For example: "A—Almighty, Alpha and Omega, I adore You for Your Authority. B—Beloved Jesus, I believe in You. Thank You for the blessings You've given me." Sometimes I pray alphabetically, thanking Jesus for the gifts He's given me, such as: "D—Dearest Divine Jesus, thank You for the gift of deliverance from death and destruction. E—Everlasting Lord Jesus, thank You for the gift of eternal life with You in heaven."

Sometimes I simply recite verses from the Bible or the names of hymns, starting with one that begins with the letter *A*, then one that begins with the letter *B*, praying through the alphabet that way. Regardless of the style of the alphabetical poem I pray, Jesus never fails to carry me into sweet slumber when I'm thanking and praising Him—a much better way to fall asleep than counting sheep. —CASSANDRA TIERSMA

FAITH STEP: *Close your eyes and try praying alphabetically, telling Jesus the ABCs of why you love Him.*

THURSDAY, SEPTEMBER 12

Brothers and sisters, we do not want you to be uninformed about those who sleep in death, so that you do not grieve like the rest of mankind, who have no hope. 1 Thessalonians 4:13 (NIV)

FROM THE OTHER END OF the phone, I heard, "He's gone. He's gone." My husband's best friend called to tell us that Jaden, his son and our beloved godson, had passed away in the hospital overnight. We were in shock. Twenty-one and a senior in college, Jaden's life was just beginning. *Why?* The news of his death hit me hard at that moment. I stood frozen in disbelief. The idea of never seeing him again was a lot to bear.

In 1 Thessalonians 4:13–17, the Apostle Paul's writing implies that Christians in the church at Thessalonica struggled with the loss of their loved ones and with that loss came much grief. Pointing to the death, resurrection, and anticipated return of Jesus, Paul sought to challenge this Christian community about their current perspective on death. They grieved as if death were the final chapter.

I sometimes want to bypass the pain and sadness I feel about death by focusing instead on the hope of reuniting with my lost loved ones when Jesus returns. But even though I'm a Jesus follower, grieving is a part of processing death. I will miss Jaden here on earth for a very long time, but I know I'll see him again in heaven. —ERICKA LOYNES

FAITH STEP: *Are you grieving a loved one? Feel your sadness and loss by writing a letter of what you wish you would have said to that person on earth or what you hope to tell that person when you are reunited in heaven.*

Friday, September 13

If any of you lacks wisdom, let him ask of God, who gives to all liberally and without reproach, and it will be given to him. James 1:5 (NKJV)

I'D NOTICED HIM ON THE first lap of my daily bike ride. A heavy-set older man I'd never seen before, plodding along the sidewalk, swinging his arms. As I zoomed past, he hollered, "Now you're making me feel bad!"

He'd said it jokingly, but it gave me pause. I'd spent my whole life endeavoring never to make anyone feel bad. *What to do, Jesus?* Did the man think I was showing off? I could slow down. But then I wouldn't complete my goal of riding 7 miles in thirty minutes. Should I go and introduce myself and ride slowly beside him? That might seem condescending. Should I just holler back, "You've got this! You're doing great! Keep up the good work!"? I'd be long past him by the time I finished saying all of that. *Jesus, I need some guidance here.*

At times in my life when I'd faced major decisions, I'd asked Jesus what to do. Sometimes I felt as if He'd answered. At other times, His answer hadn't been apparent. Then there were times when Jesus had answered eventually, but I'd had to wait for His response. Nonetheless, I'll never stop seeking the wisdom Jesus shares so willingly. All I need to do is ask.

Passing the man for the last time before I turned for home, I gave him a thumbs-up. Grinning, he gave me one too. We both were encouraged. —PAT BUTLER DYSON

FAITH STEP: *What major or minor decision can Jesus help you with today? Look for situations in which to ask for His wisdom.*

SATURDAY, SEPTEMBER 14

In the human body there are many parts and organs, each with a unique function. And so it is in the body of Christ. For though we are many, we've all been mingled into one body in Christ. This means that we are all vitally joined to one another, with each contributing to the others.
Romans 12:4–5 (TPT)

ALTHOUGH MY EYES WERE CLOSED as my five close friends and I prayed, I did a mental inventory of each lady. None of us attended the same congregation. We varied in age by twenty years. Our backgrounds, family stories, and interests were diverse. Yet we shared our love for Jesus. And that made us family.

When our former writers' group disbanded, fellow member Beth emailed me, saying she would miss seeing me. I suggested she and I meet and pray together. That was ten years and six published books ago. We now meet together, with a few others, at a central location every other week to pray. Sometimes we even discuss writing projects. But mostly we join our hearts to ask Jesus to help us raise our kids, love our husbands and parents better, and fill us with wisdom for everyday problems.

We don't debate theological differences. Our goal is to help each other know Jesus more intimately and succeed at doing life with His help.

Some glorious day we'll meet in heaven around Jesus's throne to worship Him. And that makes us family. —JEANETTE LEVELLIE

FAITH STEP: *Text a friend of a different denomination from yours. Start your message with "Dear Sister."*

SUNDAY, SEPTEMBER 15

I pray that the eyes of your heart may be enlightened so that you may know what is the hope of his calling, what is the wealth of his glorious inheritance in the saints, and what is the immeasurable greatness of his power toward us who believe. Ephesians 1:18–19 *(CSB)*

AFTER THE PASTOR FINISHED HIS sermon, he explained why the sanctuary walls were dotted with pink sticky notes. Each note contained one of fifteen different words to pray for our church. He invited us to take one off the wall. My husband slipped out of our row and randomly grabbed one. When I looked at the paper, my eyes filled with tears. The word revealed what I personally needed: *clarity.*

The next week, I read through a short workbook to prepare for a Bible study, and the word *clarity* jumped off the pages ten times. That word pinpointed a weakness in my prayer life. Sometimes, even when I'm praying *Your will be done*, I'm actually asking God to work out my life according to what I would like it to be. What I really needed was clarity to see His vision of how He wanted to use me in His work and the ability to trust that He will take care of everything else.

I still keep that sticky note at my desk. It reminds me that just as Jesus healed people of physical blindness, He is ready to give me better spiritual eyesight. Whenever I get bogged down with questions or decisions, I can ask Jesus for clarity to help me see His will more clearly. —DIANNE NEAL MATTHEWS

FAITH STEP: *Do you need Jesus to shed light on a problem or difficult decision? Ask Him to light up your path so you can follow His lead.*

MONDAY, SEPTEMBER 16

*Two are better than one, because they have a good return
for their labor. Ecclesiastes 4:9 (NIV)*

THE STRESS OF THE PREVIOUS school day had not yet melted away
when I received an email informing me of one more task for tomorrow's meeting. I sank into my chair, defeated, and the morning had
just begun. My schedule was already too full. What would I have to
sacrifice at home this evening to meet this new deadline? Time with
my family? A few loads of laundry? Much-needed rest?

My teaching teammate Christina walked into my classroom just as
I was blinking back tears. She didn't hesitate when I told her about
the email. "Let me do it for you," she offered. I protested, assuring
her I would find a way, but she surprised me with her response.
"You said in your interview that one reason you wanted to teach
here was that you wanted to be part of a team. Do you remember
that?" I nodded. "This is what a team does. We help each other.
There's no need to keep working as if you're all alone."

Her words washed over me like a warm hug. I had forgotten all
the times I'd cried out to Jesus, worn out and weary from teaching
in isolation. I'd forgotten that I'd prayed for coworkers who could
share the responsibilities of running and managing a classroom. I'd
forgotten that asking for help means being willing to accept help.

When Christina returned that afternoon with the task complete, I
thanked Jesus for the reminder that I wasn't alone. —EMILY E. RYAN

FAITH STEP: *Do you have difficulty accepting help? Ask Jesus for a lesson the
next time someone offers to help you.*

TUESDAY, SEPTEMBER 17

But we do not belong to those who shrink back and are destroyed,
but to those who have faith and are saved. Hebrews 10:39 (NIV)

I TEXTED A FRIEND TO pray for me as I worried about an upcoming conversation with Jane, a Christian colleague. She and I had differing opinions on an important issue. I wanted to talk with Jane and help her see my point rather than avoid her or get angry.

I rehearsed multiple ways the conversation could go depending on my attitude and delivery. I needed Jane to hear my concerns. Her professional position had power that could sway a decision one way or another, which I believed could end up being detrimental to many, including me.

Ding. My friend texted back that she was praying Hebrews 10:39 over me. I looked up the scripture and was surprised by the phrase "we do not belong to those who shrink back."

I often assumed Jesus wants us as Christians to be silent when we disagree. This situation, though, was potentially harmful if I did not speak up. I needed to do so the right way. I prayed the verse myself, asking Jesus to help me not shrink back, but also not speak offensively or emotionally.

I felt calm as I approached the meeting. Jane and I opened our time together in prayer. We listened to one another. She was receptive to my concerns, and I gained new perspectives from hers. Our reciprocal respect remained.

As I mirror His gentle manner and walk in His ways, I see that my humble Servant-Savior never shrank back either. —BRENDA L. YODER

FAITH STEP: *Take a moment and ponder where Jesus is asking you not to shrink back. How can you approach the situation with gentleness and grace?*

WEDNESDAY, SEPTEMBER 18

The LORD will watch over your coming and going both now and forevermore. Psalm 121:8 (NIV)

FRIENDS WITH A LARGE FAMILY live on a 10-acre wooded property. They raise poultry and goats, and they recently acquired three cows. It's a homesteader's dream, except for black bear and cougar sightings common in that area. To keep their children and animals safe, they bought two Great Pyrenees dogs.

This large species is bred to protect livestock and property. Its keen hearing and sense of smell alert it to danger, and it warns intruders with a deep *woof*. It attacks and defends if a wild animal threatens those in its care.

The children play outside unafraid, knowing their dogs keep watch. Their confidence in their pets' protective nature awakens my appreciation for Jesus's care for me.

Evil is a reality in our world, so I know I'm not immune to harm. As a result, I exercise cautions such as locking my door at night and not walking alone after dark in our marina. I use common sense even while trusting Jesus to take responsibility for me because I'm His child.

Trusting Jesus for my safety assumed new meaning when COVID-19 travel restrictions were lifted. Knowing He watches over me gave me courage to resume international travel for ministry purposes.

I'm grateful that Jesus guards me better than any watchdog can. No matter where I am, at home or abroad, fear will not tie me in knots. I'm confident in His care and free to enjoy the life He's given me. —GRACE FOX

FAITH STEP: *Think of a specific way you've felt protected by Jesus as you ponder the marvelous truth that the Creator of the universe watches over you.*

THURSDAY, SEPTEMBER 19

Do not conform to the pattern of this world, but be transformed by the renewing of your mind. Then you will be able to test and approve what God's will is—his good, pleasing and perfect will. Romans 12:2 (NIV)

MY COMPUTER IS FIVE YEARS old—which in computer years is about ninety (one human year is equal to eighteen computer years). It has been limping along. It takes ages to turn on. The lag time for connecting to the Internet is unimpressive. It's constantly buffering. The touchpad doesn't work, so I had to purchase a mouse to navigate the screen. This is problematic for a writer. My livelihood is connected to my computer. When it doesn't function well, I don't function well. My dad confirmed this. When I couldn't log in to our Zoom call, he said, "You need a new computer." I agreed. When I couldn't access our shared document, he said, "We're getting you a new computer." My mom and dad are always blessing my socks off.

My new computer arrived this week. It's a miracle! It turns on in seconds. The memory is amazing. It navigates the Internet with breathtaking speed. Everything works as it should. It is revolutionizing how I work. When Jesus entered my life, the same thing happened. He transformed my perspective and the way I lived. He renewed my mind with love, truth, and the power of the Holy Spirit. He changed my life with His grace and always blesses my socks off. With Jesus, I function so much better.
—SUSANNA FOTH AUGHTMON

FAITH STEP: *Draw a vertical line down the center of a sheet of paper. On one side, list character traits from the "old you." On the other side, list the changes that Jesus has brought into your life.*

FRIDAY, SEPTEMBER 20

He got up, rebuked the wind and said to the waves, "Quiet! Be still!"
Then the wind died down and it was completely calm. He said to
his disciples, "Why are you so afraid? Do you still have no faith?"
Mark 4:39–40 (NIV)

WHILE DRIVING TO A CONFERENCE, my husband, Ted, and I headed into some intense thunderstorms, with lightning striking all around and sheeting rain making it impossible to see the road. I huddled in the front seat praying. "Lord, just because I write epic adventures doesn't mean I want to experience them."

Many cars had parked under bridges. We pulled onto the shoulder for a while, and the storm blew past. But when we started out again, we headed right back into the downpour. As I watched the massive power of the dark skies, I thought of Jesus's sovereignty. Only He could make a way for us to go through the storm and keep us safe.

As I confronted my internal fears and the dangerous storm outside our car, I felt as if Jesus was asking me the same question He asked His disciples: "Why are you so afraid?" I realized I needed to focus on Him. I often can't control events outside myself. In the same way, I can't manipulate or control Jesus. But I can always trust Him.

Ted and I found a place to wait out more of the storm and then made it safely to the conference. I thanked Jesus for the opportunity to practice trusting Him. —SHARON HINCK

FAITH STEP: *List a few of your fears. Ask yourself, "Why am I still afraid?" then ask Jesus to deepen your hope in His love and His power by increasing your trust in Him.*

SATURDAY, SEPTEMBER 21

I am the door. If anyone enters by Me, he will be saved, and will go in and out and find pasture. John 10:9 (NKJV)

I ROAMED ALONG THE NARROW streets and brick sidewalks of Charleston, admiring ivy-covered homes from an earlier century. I stopped in front of a tiny white house with a curious entrance. The arched gray door wasn't much taller than I. It had a metal grid covering its matching window, but there was no knob. *What could be on the other side of that door?*

My thoughts jumped to children's stories about hidden entrances to special adventures. Alice followed the white rabbit down a hole into Wonderland. Lucy entered Narnia through the back of an old wardrobe. Mary found a key that unlocked the secret garden gate.

The dawn of each new morning is like that gray door swinging open—I don't know what awaits me on the other side. Might I face difficulties in the hours ahead? Maybe the day will be wondrous? My longtime, fervent prayer could receive an answer in an unexpected way. That opportunity I desire might finally become available. I might get to share the love of Jesus with someone in need.

I never discovered what was on the other side of that door, but I do know, whether difficult or wondrous, every day can be filled with hope by trusting in the beautiful words of Jesus. After all, He will open the door to His Kingdom, where I know eternal life awaits me. —BECKY ALEXANDER

FAITH STEP: *Open your front door and step across the threshold. Take a deep breath and look toward the sky. You've entered your day of unknowns and surprises. Bask in heavenly hope, trusting Jesus with whatever lies ahead.*

SUNDAY, SEPTEMBER 22

Truly I tell you, anyone who will not receive the kingdom of God like a little child will never enter it. Mark 10:15 (NIV)

I WAS WHAT WAS KNOWN as a strong-willed child. I wanted things my own way. I was always in trouble and rarely understood why. I just couldn't make sense of the world. Sometimes I knew what I was doing was wrong and deserved to be punished, but often I didn't. Above all else, I hated to be in trouble for something unintentional and so minor (at least to me) I didn't even remember doing.

As I got older, I countered with hypervigilance. I wanted to be above reproach because I was so afraid of being corrected. Those strategies later served me well in my neonatal ICU career. I kept my guard up and anticipated every possible outcome. I had to make sure nothing went wrong in order for those sick babies to grow healthy. This attitude wasn't a good lesson for walking in faith or for following Jesus, though.

Jesus says, "Come," as He calls His children to Him (Mark 10:14). And I sometimes think, *What's the catch?* But there isn't one. He loves me. He forgives me. Jesus paid for everything I ever did wrong. My best efforts to be above reproach count for nothing.

I won't get to heaven by being better or more right than anyone else. Instead, I will be with my Father for eternity by living the kind of faith that sends me running into His outstretched arms.
—SUZANNE DAVENPORT TIETJEN

FAITH STEP: *How difficult is it to let down your guard? Be honest about one of your shortcomings. Share it with Jesus as you pour your heart out to Him.*

Monday, September 23

They had argued about who was the greatest. Sitting down, Jesus called the Twelve and said, "Anyone who wants to be first must be the very last, and the servant of all." Mark 9:34–35 (NIV)

I REMEMBER WHEN MY TEEN son would wear nothing but Under Armour brand apparel and footwear. A year later, for no apparent reason, he quit wearing it, saying it was totally uncool. There was a time when fair skin was a sign of privilege; it meant you didn't have to toil in the sun. Decades later, a good tan was a status symbol, showing you had leisure time in sunny places. Once upon a time, being plump meant you were wealthy enough to eat well. More recently, light and tight suggest affluence. Sometimes status symbols are more subtle, like educational degrees, volunteer commitments, or even signs of religious piety. Obviously, what culture deems as most preferred is fickle.

Status symbols change, but the desire for them doesn't. Most people want some kind of differentiator that denotes their status so others—and they themselves—know where they stand. Many times, the outward symbol doesn't reflect reality. Even the disciples were clamoring for position, and the great equalizer, Jesus, shut them down. Jesus eschews status—most especially the fake variety—making Himself nothing by taking the nature of a servant (Philippians 2:7) for our benefit. With Jesus, I don't *need* symbolic status because He gave me His status, and that's better than a fancy clothing brand any day. —ISABELLA CAMPOLATTARO

FAITH STEP: *Jot down what you rely on for status of any kind. Ask Jesus to free you from it.*

TUESDAY, SEPTEMBER 24

But he said to me, "My grace is sufficient for you, for my power is made perfect in weakness." Therefore I will boast all the more gladly about my weaknesses, so that Christ's power may rest on me.
2 Corinthians 12:9 (NIV)

RECENTLY, I HAD TO CUT a piece of paper in half and didn't have any scissors. A friend taught me to fold the paper, wet the crease, pull the ends, and the paper would tear perfectly on the fold. It seems that wherever paper is dampened, it weakens. When the pull happens, the paper gives at its weakest point.

My heart and spiritual life are no different. Sadness, trauma, discord, or fear sometimes pull at me. If I haven't strengthened and fortified myself with prayer and Jesus's healing and protection, my heart and spirit tear. If I looked closely at that tear, I'd see it always follows the line of my weakest point.

If there's an old hurt I haven't healed, a past betrayal I haven't forgiven, a preexisting vice I haven't overcome, or a place of doubt and insecurity I haven't worked through, I remain vulnerable and susceptible to the tearing.

To strengthen my weak places and bridge my emotional gaps, I need only turn to Jesus. In His ever-gentle and consistent way, His strength fortifies my weakness. His grace knits my gaps closed, reinforces any weak places, and covers me with the power of His love and protection. Then, no matter the push, pull, tug, or tear, I remain securely in His embrace, safe and sound. —CLAIRE MCGARRY

FAITH STEP: *Fold a piece of paper in half, dampen the crease, and pull. Witness how the paper tears at the weakest point. Then discern where your weaknesses lie and turn to Jesus to fortify you.*

WEDNESDAY, SEPTEMBER 25

But those who hope in the LORD will renew their strength. They will soar on wings like eagles; they will run and not grow weary, they will walk and not be faint. Isaiah 40:31 (NIV)

WHEN I FACILITATE A CLASS or give a presentation—no matter how long I've been on my feet or how many hours have passed—my energy level rises. And it remains high long afterward because of the connections I've made with people and because of the connections I've seen people make to the content. Public speaking is my passion. I'm grateful to use the gifts Jesus gave me, but finding a job took perseverance.

Years ago, I auditioned for a college prep company looking to hire people to speak to groups of high school and first-year college students. As part of the process, I had to memorize and present a portion of a script. In the first round, I couldn't project my voice. I stumbled over words and recited things out of order. I pushed through to the end, rushed back to my seat, and held back tears.

I'd been speaking publicly for a while, so that presentation should have been easy for me to master. I decided not to lose hope and be better prepared next time by rehearsing the material to perfect my presentation. I did much better, but I wasn't hired. And then it hit me—I would have been better prepared if I'd put my trust in Jesus to help me.

I didn't give up on speaking and eventually found my dream job, thanks to Jesus never giving up on me. —ERICKA LOYNES

FAITH STEP: *Write down one thing you used to be passionate about and why you stopped doing it. Ask Jesus to renew your strength as you get back on track.*

THURSDAY, SEPTEMBER 26

... the Lord Jesus Christ, our hope. 1 Timothy 1:1 (NKJV)

MY MOM INHERITED HER FAMILY'S propensity for heart trouble. She survived almost all common and several experimental medical and surgical interventions over the course of her long battle with congestive heart failure. As if she hadn't endured enough, during a rather routine procedure, she lost her senses of taste and smell. Forever. I couldn't imagine having those two senses blanked out...until it happened to me. I emerged from a bout of COVID-19 with my lungs intact, but I lost the ability to taste or smell. I waited weeks, months, for them to kick in again. Bacon and coffee now smelled like industrial waste. Most foods tasted like cardboard. I racked my brain to remember the fragrance of my favorite cologne. I smelled smoke when it wasn't there but not when it was, which resulted in multiple slices of burned toast.

Both senses eventually returned, but the experience made me wonder, *What if I lost my ability to feel hopeful?* My thoughts about hope can be distorted by my circumstances. What would I do if I ever lost hope?

Thankfully, Jesus is my hope. Even if I lose the ability to be hopeful, there is nothing I can ever do to lose Him. He is steadfast and true; His presence isn't determined by how I feel. Jesus is always with me, in both sickness and health—and knowing this means I can never lose hope. —CYNTHIA RUCHTI

FAITH STEP: *Spray your favorite fragrance on your wrist. Thank Jesus for being your hope each time you catch a whiff as you go through the day.*

FRIDAY, SEPTEMBER 27

*Be kind and compassionate to one another, forgiving each other,
just as in Christ God forgave you. Ephesians 4:32 (NIV)*

TODAY, I MAILED A GET-WELL card to a family member who recently received a cancer diagnosis. Sending my good wishes to someone in my family doesn't sound like a big deal, except for the fact I've rarely spoken to him in decades. He's not the easiest person to get along with, in my opinion, and he's brought division to our family. Yet when I learned of his diagnosis, my heart grew tender for him. And as I prayed for his health, compassion filled me. I knew I needed to forgive him.

Jesus's forgiveness is a gift—one none of us deserves. The more I reflect on Jesus's forgiveness of me, the more willing I am to forgive those who I think don't deserve it. While it's often not easy for me to forgive others, small acts of kindness and compassion can soften the soil of my heart, allowing forgiveness to grow.

I don't believe one get-well card will erase the decades of distance I've had with this family member, yet I do hope the love of Jesus comes through. While it's always possible for healing to happen in challenging relationships, it is even more probable that true healing will occur within me. When I trust Jesus, pray for that person, and forgive, I let go of past offenses. Even if the other person does not apologize, by forgiving them I'm freed. Forgiveness is the gift I give myself. —TRICIA GOYER

FAITH STEP: *Today, commit to doing one small act of kindness toward someone you're angry with or someone who is seemingly undeserving of your consideration. Ask Jesus to help you have compassion and forgive.*

SATURDAY, SEPTEMBER 28

I praise you because I am fearfully and wonderfully made; your works are wonderful, I know that full well. Psalm 139:14 *(NIV)*

MY HUSBAND, DAVID, WAITED FOR me on the condo's balcony, enjoying the hot tub's steamy water. Before joining him, I glanced in a mirror, debating different ways I could hide my less-than-perfect figure. I stood tall and sucked in my stomach, pulling my shoulders back and tipping my head just so. I draped the towel over my swimsuit's shoulder, changed my mind, and wrapped it around my middle, attempting to disguise my waistline. And then I laughed.

This was no audition for some modeling position. I was relaxing with my husband, the man I'd been married to for four decades, the man who loves me. A meme I'd seen on social media came to mind: "Love says: I've seen the ugly parts of you and I'm staying." David has viewed every bit of me and stuck around.

Jesus has seen all my ugliness, inside and out, too, from the moment I was born. He'll witness my good, bad, and unflattering behavior until the day I die. Yet He continues to love me. This love is without condition, limitless and undeserved.

When Jesus accepted the responsibility for my sin, He proved a devotion greater than life itself. Am I grateful? Eternally. Am I self-conscious? No. Because whether I'm fat or thin, clever or naïve, selfish or sweet, He accepts me. And He's staying. —HEIDI GAUL

FAITH STEP: *Look at yourself in the mirror. Say "I love you" out loud to whatever area you feel is less than perfect. Do the same for those places inside, and thank Jesus for His unconditional love.*

SUNDAY, SEPTEMBER 29

Jesus did many other things as well. If every one of them were written down, I suppose that even the whole world would not have room for the books that would be written. John 21:25 (NIV)

I COULD SIT WITH THE hope of this verse for a long time. It's limitless.

John 21:25 refers to the things Jesus did during His three-year ministry on earth. Working three years is not a long time to fill enough books that overfill the world. That's a lot of accomplishments.

And that was more than 2,000 years ago. Imagine how much Jesus has done since His years walking the earth, without earth's limitations. I can't grasp it all.

The Apostle Paul echoed this in Ephesians 3:20–21 (NIV): "Now to him who is able to do immeasurably more than all we ask or imagine, according to his power that is at work within us, to him be glory in the church and in Christ Jesus throughout all generations, for ever and ever! Amen."

Lately, I've been looking at my to-do list each day and struggling to keep the various activities organized. Work, kids, marriage, faith, fun, bills, exercise, doctor's appointments, groceries. You know.

When I read John 21:25 and focus first on Jesus, those activities slip into place. Full disclosure, they slip back out of place repeatedly each day, but Jesus knows that.

He does not demand I fill books everywhere with my accomplishments, but instead Jesus invites me to sit and listen to Him (Luke 10:39). He invites me to experience and accept His peace (John 14:27). Being with Jesus, that's the best way to spend my time. —ERIN KEELEY MARSHALL

FAITH STEP: *Ask Jesus to surprise you with more of Himself today.*

MONDAY, SEPTEMBER 30

Why, my soul, are you downcast? Why so disturbed within me?
Put your hope in God, for I will yet praise him, my Savior
and my God. Psalm 43:5 (NIV)

I RECENTLY READ AN ARTICLE in a psychology magazine that focused on self-talk, that inner voice most of us have that offers a running commentary throughout the day. This combination of conscious thoughts and subconscious beliefs helps our brain interpret and process our experiences. Positive, encouraging self-talk can help people combat fear and grow in confidence. Negative self-talk can lead people into depression, convincing them that they are a failure and that their situation will never improve. Like many people, I tend to hear the latter.

Centuries ago, the psalm writers knew how to correct unhelpful self-talk. They often began by venting negative emotions but then deliberately shifted their focus. They rehearsed God's past goodness and His promises for the future, often ending by stating an intention to trust and praise God. Like the psalmists, I can change my self-talk and change my perspective. After admitting my fear, disappointment, or anger in prayer, I can remind myself that thanks to Jesus, I am forgiven, free, protected, and unconditionally loved. I don't have to let negative thoughts and feelings dictate my mood; I can choose to focus on truths that uplift my soul and give myself something good to talk about. —DIANNE NEAL MATTHEWS

FAITH STEP: *As you go through your day, watch for negative self-talk. Be prepared to replace each of those thoughts with a Bible verse or statement that expresses what Jesus thinks about you.*

TUESDAY, OCTOBER 1

Fruit trees of all kinds will grow on both banks of the river. Their leaves will not wither, nor will their fruit fail. Every month they will bear fruit, because the water from the sanctuary flows to them. Their fruit will serve for food and their leaves for healing. Ezekiel 47:12 (NIV)

MY TEN-YEAR-OLD DAUGHTER, JOCELYN, STARTED composting last summer. We don't really have the yard for it, so she started out small and used the large, foil-lined box her Goldfish snack comes in as her collection bin. Whenever I tried to throw away any refuse from dinner prep, she'd stop me and ask if she could have it: fruit peels, vegetable trimmings, eggshells, even coffee grounds. She cared for that pile of garbage as if it were gold, until it became so. Ultimately, she created a fertilizer, so rich my flowers bloomed with vibrant colors and hearty stems.

Jesus cares for me like I'm gold too. He collects the garbage of my life—hardships, mistakes, challenges, and stress—and draws forth the good that I'd sooner throw away. Like the leaves of the fruit trees in Ezekiel 47, Jesus can use what I wish I could discard to heal and nurture me. With Jesus, nothing is wasted. That's why I tend to grow the most from difficult circumstances. Rather than lamenting my refuse, I have to remember to trust in the process and trust in the One who tends to me with loving care. When I do, my life blossoms and I am enriched. —CLAIRE MCGARRY

FAITH STEP: *Begin a small box of compost and watch your refuse turn into fertilizer that is rich and life-giving. Thank Jesus that He uses everything to create a rich life for you too.*

WEDNESDAY, OCTOBER 2

*Where, O death, is your victory? Where, O death,
is your sting? 1 Corinthians 15:55 (NIV)*

ONE OF THE MOST ALARMING aspects of the past few years is what seemed like the moment-to-moment imminence of death from the distressingly unpredictable COVID-19 virus. I never knew who would get sick, including myself, or how severe the symptoms would be if infected. I had to come to terms with my powerlessness in the pandemic. After all, life is uncertain even when there's no highly contagious disease making its way around the globe. When I'm alive and kicking, death seems so terminal, but it's important to remember the reality of death for Christians. There is no death per se. We transition from here on earth to the heavenly realm, seamlessly.

In near-death experiences I've read (reports from those who have been revived after physically dying and had their souls continue to exist), people recount a euphorically vivid and beautiful realm, brimming with love and peace. None of those who journeyed to heaven wanted to come back. Furthermore, they report an absence of negative emotions like those we endure on earth—no grief, no fear, no judgment. Eternity, they say, is as perfect as promised.

I don't want to die an untimely death, and I don't want anyone I love to die. And they won't. In Christ, we can await heaven with joyful expectation and envision our loved ones there with confidence. Because heaven is real, I live unfettered by the fear of death that can overshadow the abundant life Christ died to give me.
—ISABELLA CAMPOLATTARO

FAITH STEP: *Use the concordance in your Bible to look up several verses about heaven. Pick one you find especially comforting and write it on an index card to keep with your daily devotionals.*

THURSDAY, OCTOBER 3

May the grace of the Lord Jesus Christ, and the love of God, and the fellowship of the Holy Spirit be with you all. 2 Corinthians 13:14 (NIV)

MY LAPTOP WAS RUNNING AS slow as molasses. Frustrated, I submitted a service request to the IT department and a video call soon came in.

"Hi, I'm Brian from IT," a cheerful voice announced. "I'm here to help and get you going." I knew immediately that Brian loved his job and people. He turned on his camera briefly so I could see his face. I told him what I do for my job and thanked him for answering my request for help. "Thank you for the job that you do," he said. "I couldn't do what you do. God gives each of us different gifts and treasures."

"Amen!" I said in agreement. I knew I was chatting with a man who knew the Lord. Within minutes, Brian identified my computer problem, told me what I needed to do to fix it, and stayed on the line until I was back in business. I was thrilled. As we ended the call, I thanked Brian again and told him to be blessed. "Amen!" he said. "God is good all the time. It's always good to connect with a fellow believer."

Despite my computer difficulties, those few minutes with Brian lifted my spirits. I was reminded about the importance of connection with others and not just others who love Jesus. Any connection is an opportunity for me to point someone to Him—and a chance for me to deepen my faith. Who knew my faulty computer could be a link between me and Jesus! —BARBRANDA LUMPKINS WALLS

FAITH STEP: *How can you connect others with Jesus? Make a paper chain, tearing one link off every day to help you remember to connect others with Jesus.*

FRIDAY, OCTOBER 4

God did this so that, by two unchangeable things in which it is impossible for God to lie, we who have fled to take hold of the hope set before us may be greatly encouraged. We have this hope as an anchor for the soul, firm and secure. Hebrews 6:18–19 (NIV)

AFTER TWO WEEKS ON A cruise ship, I was ready to go home. Bad weather had plagued us for days, with 19-foot waves and 70-mile-per-hour winds. As the lights of New York City came into view, three chimes rang out across the intercom system.

"This is your captain. Before docking at the Manhattan Cruise Terminal, we must navigate the Hudson River Channel for 6 miles. The current is unusually strong, due to prevailing storms. We will be dropping anchor here in the bay and waiting for further instructions."

The ship continued to rise and fall, lunge forward and back, tip left and right. Yet, it remained firm and secure in place because of the anchor.

The Bible describes my hope in Jesus as an anchor. The world, at times, tosses me around like a boat on an angry ocean. Circumstances can seem dark and dangerous. My heart and mind may battle fear and uncertainty. But just as I trusted our captain to get us home safely, I trust Jesus to help me navigate the rough seas of life. Jesus's two unchangeable realities—His nature and His promises—keep me grounded during the raging winds or roaring waves. I am held securely by Jesus, the Anchor of my soul. —BECKY ALEXANDER

FAITH STEP: *Are you in the midst of a storm? Draw an anchor and write the words "His Nature" and "His Promises" with the words of Hebrews 6:18–19 below it. Put the drawing where you will see it often.*

SATURDAY, OCTOBER 5

The Levites… stood to their feet to praise GOD, the God of Israel;
they praised at the top of their lungs! 2 Chronicles 20:19 (MSG)

AFTER A HARROWING DAY FOLLOWING the passing of my father the previous morning, our family was exhausted but not defeated. Three extremely important personal items that had belonged to my father were nowhere to be found. Mom, my siblings, and I looked everywhere. Suspecting that one of the items had been stolen, my brother filed a police report. Meanwhile, we were all praying for Jesus to reveal the locations of the missing items. In the course of our collective, repeated, methodical searching, the Lord revealed everything we thought was lost.

When Mom finally discovered the third missing item in a place where several of us had already looked, we were overcome with relief and joy. Mom spontaneously broke out into a praise march around her coffee table. Simultaneously, my sister and I joined in. Unable to contain our gratitude for answered prayers, we marched with upraised arms, singing at the top of our lungs: "A-men! A-men! A-men! A-men! A-men! Hallelujah!" Over and over, circling round and round, we felt overjoyed, even in the midst of our grief and sorrow, praising Jesus for His awesome goodness and faithfulness.

Since that day, I now understand what it's like to be able to rejoice in times of adversity and to praise Jesus in all situations.
—CASSANDRA TIERSMA

FAITH STEP: *Regardless of your present circumstances, trials, or adversity, stand up, raise your hands, and praise Jesus at the top of your lungs for what He has done or is going to do in your life!*

SUNDAY, OCTOBER 6

When we bless the cup at the Lord's Table, aren't we sharing in the blood of Christ? And when we break the bread, aren't we sharing in the body of Christ? 1 Corinthians 10:16 (NLT)

WHEN WE VISITED A CHURCH while on vacation last month, the pastor handed us a communion set as we entered the door. The wafer and juice came sealed together in a convenient, sterile package. What a brilliant idea.

I placed my little communion set down on a table to talk to someone and forgot about it. When the pastor's wife stood at the podium to share a few words before communion was served, I turned to my husband, Kevin. *What would I do?*

"I'll share with you," he whispered.

It was a challenge to break that wee wafer in half and sip only a little bit of the juice. But the act made me think about what the word *communion* means. Derived from the Greek word *koinonia* and the Latin word *communio,* it means "fellowship" or "sharing."

What could reflect a better picture of Jesus sharing His life with His followers than Kevin and me sharing the symbols of Jesus's body and blood?

My little mistake turned into a big blessing as I pondered the depth to which Jesus shared Himself with the world in general and with me in particular. Not just by dying in my place 2,000 years ago. But every day, every minute, He shares His wisdom, love, and power with me through the Holy Spirit indwelling my heart.

My life in Jesus. His life in mine. That's communion.
—JEANETTE LEVELLIE

FAITH STEP: *Next time you take communion, imagine Jesus living in you and you in Him. Thank Him for His constant presence and for sharing His life with you.*

MONDAY, OCTOBER 7

For in him all things were created: things in heaven and on earth, visible and invisible, whether thrones or powers or rulers or authorities; all things have been created through him and for him. Colossians 1:16 (NIV)

I STARED AT THE BRACELET I'd crafted. Loose enough to dangle without catching on things, its leaf-shaped green and blue beads made me smile. Like most of the projects I do, this one wasn't perfect. Still, it reflected my personality in a whimsical way.

Creativity isn't always easy for me. My craft room holds a closet full of quirky attempts, the shelves graced with half-finished works. But those times when my crafts come together well make all the efforts worth it. Because underneath it all, even with shaky lines and the glue blobs, it's fun.

Jesus is the King of Creation. Everything He's made is exactly the way He intended. There are no mistakes, and nothing is kept hidden in a closet or drawer. The graceful impala, the regal lion, the comical penguin—all are exactly right in His eyes. Even me.

Some days, when things aren't going according to plan, I need to remind myself that He's not finished with me yet. Parts of me might require more glue to keep from falling apart, and an ordinary place or two could benefit from sparkles. Jesus is hard at work on me and in me, and I wait with anticipation to see His finished product— me—to be revealed in heaven. —HEIDI GAUL

FAITH STEP: *Participate in a craft project. As you create your "masterpiece," reflect on the joy Jesus experiences as He constructs and refines you. Share your craft—and that joy—with others.*

TUESDAY, OCTOBER 8

"Martha, Martha," the Lord answered, "you are worried and upset about many things, but few things are needed—or indeed only one. Mary has chosen what is better, and it will not be taken away from her." Luke 10:41–42 (NIV)

IN PREPARATION FOR A WRITING assignment, I spent hours developing an outline and making extensive notes. I intended to return to my desk after the weekend to finish the assignment. But when I sat down to write, my preparatory pages were nowhere to be found. Usually when I find myself in a situation like this, I pause and pray for the Lord to direct me. But since I was already running behind schedule, I plowed full-speed ahead, frantically searching high and low, scouring my desktop, my office, the trash, and every other room of the house, to no avail. I felt more frenzied with each passing moment. Finally, I gave up. I'd need to start the project all over again.

When I returned to my desk the next morning to finish the now-late assignment, there under my left hand was the outline I'd been in a panic to find the day before. *How did that get there?* I was certain I'd looked right at that very spot time and again.

In those moments when I, like Martha of the New Testament, find myself worried and upset about something, it is *especially* then that I need to recenter my focus on Jesus, as Martha's sister, Mary, did. I was supposed to be writing about Him, but I'd let my self-imposed anxieties get in the way of the spiritual lesson the Lord wanted me to learn. —SUSAN DOWNS

FAITH STEP: *Today, whenever you are tempted to panic over your problems, turn to Jesus instead.*

WEDNESDAY, OCTOBER 9

May the God of hope fill you with all joy and peace as you trust in him, so that you may overflow with hope by the power of the Holy Spirit. Romans 15:13 (NIV)

MY DAUGHTER-IN-LAW, ERIN, BECKONED ME to a quiet corner. "I'm pregnant!" she whispered. Tears of joy filled my eyes. A year before, Erin had given birth to the baby boy she and my son, Brent, had longed for, but the child had been stillborn at twenty-nine weeks. We all prayed for this new baby, but my anxiety threatened to overcome my joy.

Kneeling in my closet, I prayed: *Jesus, I need Your promise this baby will be all right. Please help me trust that promise.* As I knelt there, a feeling of peace came over me.

I held on to Jesus's promise during Erin's first trimester, when she feared a miscarriage. In the second trimester, when Erin was diagnosed with gestational diabetes and suffered several infections, I trusted Jesus to heal her. Early in the third trimester, when Erin began to have contractions and went to the emergency room multiple times for medicine to stop the them, I prayed mightily. When Erin went into labor at thirty-one weeks and needed an emergency C-section, I cried and prayed for her and the baby. I held on to my Lord's promise and continued to trust.

When baby Betty Olivia stayed in the neonatal intensive care unit for four weeks, I visited her and trusted she would be home soon. When she came home to her loving family and I looked at her sweet face, I trusted Jesus would be with her all her life.
—PAT BUTLER DYSON

FAITH STEP: *Ask Jesus to help you trust Him in a situation where you need peace.*

THURSDAY, OCTOBER 10

Dear friends, now we are children of God, and what we will be has not yet been made known. But we know that when Christ appears, we shall be like him, for we shall see him as he is. 1 John 3:2 (NIV)

MY MIDDLE SON, WILL, HAS strong hands just like my husband, Scott. Scott loves that connection with Will. My oldest son, Jack, and my youngest son, Addison, have soft hands like mine. I love that their hands come from my side of the family. However, I am thankful that I have not passed on my poor vision. I have had to wear glasses or contacts since I was four years old. My boys are glasses-free and follow in Scott's genetic footsteps with blue eyes and 20/20 vision.

Much of who I am is because of my ancestors. My DNA determines many of my family traits, but I also have a spiritual heritage. My parents instilled godly values in me by trusting Jesus and modeling their lives after Him. Jesus passed along His family traits to me as well. I'm made in His image (Genesis 1:27), and when I accepted Jesus as my Savior, I became part of His family—a daughter of the King (John 1:12).

Unlike the unchangeable DNA assigned to me at birth, I can grow in my likeness to Christ. The more time I spend with Jesus, the more I become like Him. Knowing Him and keeping Him present in my life are traits I strive to pass along to my boys, friends, and family—a spiritual DNA to be shared by all. —SUSANNA FOTH AUGHTMON

FAITH STEP: *Note the family traits you can see in yourself, then identify traits you've inherited from Jesus as He's reshaped your heart, mind, and spirit.*

FRIDAY, OCTOBER 11

Shout joyfully to the LORD, all the earth; Break forth in song, rejoice, and sing praises. Psalm 98:4 (NKJV)

"WERE YOU SINGING?" MY HUSBAND, Jeff, asked me as I straggled into the kitchen early one morning.

I couldn't imagine what he was talking about. I don't talk, much less sing, before my coffee, but he insisted.

"Something about joy in the house of the Lord?" said Jeff.

I thought for a moment. I'd awakened with the song "House of the Lord" in my head from a dream. *But how could I not realize I was singing?* Perhaps because these days, I carry a song in my heart.

It hadn't always been that way. For years, I'd listened to talk radio or news, mostly by force of habit. People who called in to talk shows were usually angry. The news was generally bad. I never felt uplifted. One day when I switched the dial to a Christian radio station, I heard a song we sang in church and I kept listening. That was decades ago.

Every day, I hear music that reflects the way I'm feeling. Some of the songs are so touching that they make me cry. Some are so joyful I want to dance. When I sing along, I feel so close to Him.

At night, when I am worried and fearful, Jesus plants a song in my mind to lull me to sleep. The joy, hope, and peace Christian music has brought me has changed my life. And that's truly something to sing about. —PAT BUTLER DYSON

FAITH STEP: *Play your favorite praise song and worship Jesus. Sing along, if you'd like.*

SATURDAY, OCTOBER 12

In his great mercy he has given us new birth into a living hope through the resurrection of Jesus Christ from the dead. 1 Peter 1:3 *(NIV)*

ON A RECENT TRIP BACK to my hometown—a trek I hadn't taken for too long—I noted some familiar landmarks that hadn't changed much, but many had changed radically. *When had they torn down that old barn and replaced it with a cheese factory? What happened to the car dealership that used to dominate that intersection?* The most profound sites for me were the older, once-occupied homes that—vacant for decades—had lost their ability to keep standing.

What happens to a home with no breath? When a house no longer has humans caring for it, living and breathing inside it, the building more quickly crumbles. Seeing those abandoned houses made me wonder: what happens to a human heart that seems to have lost its breath of hope? If uncared for, would it experience the same accelerated crumbling?

The picture of that heart became startlingly clear. A heart without hope quickly falls apart. The presence of Jesus—our eternal hope—breathes life into abandoned, broken, neglected, struggling hearts. As surely as Christ's first post-death breath changed the tomb from a symbol of supposed defeat and decay to a scene of glorious victory, His breath within me transforms whatever surrounds me too.
—CYNTHIA RUCHTI

FAITH STEP: *Consider someone who appears to be crumbling like an uncared-for house. Send a card, text, or call and share Jesus, your eternal hope.*

SUNDAY, OCTOBER 13

---

*Peace I leave with you; my peace I give you. I do not give
to you as the world gives. Do not let your hearts be troubled
and do not be afraid. John 14:27 (NIV)*

ONE MORNING, I WATCHED AN avalanche of clouds crawl over the mountains. A few minutes later, I was in the midst of an outrageous storm. The clouds consumed the blue sky, and a dense, dark fog settled in. The wind whipped up to 91 miles per hour. Sheets of rain, blowing sideways, pounded our house. Friends texted messages asking if we saw the clouds coming and commented on how ominous it looked.

It might have looked ominous, but while the storm raged, I sat in my warm home reading a book and sipping tea. It reminded me of a contest I had heard about for artists who were asked to create an image of peace. One painted a green field with a brook flowing through. Another painted a still lake at the foot of a majestic mountain. My favorite was a painting of a raging waterfall, with a tree limb protruding out. On the branch sat a nest that held a calm mother bird and three chicks. This painting won.

Jesus's parting words were His promise of the peace He gives. He never guaranteed a life without storms, but thanks to Jesus, we can experience an unexplainable peace (Philippians 4:7). The storm outside eventually passed but left me with a sweet memory of feeling His peace in the midst of it. My own perfect picture of peace from the Master Artist. —JEANNIE BLACKMER

FAITH STEP: *Are you facing a storm? Look through some magazines and find an image that most reminds you of Jesus's peace and place it somewhere in your home.*

MONDAY, OCTOBER 14

Humble yourselves, therefore, under God's mighty hand, that he may lift you up in due time. Cast all your anxiety on him because he cares for you. 1 Peter 5:6–7 (NIV)

I'M RECOVERING FROM SURGERY ON two joints in my right hand. A third joint, which was fine before surgery, is swollen with decreased range of motion. Two months out, my hand doesn't work well. I write left-handed, but I didn't realize how otherwise right-handed I am.

I can't open jars. I drop things without warning. And I'm so irritable I wouldn't spend time in my own company if I could possibly avoid it. So, when the story of Jesus cursing the barren fig tree came up in my Bible reading (Matthew 21:19), I thought, *Irritable Jesus! Yes!* I was happy to think that Jesus was occasionally out of sorts.

I studied some scripture references and I'm reevaluating. My irritability is self-centered and demanding in nature. Jesus, however, wasn't selfish or out of control, even though He sometimes got angry. When He cleansed the temple early in His ministry, Jesus assembled a whip before turning over any tables (John 2:15). He wasn't pitching a fit like a spoiled child (or like me). He didn't lose His temper, and He hadn't made some snap decision. Jesus's zeal for His Father's house filled Him with holy wrath (John 2:17).

My irritability caused by my hand surgery has no excuse. Humbled under His mighty hand, I can take my problems to Jesus, who cares for me. —SUZANNE DAVENPORT TIETJEN

FAITH STEP: *Do you have a short fuse too? Today, stop short before throwing a fit (or anything else). Find a quiet spot and hand your cares to Jesus. Picture that transaction in your mind.*

Tuesday, October 15

Let us hold unswervingly to the hope we profess, for he who promised is faithful. Hebrews 10:23 (NIV)

IT'S MOVING DAY FOR MY daughter. She had made arrangements with a company that provides a truck and movers. Last night, a representative called her to say that due to labor issues, they couldn't do the job. With some scrambling, she arranged to hire the truck and driver while we recruited volunteers to do the heavy lifting. The moral of the story is that people aren't always dependable.

The stress of this move showed me the sharp contrast between human promises and the promises of Jesus. When He said He would die and rise again, He did. When He said He will never forsake us, He remains faithful. When He told us that He is going to prepare a place for us, we can count on His pledge.

I'm a bit of an idealist, so when life doesn't go along on a smooth and sunny path, I can feel let down. But then I remember that I'm also one of those humans who isn't always faithful. I, too, have let others down and realize there is no need to fume about those who are undependable. Instead, I can take comfort in the reminder that there is One I can always fully count on.

Jesus knows that fallen men and women can be untrustworthy (John 2:24). But when it comes time for us to make the move to heaven, we don't have to rely on a local moving company. Jesus will keep His promise and welcome us into His kingdom.
—SHARON HINCK

FAITH STEP: *Make a list of the promises that Jesus has fulfilled in your life. Thank Him for being faithful.*

WEDNESDAY, OCTOBER 16

But as for me, I watch in hope for the LORD, I wait for God my Savior; my God will hear me. Micah 7:7 (NIV)

ONE CAN ONLY HOPE. I read this line of dialogue in a novel recently, and it made me think about that expression. Our culture typically uses *hope* to mean that we wish for something to happen, but it often conveys an element of doubt.

What a far cry from the Hebrew and Greek words translated as *hope* in the Bible. Hebrews 11:1 (NKJV) includes hope in a succinct definition of faith: "…the substance of things hoped for, the evidence of things not seen." Even devoted Christ followers can have bouts of doubt, but deep down we know what we hope for is a sure thing.

When the object of my hope is Jesus, it's more than a feeling; it's a reality—one that affects my past, present, and future. When I cringe at something shameful from my past, I don't have to hope it's been forgiven. I have the promise that when I confess, He forgives (1 John 1:9). When worries about my present circumstances invade my thoughts, there's no need to simply hope things will get better. I can rest in the assurance that God will work everything out for my good (Romans 8:28). Any anxiety about the unknown future can be soothed by remembering that Jesus is preparing an eternal home for me (Revelation 21). In light of all these promises, a better expression would be: *one can only believe.* —DIANNE NEAL MATTHEWS

FAITH STEP: *What situation in your life makes you feel hopeless? Read Micah 7:7 as a prayer to Jesus. Ask Him to make this promise the foundation of your life.*

THURSDAY, OCTOBER 17

For we do not have a high priest who is unable to empathize with our weaknesses, but we have one who has been tempted in every way, just as we are—yet he did not sin. Hebrews 4:15 (NIV)

IN PREPARING TO FACILITATE A corporate training course on emotional intelligence, I was surprised by the difference between empathy and sympathy. Sympathy is staying where I am and acknowledging from a distance that someone else's situation is bad. Empathy is moving closer and trying to feel what someone else is feeling. Where a sympathetic person attempts to make someone feel better with words, an empathetic person listens, stays present with someone in their space, and accepts all emotions.

We have a high priest who has experienced everything necessary as a human being in order to understand all of our struggles. Jesus is sympathetic because He sees the rough situations I'm in and provides a divine perspective of my circumstances. But He is also empathetic. He desires to connect with me (Revelation 3:20) and is willing to meet me where I am to comfort me and ease my burden (Matthew 11:28–29). Jesus is also compassionate. He steps in to address my needs (Matthew 14:14).

When people share their pain with me, I tend to stay in the safe place of sympathy. I want to pull them out of their dark space and brush aside their feelings. But Jesus, as my high priest, empathizes with me when I share my pain and weaknesses. My hope is to reflect His example and demonstrate that same empathy to others. —ERICKA LOYNES

FAITH STEP: *The next time someone shares their hurt with you, try putting yourself in their shoes, feeling their emotions and listening to their thoughts.*

FRIDAY, OCTOBER 18

Your beauty should not come from outward adornment, such as elaborate hairstyles and the wearing of gold jewelry or fine clothes. 1 Peter 3:3 (NIV)

FOR MONTHS, I DROVE BY a house while the owner built a shed on his front lawn. I'd never seen a small project take so long, nor a utility building so equipped and beautifully adorned. Maybe he went all out because it's visible from the street. It has electricity for the beautiful lanterns that hang near the front door, plumbing for a spigot to water the bright flowers in boxes placed beneath the windows and shutters, and a fancy copper weather vane perched on the cupola that glistens in the sun.

What's even more perplexing is that even though the shed is so detailed, the owner never bothered to build a solid foundation underneath it. Instead, it sits on concrete pylons placed under the frame.

I can't help but compare that masterpiece to what our culture has become with so much emphasis on outward appearance. A solid foundation seems to be a forgotten detail, an afterthought. I know lasting happiness is as elusive as the wind when my focus is on outward, shallow things.

As a believer, I strive to build the foundation of my life on Jesus and His teachings. My Redeemer is solid and true, trustworthy and strong. When my choices are made while looking through the lens of His love and faithfulness, outward appearances, even outer circumstances, don't seem to matter. Instead, faith, hope, and love are built in my heart, soul, and mind—beautiful adornments for others to see. —CLAIRE MCGARRY

FAITH STEP: *When applying your makeup or putting on your jewelry today, think of the beautiful things Jesus is adorning your heart with. Be sure to thank Him.*

SATURDAY, OCTOBER 19

He who believes in Me, as the Scripture has said, out of his heart will flow rivers of living water. John 7:38 (NKJV)

AFTER PACKING OUR LUNCH, MY husband and I drove to one of our favorite parks to picnic. A rustic table welcomed us to rest under a canopy of tall firs. The scent of cedar mixed with loamy soil teased our senses. Birds flitted from tree to tree, and a cheeky squirrel scampered along branches. It was an idyllic scene.

When we'd finished our meal, we hiked to the banks of a nearby stream. I zipped my windbreaker against the chilled air and listened. The water rushed and gurgled like a thousand voices, lulling me to a place of peace. My fingers dipped into the water.

Leonardo da Vinci's thoughts on the movement of water came to mind: "When you put your hand in a flowing stream, you touch the last that has gone before and the first of what is still to come." As I listen to the rushing waters, I realize my river of life flows with constant change. The knowledge that this moment I have right now—this tiny unit of time—is all I have. I don't live in what has gone by, though most of the memories are beautiful. The future is in Jesus's hands. Like a tiny drop in a creek, I am swept by the current of an ever-changing world.

But there is more than that for believers. My life reflects Jesus. His love flows from my heart like a river. Its course and depth change constantly as I listen to Him, but it will never run dry. —HEIDI GAUL

FAITH STEP: *Sit by a stream, river, or another body of water and spend time with Jesus praying, but mostly listening.*

SUNDAY, OCTOBER 20

And the crowds that went before him and that followed him were shouting, "Hosanna to the Son of David! Blessed is he who comes in the name of the Lord! Hosanna in the highest!" Matthew 21:9 (ESV)

MY HUSBAND AND I TRAVELED to Istanbul to attend our ministry's staff conference. Several years had passed since we'd last seen our national coworkers, and we thoroughly enjoyed catching up with their news over a meal and in one-on-one conversations. We listened to their stories about introducing others to Jesus, encouraged those who felt work-weary, rejoiced with those who'd experienced spiritual breakthroughs in their ministry, and prayed with them all.

Those things brought me great joy, but the greatest joy of all came when we sang worship songs together. The American pastor of a Hungarian congregation led the singing and played guitar. A Lebanese fellow played the drums. Voices from Ukraine, Romania, Poland, Slovakia, Uganda, Egypt, Germany, and North America blended to praise Jesus.

At one point, the worship leader asked everyone to sing, in unison, a specific chorus in their native language. It felt to me like the heavens opened to reveal a sneak peek of the sacred hope that lies ahead.

Someday racial discrimination will end. Doctrinal differences and family divisions will cease to exist. Someday soon we'll stand before Jesus with people from every tribe and nation and sing praises with one voice to Him, the Savior of the world. What a glorious day that will be! —GRACE FOX

FAITH STEP: *Go to YouTube and listen to a worship song in a language other than your own.*

MONDAY, OCTOBER 21

When I consider your heavens, the work of your fingers, the moon and the stars, which you have set in place, what is mankind that you are mindful of them, human beings that you care for them? Psalm 8:3–4 (NIV)

THE BEST PART ABOUT MY daily commute is that it brings me past NASA's Johnson Space Center in Houston. At the entrance, twin T-38 Talon jets point toward the clouds as if they're about to launch into the heavens with the next crew of astronauts in training. Behind the tree line, the space shuttle replica *Independence* is perched atop a carrier aircraft, where just a glimpse of it causes older generations to reminisce and younger generations to dream.

Most mornings, I can't help but slow down when I pass the NASA complex. The evidence of man's relationship with space exploration reminds me of our place in the universe that Jesus created. I can't help but consider the heavens, as David did in Psalm 8, and marvel that every planet, moon, star, and galaxy are the work of His fingers, hung perfectly into place as if dangling from a baby's mobile. When I remember how capable Jesus is to care for the entire universe, it helps me trust Him to care for me.

But other mornings, when my mind is distracted, I drive past NASA without noticing the familiar landmarks. On those days, my problems seem bigger and more unmanageable until I remember to stop, look up at the sky, and consider the heavens once again. If Jesus can care for the universe, He can certainly take care of me.
—EMILY E. RYAN

FAITH STEP: *Remember Jesus's care for you by looking at the sky or exploring the vast library of outer space photos available on NASA's website.*

TUESDAY, OCTOBER 22

He wakens me morning by morning, wakens my ear to listen
like one being instructed. Isaiah 50:4 (NIV)

I LAY IN BED WIDE awake and gazed at the clock. *1:00 a.m.* It was still hours away from my 5:00 a.m. alarm. I grabbed my cell phone, wondering if I'd received any late-night texts or emails. I scrolled social media and read the news. Before I knew it, an hour had passed. I put my phone aside, but my mind raced about daytime problems. I was still fully awake when my alarm went off. I'd wasted both sleep and a sound mind.

As an elementary school counselor, I know better than to use my phone in the middle of the night. I've taught my students that using electronic devices after bedtime is unhealthy sleep hygiene. A device's screen light stimulates the brain, making it hard to sleep. I didn't listen to my own advice.

I wasn't listening to Jesus either. I gave my best energy to technology instead of Him when I grabbed my phone at night. That time could have been better used for prayer, worship, or sleep. Later, I read Isaiah 50, which says God gives me a listening ear when He wakes me in the morning. I prayed for self-control and asked Jesus to remind me to reach for Him when I can't sleep—for it is only with Him that I will receive true rest. —BRENDA L. YODER

FAITH STEP: *Do you reach for technology when you can't sleep? Instead, place your Bible on your nightstand and ask Jesus to help you reach for it—and Him—instead.*

WEDNESDAY, OCTOBER 23

He is faithful and just to forgive us our sins and to cleanse us from all unrighteousness. 1 John 1:9 (NKJV)

ONE FALL EVENING WHILE SEVERE storms and tornadoes ravaged our community, a friend called. "Charlie's family is fine, but their house is destroyed." Chills raced through me as I tried to imagine the devastation the family must be experiencing.

The next day, I joined crowds of people and combed through the destruction of Charlie's home, salvaging a kitchen utensil near the woodline, a left shoe in the field, and a wedding ring near the creek. I gathered clothing, stuffing garbage bags full of sopping items that had been pummeled into the mud by rain and hail. "Those will never come clean," Charlie's wife said as I loaded ten bags into my car, determined to put my laundry skills to the test.

On my patio, I unpacked the first bag and laid out each item. There was so much mud, I doubted half the clothes could be saved. I traded the bottle of stain remover in my hand for a water hose and set the nozzle to the highest pressure. Amazed, I watched the powerful spray separate ground-in dirt from clothing fibers.

Like those muddy clothes, I once saw myself as unsalvageable. I searched for a stain remover, believing I had to make myself clean. I went to church, tried to read my Bible, and prayed, but a shadow of shame always remained. Finally, I accepted the full force of love and grace Jesus had been trying to wash over me. He has proven to be the most powerful stain remover of all. —KAREN SARGENT

FAITH STEP: *What stain are you trying to remove by yourself? Stop trying and let Jesus wash it white as snow.*

THURSDAY, OCTOBER 24

Do not judge, or you too will be judged. For in the same way you judge others, you will be judged, and with the measure you use, it will be measured to you. Matthew 7:1–2 (NIV)

I CAN ALMOST SEE THE woman cowering, head hung in hot-faced shame. The gathering crowd of religious folks are looming, glaring in judgment, raising their stones and voices in condemnation. I imagine she was feeling frightened and ashamed, her very life in the hands of powerful, angry men (John 8:3–11, NIV).

Jesus shut them down. "Let any one of you who is without sin be the first to throw a stone at her." He didn't qualify or quantify the sin—sin was sin, none better, none worse. Clearly, those wielding the stones so viciously had secrets themselves. They were wise enough to drop their weapons, shut up, and leave. Jesus sounds light and gentle as He sends the woman on her way, saying, "Go now and leave your life of sin."

I've both cowered in sin-filled shame for my mistakes and wielded stones eager to condemn someone I deem has done wrong. I've repeated sins and snubs, and I have repented countless times. I've collected stones, storing some, hurling others, realizing all too late I should just drop my weapon, shut up, and walk away. I am learning, more slowly than most maybe, to leave judgment to the only righteous judge: Jesus. —ISABELLA CAMPOLATTARO

FAITH STEP: *Find a smooth pebble and inscribe it with Jesus's words in John 8:7 (NIV): "Let any one of you who is without sin be the first to throw a stone." Carry it in your purse or pocket and touch it as needed for a gentle reminder.*

FRIDAY, OCTOBER 25

Blessed is the one who does not walk in step with the wicked or stand in the way that sinners take or sit in the company of mockers, but whose delight is in the law of the LORD, and who meditates on his law day and night. Psalm 1:1–2 (NIV)

ONE OF THE FAVORITE GAMES my elementary-school-aged children like to play with their niece, my three-year-old granddaughter, Amelia, is hide-and-seek. It's darling when Amelia is hiding and the seekers, my children, walk close to her. She starts to giggle, but my older kids pretend they can't see her sitting under the dining room table or behind the curtain. Yet the game wouldn't be fun if my children didn't playfully pursue Amelia and allow her to think she was happily hiding from view.

Happiness in the Bible is often translated as "blessed." Yet this blessing is often different from what we think of. The Hebrew root of blessed in this context is *ashar,* which means "straight" or "right," as if seeking the right way. It doesn't entail just sitting around and hoping God will send a good gift down to us. Instead, it's choosing to take the proper steps toward Jesus. It's deciding to seek Him above everything else—and finding happiness there.

As much as Amelia likes hide-and-seek, the good news is that Jesus doesn't play games. He shows Himself to all who seek Him, and in the same way, none are able to hide from Him. —TRICIA GOYER

FAITH STEP: *Find a quiet place and ask yourself if you are trying to hide something from Jesus. What active step can you take to come out in the open and be found by Him?*

SATURDAY, OCTOBER 26

But in all these things we overwhelmingly conquer through Him who loved us. Romans 8:37 (NASB)

AFTER FINISHING A BOOK ABOUT a woman's true story, I sank my head into my pillow and sobbed. I recalled similar hurtful experiences like those she'd described. After calming down, I took her advice. I walked to the bathroom, looked in the mirror, and said aloud, "I am a survivor of childhood sexual and verbal abuse."

How could it be that now—in my fifties, married to a kindhearted husband, and mom to three grown, loving children—the suffering of my childhood still had power over me? It had come up before, but in the busyness of raising a family, I was able to shove the past away. Now, decades later, the Lord shone His light on years of abuse I'd endured from two close family members, which had left me feeling insecure, fearful, and lacking confidence in adulthood.

In the weeks that followed, clinging to Jesus my Savior, every morning I'd remind myself I was no longer a victim but a survivor, as I'd say aloud, "Lord, thank You that I'm Your precious daughter, so beloved by You and so cherished by You." I began to feel a desire and growing sense of hope for Jesus's tender healing touch and wholeness.

Recently at the close of a church service, my husband and I approached one of the prayer team couples up front. I told them about my traumatic childhood abuse. Their Spirit-led prayers strengthened my newfound hope; I verbally forgave my abusers and asked Jesus to restore me. I know this journey to complete emotional healing is a process, but thanks to Jesus, I am a survivor. I trust He will finish it. —JENNIFER ANNE F. MESSING

FAITH STEP: *Ask a close friend to pray with you for hope, healing, and wholeness.*

SUNDAY, OCTOBER 27

He has made everything beautiful in its time. Ecclesiastes 3:11 (NKJV)

AN ART GALLERY IS ALWAYS carefully planned. What will patrons see first? Last? What atmosphere will each room or alcove evoke? The pop-up artists gallery our church hosted recently was as well planned as any created by a professional curator. The first piece visitors viewed was an intriguing pottery vase—creamy white with distinct, but seemingly random, charcoal-colored veins. Some call it horsehair pottery, a form of raku in which hairs from the tail or mane of a horse are applied to hot clay pots newly removed from a kiln.

But no horsehairs were used in creating this vessel. The potter had saved hairs that fell from his beloved wife's head during her battle with cancer. He made art from one of the most dehumanizing moments of her painful sojourn. His wife survived. The pottery reminds them both—and anyone who purchases one of the pieces—that Jesus can do more than redeem. He can make beauty from pain.

During the art display at church, a woman tentatively entered the doors with her family. She had not wanted to come, she said, since she and Jesus had not been speaking for a long time. Then her eyes landed on that piece of pottery. She was confronted with evidence that pain-fired beauty was possible in Jesus's hands. The woman said that the moment she read the placard explanation, something leapt in her heart. The pottery seemed to have been placed there for her. Jesus loved her. This she knew. —CYNTHIA RUCHTI

FAITH STEP: *Find an image or article about horsehair raku pottery and put it somewhere visible this week as a reminder of the beauty Jesus has created from your pain.*

MONDAY, OCTOBER 28

Submit yourselves therefore to God. Resist the devil,
and he will flee from you. James 4:7 (KJV)

I'VE WORKED FROM HOME FOR a lot of years, but I frequently take my at-home office on the road to fit it in among mom responsibilities and other errands.

A surprising number of tasks can be done in the car. Drive time is prime time to accomplish "filler" activities like listening to podcasts or audiobooks. I can also dictate notes for an assignment while waiting in the carpool line or at a sports practice.

But time in the car can create a messy vehicle. Recently, I looked down and felt ashamed about the state of the floor mats. The layers of dirt and debris were gross. I was tidier than that, usually. I figured all they needed was a good shake. Within five minutes, it was done and the environment of the whole vehicle felt better.

When one part of a space is messy, the whole space feels filthy. Spiritual battles can have a similar effect on my heart and mind. When the enemy attacks me in one area—finances, health, recurring sins, family relationships—my fear and struggle can carry over into other areas.

But James 4:7 encourages me toward consistent, thorough victory. When I resist the devil, he flees. He has to leave. Jesus's name holds the power to shake off Satan's tactics completely.

In Jesus, I have the authority to shake off enemy attacks. And when he flees, the entire environment of my life is fresher and cleaner. —ERIN KEELEY MARSHALL

FAITH STEP: *Make a list of the enemy's tactics against you lately. Speak Jesus's name over it, and practice the spiritual shake-off.*

Tuesday, October 29

Sensible people will see trouble coming and avoid it, but an unthinking person will walk right into it and regret it later. Proverbs 22:3 (GNT)

It was a cold, snowy day in the mountains. A sign at the side of the road read, "Warning: Long, Steep Downgrade Ahead." Seeing that sign, I thought, *Where was that sign when I needed it?* Recalling a number of challenging times in my life, I wished I'd been given such a warning prior to all the metaphorical long, steep downgrades of life. Had I been forewarned that those impending "downgrades" were going to be lo-o-ong *and* steep, maybe I could've avoided them or geared up for them. They might have been easier to endure.

Sooner or later, everyone experiences an unexpected long, steep downgrade in life. But downturns needn't catch anyone off guard; Jesus said troubles in this life are inevitable (John 16:33).

No matter where I travel on the road of life, I can take heart. Jesus offers peace. Whether the road ahead is an uphill struggle or a steep downgrade, Jesus has already overcome the world—including any troubled roads of my past or unforeseen ups and downs on the road ahead. —Cassandra Tiersma

Faith Step: *The next time you get in your car and buckle your seat belt, remember to ask Jesus for the sense to see trouble coming and avoid it. Ask Him to fill you with peace for the road ahead.*

WEDNESDAY, OCTOBER 30

The kingdom of heaven is like a mustard seed, which a man took and planted in his field. Though it is the smallest of all seeds, yet when it grows, it is the largest of garden plants and becomes a tree, so that the birds come and perch in its branches. Matthew 13:31–32 (NIV)

EVER SINCE I GOT PIERCED ears, I've struggled to keep both earrings in. It seemed one earring or the other was always coming out, sometimes dropping where I wouldn't notice it or was unable to retrieve it. Like wayward socks that vanish in the black hole of the dryer, my earrings go missing and never come back.

Recently, I discovered rubber backings. They are the tiniest, littlest bits of rubber with a hole through the middle and are so small, it's sometimes hard to get a good grip on them. Yet, once I slide them onto the back of my earring posts, my earrings are anchored in place.

I used to think that following Jesus meant hours and hours of quiet meditation, soaking in scripture and abiding in His presence. It's taken me a long time to realize that tiny actions, like unusual kindness from someone or a small prayer whispered quickly, keep my heart anchored in His. Even a song of praise and seeing something in nature can keep me connected to Jesus and away from the black hole of lost hope and hidden joy. Remaining constantly mindful of the good He works in my life, I joyfully remain anchored in place with Him. —CLAIRE MCGARRY

FAITH STEP: *Is there a small item in your life that has become invaluable? Each time you use it, say a prayer to anchor yourself in Jesus.*

Thursday, October 31

Never stop praying, especially for others. Always pray by the power of the Spirit. Stay alert and keep praying for God's people. Ephesians 6:18 (CEV)

I OFTEN CHAT WITH A coworker about what's going on in our lives. One morning, a friend shared with me that his brother was going through some health and personal struggles. I asked his brother's name and he told me it was Paul. "OK," I said. "I'll be praying for Paul."

About a week later, I inquired about my colleague's sibling. "Hey, how's Paul doing?" I asked. My coworker promptly gave me an update and assured me that his brother was making progress. "Thanks for praying for him," he said. "And thanks for asking about him by name."

It struck me in that moment what an encouragement it was to my friend to know that I had prayed for his loved one—and had called out his name to Jesus.

The Apostle Paul instructed the church at Ephesus never to stop praying for others. There are so many people I strive to remember and pray for by name. Family and friends, coworkers and neighbors, and even people I hear about in daily newscasts are those I pray for. Some stand in need of healing. Others need encouragement or guidance. And still others need financial blessings or strength to keep pushing onward. Of course, Jesus knows who they are and what they need, but it certainly doesn't hurt to tell Him. In fact, that's what we are called to do. —BARBRANDA LUMPKINS WALLS

FAITH STEP: *List at least three people you want to remember as you pray today. Be sure to call out their names and specific requests to Jesus. And let them know that you are praying for them.*

FRIDAY, NOVEMBER 1

Again, truly I tell you that if two of you on earth agree about anything they ask for, it will be done for them by my Father in heaven. Matthew 18:19 (NIV)

TODAY, MY BACK HURT, AND my husband suggested I take an aspirin. "Nope," I said. "I'll wait until it's really bad." I have this crazy philosophy of not taking pain meds until the pain is the worst it will ever be and I truly can't stand it any longer. Not a smart approach.

Sadly, I sometimes apply the same theory to asking for prayer support. Recently, I was struggling with depression. I wanted to ask a few trusted friends to pray for me, but I decided my situation wasn't really bad enough yet. I'd wait until the misery got unbearable before bothering anyone.

Medical professionals say that when treating pain, it's important to stay ahead of it. My philosophy of waiting until I'm sure it's the worst it will ever be is the wrong approach. Equally, hesitating to ask for prayer support is not the best approach since Jesus calls believers to join in prayer for each other. I finally reached out to a few friends and confessed that depression was digging its claws into me and I needed help. Their prayers, supportive emails, and compassion lifted me over the deepest emotional potholes.

Each time I am prayed for by others, my hope is rekindled and I witness the change Jesus brings. Each time I pray for friends, I rejoice in being part of His answer for them. It's a beautiful dose of pain relief that can be administered early and often—no prescription required. —SHARON HINCK

FAITH STEP: *Tell a friend about a hurt or need and ask her to lift you in prayer.*

SATURDAY, NOVEMBER 2

Therefore God exalted him to the highest place and gave him
the name that is above every name, that at the name of Jesus every knee
should bow, in heaven and on earth and under the earth, and every tongue
acknowledge that Jesus Christ is Lord, to the glory of God the Father.
Philippians 2:9—11 (NIV)

I WOKE UP KNOWING IT would be a difficult day. For many hours, I would be in a room with people who are sometimes hard to love, and I wasn't sure how I would handle the situation. The group was known for being unruly, immature, vulgar, and disrespectful—on their good days. I knew I couldn't manage without Jesus's help.

I arrived early and spent time praying over the room where we would gather. I spoke the name of Jesus aloud several times, hopeful His presence would calm attitudes, diffuse anger, and pacify dissension. Then I waited.

At the end of the day, however, I drove home disappointed. I couldn't understand why nothing had changed in the words or actions of the group when I had specifically called on the name of Jesus for help. Wasn't He listening?

It wasn't long before Jesus, in His mercy, showed me where I had erred in my expectations. I had used the name of Jesus as if it were the name of a genie, ready to grant my wishes and meet my demands. Not once had I spoken His name as a declaration of His preeminence in my life. I had asked Jesus to change the hearts of others when I should have asked Him to change my own.
—EMILY E. RYAN

FAITH STEP: *As you pray today, speak the name of Jesus out loud to acknowledge His place as Lord in your life.*

SUNDAY, NOVEMBER 3

---

*And let us consider how we may spur one another on toward love
and good deeds, not giving up meeting together, as some are in the habit
of doing, but encouraging one another—and all the more as you see
the Day approaching. Hebrews 10:24–25 (NIV)*

WHEN A MINISTRY OPPORTUNITY AROSE today, I fought the urge to say no. I had a host of valid reasons to give as a way out. It meant an Uber ride across town in heavy traffic. And I had a number of pressing deadlines breathing down my neck. Plus, I would be called upon to use my rusty Korean language skills—a prospect that is fraught with the potential of embarrassment since so many years have passed since our family returned to the United States from Korea. Yet, despite all my excuses to stay home, I agreed to go and meet with a group of international visitors.

Once there, making new friends and getting reacquainted with old ones, I was glad I'd made the effort to go. My heart was truly stirred to hear their stories of God's protection and provision. Despite the hardships they'd endured, these Christ followers held strong to their faith in Jesus. I was reminded, yet again, that Jesus is still in the business of changing lives.

When I stepped outside my own little challenge-filled realm, I gained a broader perspective of the way God is moving and working, not only in my little corner but also all around the world. And my Korean wasn't as rusty as I'd feared! —SUSAN DOWNS

FAITH STEP: *Seize an opportunity to step outside your comfort zone to bless someone today. You may very well find that the greater blessing is yours.*

MONDAY, NOVEMBER 4

You are my hiding place; you will protect me from trouble and surround me with songs of deliverance. Psalm 32:7 (NIV)

ONE EVENING, I TUNED IN to a Facebook Live program that featured panelists who doled out advice to people facing all types of situations. The show's guests are often friends of mine who are funny and witty, and I enjoy their banter as they respond to viewers who want solutions to their problems.

One woman sought guidance about an old boyfriend who had broken up with her years ago and had reentered her life. As the panelists debated what the woman should do, one of them said, "Rejection is God's protection." Whoa! Those words really resonated with me. I immediately thought about the times I had been rejected. There were jobs I had sought and after several interviews, I didn't get them. Work assignments I wanted and wasn't chosen. Even romantic relationships that ended and left me wondering what went wrong.

But looking back at those experiences, I recognize that it was God protecting me from mistakes, heartache, and probably more than I could ever imagine. That job I wanted so badly and didn't get? I later found out that it would have been more headaches than I bargained for. The relationship that didn't pan out the way I had hoped? It was because the Lord had someone better for me (my husband!). So, now whenever I encounter rejection, even though I may be hurt or disappointed at the time, I view it as a good thing: Jesus's protective hand at work in my life. Once again, He has delivered me. —BARBRANDA LUMPKINS WALLS

FAITH STEP: *Think of an instance when your rejection was God's protection. Share that story to encourage someone today.*

TUESDAY, NOVEMBER 5

For we are to God the pleasing aroma of Christ among those who are being saved and those who are perishing. 2 Corinthians 2:15 *(NIV)*

I WAS TYPING AT MY computer one morning when a pungent scent wrinkled my nose. Hurrying from my chair, I reached the kitchen in a few steps and yanked open the oven door. Sure enough, my cherry pie had oozed over the pan. A blob of filling was bubbling on the bottom of the oven.

I waved a hot pad to disperse the smoke and grabbed a spatula to scrape up the burning mess. Then I opened two windows to create a draft to pull the haze out of the house.

Someone told me years ago it takes two open windows to pull bad air from a space. If only one is open, most of the air sits still.

It occurred to me that relationships are similar. Healthy communicating involves two people open to take in what the other is saying. One-way communication doesn't do much except create an environment for stagnancy.

Relating with Jesus is like any other relationship. When He speaks to me, I take in His words and get to know His heart. When I in turn share my heart with Him, He draws me to Him. Staying open to Jesus casts away any toxicity that clouds my heart. Consistent back-and-forth communication with Him clears the air for me to see more clearly and respond to Him. Openness with Jesus—that's sweeter than cherry pie. —ERIN KEELEY MARSHALL

FAITH STEP: *Bake a sweet treat, either homemade or store-bought from the freezer section. Practice back-and-forth communication with Jesus as you breathe in the pleasing aroma.*

WEDNESDAY, NOVEMBER 6

Give thanks to the LORD with the lyre; make melody to him with the harp of ten strings! Psalm 33:2 (ESV)

ALTHOUGH MY HARP IS NOT the type that King David, the author of Psalm 33, played, I also play an ancient instrument. My vintage Oscar Schmidt autoharp (in the zither family) has more than three times as many strings as David's U-shaped lyre of antiquity. Tuning a thirty-six-string instrument on a cold Sunday morning before church music rehearsal can be time-consuming. To put it into perspective, it's the equivalent of tuning six guitars.

I've recently noticed that while hurriedly tuning each of those steel strings, anxious to get to music rehearsal on time, I find myself praying quick, brief prayers of gratitude as each string comes into tune true to its note. "Thank You, Jesus!...Thank You, Jesus!...Thank You, Jesus!" When it dawned on me what I was doing, I began to refer to tuning my instrument as a thirty-six-string prayer.

That's really what this song of life is about, isn't it? Seeking God's blessing, praying that He will bring the individual notes of my life into resonance with His plan, and thanking Him when situations and events are in harmony with His will. I'm thankful that Jesus fine-tunes me each and every day; no doubt my praise of thanks to Him is music to His ears. —CASSANDRA TIERSMA

FAITH STEP: *Give thanks to the Lord with your own ten-string or thirty-six-string prayer. On a blank sheet of paper, write ten or thirty-six items for which you are grateful. Make a melody to Him by reading the list aloud, proclaiming over each blessing: "Thank You, Jesus!"*

THURSDAY, NOVEMBER 7

There is no fear in love. But perfect love drives out fear, because fear has to do with punishment. The one who fears is not made perfect in love. We love because he first loved us. 1 John 4:18–19 (NIV)

THE LAST FEW MONTHS, I'VE been waking up at 3:00 a.m., wide awake. I mull over unfinished work, college tuition bills, and mistakes I've made that day or over my lifetime. Then I worry about my boys. *How is Addie really doing?* At fifteen, he likes to keep his thoughts to himself. *Do Jack and Will have everything they need at college?* My wondering jumps to catastrophe thinking. *They haven't texted in a while. What if something happened to them?* These early-morning thoughts have a way of spiraling into worry and fear.

I've started combating these anxiety-producing thoughts with words of truth. I let myself be lulled back to sleep by remembering the themes of hope-filled sermons, reciting the truth of scripture, and singing lyrics of worship songs in my mind. The enemy of my soul would like me to feel alone and afraid, apprehensive about life, but I invite the love of Jesus to surround me. In Him I am completely loved and made perfect in His love. He is my Protector and Provider. In Jesus's presence, I have no fear. None.

And with those calming thoughts, I can sleep soundly. —SUSANNA FOTH AUGHTMON

FAITH STEP: *What keeps you up at night? Combat the worries and fears that crowd your mind with the hope and truth of Jesus. Write out 1 John 4:18–19 on a note card and memorize it. Repeat it in your mind the next time worry won't let you sleep.*

FRIDAY, NOVEMBER 8

Do all things without complaining and disputing, that you may become blameless and harmless, children of God without fault in the midst of a crooked and perverse generation, among whom you shine as lights in the world. Philippians 2:14–15 (NKJV)

"How is Sophie?" I asked Ben, the electrician who services my workplace. I remembered that his wife struggled with several health issues.

Ben told me she was doing fantastic but that she'd have a feeding tube for the remainder of her life. The cancer Sophie experienced in her thyroid several years ago had moved to her jaw and damaged the bones. The doctor replaced the missing bones with metal strips. Even so, Ben said Sophie remained cheerful, impervious to the sunken cheek and unbalanced look of her face. She'd decided that looks aren't everything. So she continued to attend all her usual clubs, meetings, and church functions.

"A few days ago, some more bones just fell out," Ben said, his voice cracking. "But the doctor told us to expect that."

All of a sudden, my little shoulder and back issues became a grain of sand compared to Sophie's problems. I asked Jesus to forgive me for all the whining I did and the many pity parties I'd hosted for myself over the years.

Jesus doesn't cause sickness. He's the Healer. But He does sometimes show me an individual who's far worse off than I am, not so I'll feel ashamed, but so I'll remember that other people also have problems, some that are bigger than mine. And He reminds me that because of their faith, my faith can grow as I pray for their healing.
—Jeanette Levellie

Faith Step: *Visit, text, or call a friend whose life is harder than yours. Pray for her.*

SATURDAY, NOVEMBER 9

A generous person will prosper; whoever refreshes others will be refreshed. Proverbs 11:25 (NIV)

ON MY WAY HOME FROM helping my daughter paint her kitchen, it dawned on me I was low on two staples—milk and cat food. I'd have to pop into the grocery store. Looking down at my paint-splattered clothes, I checked the mirror for the rest of me. My grandson Jameson had a new helicopter toy he'd used to rearrange my hair. Any makeup I'd applied earlier had worn off. *Jesus, don't let me run into anyone I know.*

Yes! I made it to the register with no one seeing me and there was no line. When I handed the cashier my store rewards card, she smirked. "What's this?"

It was my library card. "I know it's here somewhere," I said, scrabbling through a wad of cards in my billfold. My compulsiveness and the possibility of winning a free turkey kept me searching. As the cashier joined the hunt, I noticed a line forming behind me.

Suddenly, a petite white-haired woman brushed past me, inserted her card in the reader and marched back past me.

"I got it," she said. I thanked her profusely, suddenly realizing she thought I didn't have any money. Mortified, I left the store but waited for the woman to come out. When she did, I said, "Ma'am, I appreciate what you did, but I had the money. I was just—"

The woman raised her dainty hand like a policeman ordering HALT and said, "I did it for me!"

I thanked her again and asked Jesus to forgive my pride for not allowing a stranger the joy of giving. —PAT BUTLER DYSON

FAITH STEP: *Ask Jesus to help you receive as joyfully as you give.*

SUNDAY, NOVEMBER 10

Now to him who is able to do immeasurably more than all we ask or imagine, according to his power that is at work within us, to him be glory in the church and in Christ Jesus throughout all generations, for ever and ever! Amen. Ephesians 3:20–21 (NIV)

I'VE ALWAYS USED A SMALL shoulder purse that lets me be hands-free. And there's no need to set it down in a shopping cart or public bathroom. People have occasionally laughed at the size of my purse, questioning how I can carry everything I might need. They're amazed at what I have packed in it when I pull out all the essentials plus extras: tissue, pen, Band-Aid, cough drop, and a mini nail file.

I'm often amazed at how much truth can be packed into one or two Bible verses. The few lines of Ephesians 3:20–21 tell so much about the who, what, how, and why of our relationship with God. The words say He can do far beyond anything we might think up, using His own power working in and through us, so that Jesus and His church will receive the glory.

Jesus's public ministry lasted only three years, but He packed a lot into that time: teaching, healing, comforting, guiding, loving, and—most importantly—dying for our sins. Through Him, those early disciples saw and experienced things they'd never imagined possible. I think Jesus still likes to amaze His followers like that. As I learn to pack lighter for my life journey by letting Him carry my burdens, my hands will be free to praise Him for doing more than I can imagine. —DIANNE NEAL MATTHEWS

FAITH STEP: *Choose a Bible verse that has a lot of personal meaning. Memorize it so that you can always carry it with you, hands-free.*

VETERANS DAY, MONDAY, NOVEMBER 11

*But I say to you, love your enemies, bless those who curse you,
do good to those who hate you, and pray for those who spitefully
use you and persecute you. Matthew 5:44 (NKJV)*

DANIEL JAMES BROWN'S BOOK *Facing the Mountain* opened my eyes about the Japanese-American WWII heroes. After Japan's bombing of Pearl Harbor, some Americans experienced anger and a deep distrust of all Japanese, including those who were born and living in the United States. To quell the US government's fears, 120,000 people of Japanese ancestry, including US citizens, were imprisoned in internment camps. Mistakenly singled out as "alien enemies," their lives changed irrevocably the day they boarded buses to unknown, desolate destinations.

Despite hatred and prejudice, young men from Hawaii and the camps remained patriotic. They chose to enlist, fight, and give their lives for a country that no longer wanted them. Brown's book is about the bravery and dedication of the 442nd Infantry Regiment, composed almost entirely of second-generation American soldiers of Japanese ancestry and one of the most decorated military units of its size and length of service in US history.

As these men prayed during battle, they were met by One who understood. Jesus, too, lived with humiliation and suffering. He responded with courage, love, and a dedication to die for people who rejected Him.

Today, we honor those who have fought for our country and the One who fought for our souls. Through them, we've all won. —HEIDI GAUL

FAITH STEP: *Research history to discover the sacrifices our armed forces have made, protecting our way of life. Find some way to honor them today.*

TUESDAY, NOVEMBER 12

God has filled him with his power and given him skill, ability, and understanding for every kind of artistic work. Exodus 35:31 (GNT)

As a writer, I'm in continual need of ideas for worthwhile things to write about. I pray constantly for inspiration. And as someone who takes a lot of creative risks—whether in writing or in performance art or simply by experimenting with my hair or wardrobe—courage is frequently required.

This morning, I listened to a video in which a woman was advocating the importance of being courageous in our creativity. She was so enthusiastic about this idea that in an earnest slip of the tongue, she got her words tangled up. "Creative" and "courageous" accidentally came out as one word when she declared, "We need to be creageous."

"Creageous." That perfectly describes how I want to be—not just creative but also courageous—"creageous." As a person made in the image and likeness of our Creator, who continually inspires creativity in me, I can also be filled with the courage needed to carry out inspired plans, projects, and ideas.

From now on, whenever I'm praying for inspiration, I'll also be asking Jesus to make me "creageous"! —CASSANDRA TIERSMA

FAITH STEP: *What aspect of your creativity could use a boost of courage? Read Exodus 35:31—35 and be inspired, for it's the Lord Himself who fills you with His Spirit, skills, and ideas to do creative and artistic things to glorify Him. Ask Jesus to make you "creageous."*

WEDNESDAY, NOVEMBER 13

*May the favor of the Lord our God rest on us; establish
the work of our hands for us. Psalm 90:17 (NIV)*

MY FOURTH-GRADE STUDENTS ASKED WHY I was crying as they lined up in the hallway. They had put sticky notes on a wall in the entryway of the school where I work as an elementary school counselor. Each student, from kindergarten through fourth grade, had written something about kindness throughout the month and posted it on what we called the Kindness Wall.

I asked the fourth graders what they had learned from the activity. A dozen students raised their hands. One said he hoped people of different colors would stop hating each other. Another said kindness can help someone who is depressed. One girl said when you include someone, you make a difference in their life.

Their words were powerful. My tears were happy tears, I told them. Inwardly, I praised Jesus for showing up in such an unexpected way at my job. Rarely do I make time to pray during my workday. Too often I read my morning devotional and rush off to work, disconnecting Jesus from my daily activities. Would Jesus show up even more if I asked Him to do so?

The experience challenged me to make a habit of praying through my workday. Now I'm more aware of where Jesus is working and how He may show up, using His powerful presence to move me to tears. —BRENDA L. YODER

FAITH STEP: *Invite Jesus to join you in your daily activities at work, at home, or in your community by praying throughout the day. Make note of how you experience His presence in both big and small ways.*

THURSDAY, NOVEMBER 14

Gracious words are a honeycomb, sweet to the soul and healing to the bones. Proverbs 16:24 *(NIV)*

A FEW DAYS AGO, MY husband, Michael, arrived home from work looking tired and hungry. While he hung up his coat, I asked him if he had remembered to call our mortgage broker.

"No, I forgot," he answered.

"You never make it a priority to do what I've asked you to do!" I exclaimed in frustration. I really wanted our refinance application to get finalized.

"To say that I *never* make your requests important is a little bit harsh, Jennifer Anne," he said.

As I reflected on Michael's response, conviction filled my heart. Proverbs 11:16 (NASB) came to mind: "A gracious woman attains honor." Graciousness is honorable because it is truly difficult to be gracious—meaning kind, courteous, and merciful—in every situation.

I purposed to make a conscious effort to be gracious in my speech by speaking encouraging and uplifting words to my husband, my kids, and my friends; in my attitude by striving to be more patient and forgiving when people make mistakes; and in my actions by giving people a smile or friendly greeting.

At dinner that night, I offered Michael a heartfelt apology. He graciously forgave me. By relying on Jesus's strength and with the Holy Spirit's guidance, my words can be sweet, healing, and graceful in every situation and with everyone I encounter each day.
—JENNIFER ANNE F. MESSING

FAITH STEP: *How gracious is your speech? If you're about to think or speak unkind words, with Jesus's help, consciously replace them with tenderhearted, loving words instead.*

FRIDAY, NOVEMBER 15

My command is this: Love each other as I have loved you. John 15:12 (NIV)

I'M CROCHETING A RUANA, WHICH is a cross between a cape and a poncho, for my daughter. The pattern I chose involves four multicolored pastel panels, about the width and length of table runners, sewn together at one end and in the back.

This cozy garment will fit no matter her size or age and can be worn with dresses or jeans. It matches my love for her—always available, never constricting. Since we live an hour apart, I hope this gift will remind her of a comforting, reassuring hug from Mom whenever she needs it. I want her to know that whether she can see me or not, my love is there with her—always.

When I first found my way to Jesus, the concept of unconditional love was foreign to me. Just as with all my human relationships, I believed there must be some sort of behavior that would trigger His wrath. But He never tired of my questions and never lost patience with my endless mistakes. His love for me is perpetual, His forgiveness limitless. And though I can't see my Lord, I sense His eternal presence guiding me.

The affection I feel for my beloved daughter is but a tiny reflection of the depth of Jesus's love. I look forward to the blessing of sharing it in these few skeins of intertwined yarn. —HEIDI GAUL

FAITH STEP: *Make a gift for a loved one. If you're not crafty, write a letter or note instead. Pray over that person as you work on her gift.*

SATURDAY, NOVEMBER 16

The LORD is my shepherd, I lack nothing. He makes me lie down in green pastures, he leads me beside quiet waters. Psalm 23:1–2 (NIV)

MY YOUNGEST DAUGHTER, KIM, AND her two little ones lived about an hour's drive away for ten months while her husband, a fourth-year medical student, worked in various hospitals across the province. I jumped at the opportunity to lend Kim a hand whenever she was on her own.

Watching Kim engage with her children blessed my heart. For everyone's sake, she arranged their daily schedule to ensure an afternoon of quiet time. Two-year-old Lexi didn't always feel the need to rest in her bedroom after lunch, so she did her best to stall, but Kim vetoed her tactics. She understood her daughter, and she knew Lexi would benefit from a quiet space to relax. She might not sleep, but resting and reading books in bed refreshed her for the remainder of the day.

Just as a mother understands her child's need for rest, Jesus knows I need to recharge. But like Lexi, I don't always want to. Sometimes I feel guilty about taking a break. I fear disappointing someone, appearing irresponsible, or missing an opportunity that might not present itself again. But giving myself the grace and space to rest is neither wrong nor a sign of weakness. It's a wise discipline, and one that Jesus acknowledged when He took on human form (Mark 6:31). Since Jesus recognized the value of rest in the midst of His busy life, shouldn't I? —GRACE FOX

FAITH STEP: *Give yourself the gift of a ten-minute rest today. Lie down, put your feet up, close your eyes, and enjoy.*

SUNDAY, NOVEMBER 17

*They begged him to let them touch even the edge of his cloak,
and all who touched it were healed. Mark 6:56 (NIV)*

I BOUGHT A NEW BLACK dress for my eleven-year-old daughter for her violin concert. She looked so elegant and grown-up when she put it on at home. Yet, when she walked on stage with the rest of the orchestra, part of the skirt was hiked up a bit, clinging to her tights from static electricity.

As I sat in the school auditorium, I tried to will her to pull it down with my mental telepathy. Since I don't have any, she continued on without noticing. My fingers itched the entire concert, begging me to reach out and tug on the hem of her dress to release it from her tights so it could flow around her the way that it should. I was simply too far away.

I've had phases in my life when I've been too far away from Jesus too. With a stubborn streak that runs deep, I try to do things all on my own, blazing my own trail, performing for the crowd. Even when things do go my way, there's always a bit of unrest in my heart as I cling to my own will, not His. It's as if my heart doesn't flow the way that it should.

That's when I know I need more time with Jesus. Moving close to Him, I envision myself reaching out to touch His cloak. When I do, that unrest in my heart is healed. I am at peace, and everything flows as it should. —CLAIRE MCGARRY

FAITH STEP: *Close your eyes and imagine you're reaching out to touch the edge of Jesus's cloak. What changes happen in your heart?*

MONDAY, NOVEMBER 18

Until now you have asked nothing in My name. Ask, and you will receive, that your joy may be full. John 16:24 (NKJV)

WHEN MY SON, DJ, WAS in his first year of college and hoping to secure an internship in the film and television industry, my husband and I did our best to advise him. We shared the importance of building a personal and professional network, drafting a strong cover letter, and creating an outstanding résumé. Most importantly, we reminded him of something we taught him when he was younger—to be bold and ask for what you need.

Good advice for DJ, but I have to admit that I don't always ask for what I need. I'm rarely bold in stating my desires, even with Jesus. Jesus doesn't discourage me from hoping for the things I want, but He makes it clear that whatever my desire, I need to ask for it in His name. So why don't I? Maybe I fear that what I'm asking for is too much. Perhaps I hesitate because I wonder if it's really His will for me. Hope is good, but my hope needs to be activated with asking so that Jesus can fulfill my desires.

To his delight, DJ secured an internship with the Memphis & Shelby County Film and Television Commission. Because I love my son, I always want him to have what he hopes for. Because Jesus loves me, He wants me to have the things I hope for too. And like DJ, I only have to ask. —ERICKA LOYNES

FAITH STEP: *Create a list and take it to Jesus, boldly asking for what you want in His name. Pray over it daily for the next two weeks and write the date when Jesus answers.*

TUESDAY, NOVEMBER 19

Jacob, the LORD created you. Israel, he made you, and now he says, "Don't be afraid. I saved you. I named you. You are mine." Isaiah 43:1 (ERV)

ON OUR GRANDSON'S RECENT BIRTHDAY, my husband, Jeff, and I reminisced about the joy we'd experienced when we learned we'd be grandparents. How we praised Jesus! I had asked our son and daughter-in-law if they'd chosen a name for their baby boy, and they hadn't, so I decided to help.

I made a list of tips for choosing a baby's name. Family names are good, but be careful not to favor one family over the other or feelings may be hurt. Be sure the child's initials don't spell anything weird. Make certain the baby's name doesn't rhyme with something that other kids can tease about. Find out the meaning of the name. A name that means "lazy" or "homely" will never do. As my list grew longer, I recalled what had happened to my friend Janis. She'd given her kids a lovely book of baby names in which she'd highlighted all her preferences. Shockingly, none of her favorites was chosen. I didn't want to interfere, but at this point, I couldn't help myself.

Biblical names are always excellent choices. *Jacob* is a wonderful name for a boy. Scanning my Bible concordance for references, I came across the verse above from Isaiah 43. I let the words sink in. Then I wadded up my carefully prepared list for choosing baby names and pitched it in the trash.

It didn't matter what the baby would be called. What mattered was that Jesus knew his name. And he was His. —PAT BUTLER DYSON

FAITH STEP: *Read Isaiah 43:1 aloud. Substitute your own name for Jacob/ Israel.*

Wednesday, November 20

You, Lord, are my lamp; the Lord turns my darkness into light.
2 Samuel 22:29 (NIV)

Although I was raised in a flat, irrigated valley with a sunny, hot climate conducive to vineyards, fig trees, and olive groves, I prefer green rolling hills landscaped by God with lush ferns, evergreens, and wild berries. Therefore, I've lived most of my adult life at the higher latitudes of the Pacific Northwest with four distinct seasons and generous precipitation. Consequently, I learned firsthand about seasonal affective disorder (SAD) from living in a region with short days and long winters.

Seeking the blessing of additional natural light during the dark months of winter, I replaced our light bulbs with full-spectrum bulbs. But the game changer was a special therapeutic light fixture I call my "happy lamp." Without adequate daylight, I lose my sunny outlook on life. Soaking up simulated sunshine from my "happy lamp" helps to curb my winter blues when spring seems an eternity away.

God, in His infinite wisdom, didn't just provide physical light from the sun. He gave us the life-giving eternal Light of the World, His Son, Jesus. Using my "happy lamp" reminds me of the biblical declarations that the Lord is my light. His Word is a lamp for my feet, a light on my path (Psalm 119:105). Jesus is the Light of the World, and whoever follows Him will have the light of life (John 8:12). Thus, I'm reminded daily that Jesus is my true lamp. It's Jesus who turns my darkness into light. —Cassandra Tiersma

Faith Step: *Do you have a favorite lamp? Clip a copy of 2 Samuel 22:29 onto the shade. Thank Jesus for turning your darkness into light each time you turn on your lamp.*

THURSDAY, NOVEMBER 21

You hem me in behind and before, and you lay your hand upon me. Psalm 139:5 (NIV)

I TRIED OPENING MY WEBSITE and found this greeting: "There has been a critical error on this website." The message is known as "the white screen of death," and it's the last thing one wants to see when she has pieces of her soul invested in the World Wide Web. But it was also a perfect reflection of what I'd been feeling lately.

A career change made much of the year feel like a critical error. A blank screen. A forgotten promise. It felt as if I spent more days looking for Jesus than seeing Him.

I knew that troubleshooting my website would take more time than I had at that moment, so I closed my computer and picked up my phone, determined to find evidence of Jesus in the months that seemed so desolate. I opened my photo archive and let the moments and memories scroll past my fingertips. As the images appeared, a new perspective emerged.

Instead of challenges, I found stories our children will laugh about for years. Instead of months of hard work, I found moments of celebration. Instead of disappointments, I found answered prayers. But best of all, instead of an absent Lord, I found Jesus, who was present in every photo, hemming me in behind and before. Always working. Always caring. Always creating. Always loving.

I'd been tempted to write the entire year off as one big critical error. But as I chose to reflect more intentionally, I saw the year was actually one of my best ones yet. Jesus had been by my side.
—EMILY E. RYAN

FAITH STEP: *Look through your photos and ask Jesus to reveal His presence in your moments and memories.*

FRIDAY, NOVEMBER 22

"For I know the plans I have for you," declares the LORD, "plans to prosper you and not to harm you, plans to give you hope and a future."
Jeremiah 29:11 (NIV)

I STOOD ON THE SCORCHED foundation and looked at what had been, the day before, our beautiful home. The house had burned to the ground; all that remained were twisted blackened metal scraps, ashes strewn everywhere, and piles of charred rubble. I choked back a sob. We'd had to evacuate due to a raging wildfire, and all our possessions, except our dog, Ody, and the clothes on our backs, were gone.

Turning away from the painful sight, I decided to check my beehives. The ground was black, and the lilac bushes behind them had burned. One of my hives lay toppled on the ground. The other still stood, but soot covered its lid. I asked Zane, my husband, and my son, Josh, to pick up the fallen hive and set it back on the cinder blocks. When they did, bees started flying out. They had miraculously survived!

As I watched my bees buzzing in and out of their home, hope stirred in me. Jeremiah 29:11 is a verse I've clung to throughout my life. Jesus promises a hope and a future. I know I have an eternal home in paradise with Him to look forward to. Yet I also believed He gives me hope here and now. At that moment, I chose to believe Jesus would bring good from this painful experience. Our home was destroyed and I didn't have a clear vision of our future, but I still had an inkling of hope buzzing in my soul. —JEANNIE BLACKMER

FAITH STEP: *Write in your journal about a time when all seemed lost, yet you put your hope in Jesus.*

SATURDAY, NOVEMBER 23

Even to your old age and gray hairs I am he, I am he who will sustain you. I have made you and I will carry you; I will sustain you and I will rescue you. Isaiah 46:4 (NIV)

MY SMALL GROUP BIBLE STUDY friends and I have had a year of caring for elderly relatives and navigating their end-of-life decisions. Not only have the struggles and losses been painful and difficult, but they have also forced me to think about my own aging and health challenges and how long I will be granted independence. I found myself battling fear that paints worst-case scenarios in vibrant colors across my mind. I thought I'd learned to trust Jesus in various situations throughout my life, but lately I've wondered where my trust has gone.

To help me escape mentally, I enjoy a fantasy computer game in which I gain skills and solve puzzles to get to another level with new virtual places to explore. With each level I conquer, I collect an on-screen treasure. While playing one day, I realized Jesus accompanies me into my real-life next level with the challenges of aging now frequently popping up. He sustained me during other life stages—in school, as a young married woman, in parenting, and in various careers. I had followed Him through vocational hurdles, relationship conflicts, and financial problems. Jesus proved Himself faithful over and over.

As I stand on the threshold of my advanced level in life that has new puzzles to solve and different places to explore, Jesus's faithfulness outshines my fear. Knowing He will sustain me makes aging less frightening, especially when I consider the best treasure of all awaits me at the end—eternity with Him. —SHARON HINCK

FAITH STEP: *Draw the levels or phases of your life. What new area or challenge is before you? Tell Jesus you will trust Him as you step forward.*

SUNDAY, NOVEMBER 24

I have not stopped giving thanks for you, remembering you in my prayers. I keep asking that the God of our Lord Jesus Christ, the glorious Father, may give you the Spirit of wisdom and revelation, so that you may know him better. Ephesians 1:16—17 (NIV)

OUR OLDEST SON, JACK, IS a junior in college. He has a beautiful brain and is using it. He is earning a double major in business management and humanities and a double minor in psychology and pre-law. He plans to graduate next year and attend law school. His knowledge and drive are impressive. Especially to his dad and me. We didn't navigate college in quite the same way. I took four and a half years of classes over six years before graduating. My husband, Scott, spent several years in college studying art before majoring in church leadership. We took a long and varied path in our journeys of knowledge.

I have taken a long and varied path in my journey of knowing Jesus too. I am still learning about Him every day. He is the One who knows me and loves me completely. This knowledge can be too much for my brain. I can't fully grasp His omniscience and omnipotence. But I want to know the fullness of His love and goodness. Moment by moment, He builds out my faith, teaching me about grace and revealing His incredible care for me.

I want to keep learning about Him for the rest of my days. —SUSANNA FOTH AUGHTMON

FAITH STEP: *In what ways do you want to know Jesus better? Spend time today in prayer, then write down one or two lessons you want to learn from Him by finishing the phrase: Jesus, I'm ready for You to teach me _____.*

MONDAY, NOVEMBER 25

But the Lord answered and said to her, "Martha, Martha, you are worried and distracted by many things; but only one thing is necessary; for Mary has chosen the good part, which shall not be taken away from her." Luke 10:41–42 (NASB)

I WASTED MUCH OF THIS morning trying to track down some missing medications that had been mailed but not received. The shipper said it had transferred them to the postal service a few days before, and the postal service said the package hadn't been scanned in. The customer service rep said the package was in Grand Prairie, Texas (after having visited Denver twice).

My husband and I live in middle-of-nowhere, Wyoming, and this kind of thing happens often. No one seems very concerned about this, so I've decided I won't be either. I'll be fine without these particular pills for a while.

I like things to be managed and "done right." I work my to-do list. In these ways, I'm often more like Martha than Mary. Still, I take what Jesus told Martha in Luke 10 as if He were saying it to me. I do get worried and distracted about so many things. Martha spent herself in activity, while Mary listened to what Jesus was saying as if it was the only thing that mattered. Because it was.

I'm praying that Jesus will help me spend my time, attention, and energy on what matters most. Just because technology makes it possible to know where a package is at any moment in time doesn't mean I need to track it moment by moment. Instead, I want to be like Mary—filling my moments with Jesus. —SUZANNE DAVENPORT TIETJEN

FAITH STEP: *Do you feel as though everything depends on you? Stop your busyness for five minutes to be still before the Lord.*

TUESDAY, NOVEMBER 26

Giving thanks always and for everything to God the Father in the name of our Lord Jesus Christ. Ephesians 5:20 (ESV)

MY SON ISAAC IS UNUSUALLY and perpetually grateful. He isn't a Down syndrome stereotype of nonstop love and laughter per se, but he does excel at positivity and affection in a big way. I believe he has a special connection with Jesus and the heavenly realms, and he seems to understand and live this verse to the fullest.

Isaac routinely thanks me for the smallest things. For instance, moments after waking, he might suddenly say, "Thank you for my dinner, Mommy," with genuine gratitude, as though I'd just served him his favorite meal that very moment. He thanks me for picking him up from school and dropping him off at his dad's. He thanks me for the packaging of his gifts as much as for the gift itself.

Isaac often embodies an attitude of gratitude.

I'm a pretty grateful person, but it's a discipline I've cultivated with intention over years. I've also become more grateful after losing things for which I was not grateful at the time. My gratitude is practiced and deliberate. In fact, I exchange a daily gratitude email with a few friends. It helps keep my glass half-full.

I've learned a lot from Isaac. Because I'm analytical, I've tried to understand why he's always so thankful. Perhaps Isaac is so grateful in part because he *isn't* analytical. He accepts and enjoys what is without questioning, comparing, assessing, or projecting. He receives what is provided as good and plenty—a lesson I am grateful for. —ISABELLA CAMPOLATTARO

FAITH STEP: *Commit to exchanging a short daily gratitude list with a friend, then work to embody an attitude of gratitude by inviting other friends to join the exchange.*

WEDNESDAY, NOVEMBER 27

See, I am doing a new thing! Now it springs up; do you not perceive it? I am making a way in the wilderness and streams in the wasteland. Isaiah 43:19 (NIV)

KAUAI IS NICKNAMED THE GARDEN Island for good reason. Vast amounts of rain fall on this Hawaiian island annually, leaving the meadows a lush green and the trees entwined with blossoms. Yet there's a backstory to this peaceful land that looks like a storybook fairy tale.

Long ago, a fiery eruption of great magnitude spewed forth enough lava to form this place with dramatic cliffs and jagged mountains. A desolate, hot, unforgiving landscape was born. But this morning, as I reviewed our anniversary vacation photos of Kauai, all I saw was serene beauty—white sand beaches, majestic peaks, cascading waterfalls, breathtaking sunsets, and tropical rain forests—an inspirational paradise.

When I think of my life before I found Jesus, I see the same brutal force at work, the raging, the destruction—the ugliness. If I dig deep enough, I can still find evidence of my turbulent past. But I choose not to, and instead I choose to look at the beautiful way Jesus transformed my life. He has lavished His love on me, healing my soul.

Just as the island once bore the mark of damage but with time turned into paradise, Jesus sees my sin but offers me His eternal paradise. Like Kauai's spired mountains and trees stretching to the sky, because of Jesus, I, too, have been remade. Today, I am strong, beautiful, and filled with His peace. Jesus is the Creator and Hero of my real-life transformation story. —HEIDI GAUL

FAITH STEP: *Think about how Jesus has remade you into something beautiful. Collect nature photos that reflect the tranquility you feel through Jesus and place them where you can see them throughout the day.*

THANKSGIVING DAY,
THURSDAY, NOVEMBER 28

But now, Lord, what do I look for? My hope is in you. Psalm 39:7 *(NIV)*

As I ASSEMBLED INGREDIENTS FOR pumpkin pie, my thoughts drifted to past Thanksgivings: waking to the aroma of Dad's turkey roasting, setting the table with the good china, and mingling with kinfolk. But my most poignant Thanksgiving memory was when Jesus restored my hope.

Our three-year-old son, Blake, had died suddenly of meningitis that October. Unwilling to face the traditional Thanksgiving celebration, my husband, our two sons, and I went to my Uncle O.D.'s home. I stared out the car window at the bleak November landscape, a fitting reflection of my soul. *Why, Jesus?* I cried, for the thousandth time.

We attended a Thanksgiving Day football game, but I couldn't concentrate. Blake had loved football, but I would never watch him play. Nor would I see him grow up, marry, or have children. Death had robbed me of my hopes and dreams for my youngest son. *Why, Jesus?*

By afternoon, I was ready to leave, but O.D. suggested we accompany him to his farm to feed the animals. While the boys fed the horses, O.D. pointed to the back pasture where his cow was giving birth. Fascinated, we marveled as the calf emerged and, eventually, stood on wobbly legs.

Tears filled my eyes and some of the heaviness inside of me lifted. New life—a reason for hope. *Thank You for arranging this for me, Jesus. My hope remains in You.*

Two Thanksgivings later, the hope that had been birthed in Uncle O.D.'s pasture was manifested when we adopted our baby daughter, Melissa. —PAT BUTLER DYSON

FAITH STEP: *When you are at your lowest point, beseech Jesus to show you a sign that will restore your hope.*

FRIDAY, NOVEMBER 29

And God raised us up with Christ and seated us with him in the heavenly realms in Christ Jesus, in order that in the coming ages he might show the incomparable riches of his grace, expressed in his kindness to us in Christ Jesus. Ephesians 2:6–7 (NIV)

FOR TWO MONTHS, I RACKED my brain, wondering how I could lose a wool coat. Living in the Deep South, I seldom needed a heavy coat. But it would have been great to have while visiting family who lived farther north, especially my daughter's family in northern Indiana. I finally gave up, blaming the loss on our frequent moves. Then one day I discovered the coat in the bedroom closet of my adult son who had lived with us the past few years. Hanging beside it was a warm hooded parka that I thought I'd given away, an all-weather coat that I'd bought for business events and forgotten about, and a corduroy jacket.

Like a kid at Christmas, I threw the coats on my bed and tried on each one, occasionally exclaiming to my husband, "I feel so *rich*!" The last time those words left my mouth, I began to feel sheepish. Why wouldn't I feel that way every day?

Different Bible translations describe the riches we have in Christ as incomparable, immeasurable, surpassing, and exceeding. But even those words fail to express all that Jesus offers: forgiveness for sins, unconditional love, and the power to live a godly life. Because of Christ's abiding presence within me and the promise of eternal life with Him, I am beyond rich. —DIANNE NEAL MATTHEWS

FAITH STEP: *Mentally list your most valuable possessions. Now compare them with the riches Jesus has provided for you, both here on earth and in your eternal heavenly home.*

SATURDAY, NOVEMBER 30

Give, and it will be given to you. A good measure, pressed down, shaken together and running over, will be poured into your lap. For with the measure you use, it will be measured to you. Luke 6:38 (NIV)

TWENTY-FIVE SHOEBOXES OF GIFTS FOR kids in need—a challenging yet reasonable goal for my immediate family and closest friends. I planned a packing party and sent email invitations 327 days before Christmas. Every two months, I shared an inspiring video about Operation Christmas Child and made suggestions for items to purchase for the boxes.

As our November event approached, several people called to let me know they couldn't attend. I felt a tinge of disappointment, fearing my goal might slip out of reach. But then, the floodgates of heaven opened. Someone handed me cash to buy toys and picture books. Five boxes arrived by mail from out-of-state relatives, filled with reusable drink containers, whistles, handmade hats, harmonicas, sunglasses, and socks. Friends dropped off bags of stuffed animals, Matchbox cars, games, and deflated soccer balls with pumps. And the evening of the packing party? Well, so many sweet volunteers showed up to help that I lost count.

We didn't meet my goal of twenty-five—we shot right past it to ninety-three! Witnessing the generosity of fellow believers lights my heart like a Christmas tree. Because they gave, almost 100 children will hear the message of salvation through Jesus. For many kids, the shoebox will be the only gift they get this holiday season. For some, it'll be the first present they've ever received in their lives.

I'm already planning a packing party for next November. Would you like to come? —BECKY ALEXANDER

FAITH STEP: *Give to a ministry that presents the hope of Jesus to children in need.*

FIRST SUNDAY OF ADVENT, DECEMBER 1

He will be raised and lifted up and highly exalted. Isaiah 52:13 (NIV)

I HAVE CHRISTMAS GLASSES THAT don't sharpen your vision; they distort it. When I put on the cardboard frames and look at Christmas lights, the plastic lenses shape the lights into objects. If I'm wearing the angel glasses, each light will be reflected as an angel. Put on the snowflake glasses and the entire Christmas tree is covered in snowflake lights. I have several different pairs, and our family enjoys passing them around, declaring which is their favorite.

Even without the nifty glasses, my view at Christmas has been distorted. Growing up, my children celebrated the Savior's birthday. We sang Christmas hymns, donated gifts, and attended Christmas services. But commercialism, Santa Claus, and characters in holiday movies had the stronger attraction. Keeping Christ at the center of Christmas required effort.

A few seasons ago while listening to a favorite podcast, I learned about Advent. My church doesn't observe the season, so I didn't really know much about it. The podcast guest explained why believers celebrate Advent and how her book would guide readers through the weeks leading up to Christmas. I decided to give it a try and ordered her book.

Beginning the first Sunday of Advent, I followed through scripture, prayers, hymns, and activities, remembering the profound need for, and miracle of, the Messiah. Each day immersed me deeper into anticipating Jesus's birth and further from a distorted worldly holiday. When Christmas morning arrived, my heart had prepared room for Baby Jesus. The lens of Advent cleared up my view by shining a bright light on Christ and exalting Him at the center of Christmas. —KAREN SARGENT

FAITH STEP: *Invite a friend who hasn't experienced Advent to observe the holiday with you this Christmas.*

MONDAY, DECEMBER 2

The kingdom of heaven is like a mustard seed, which a man took and planted in his field. Though it is the smallest of all seeds, yet when it grows, it is the largest of garden plants and becomes a tree, so that the birds come and perch in its branches. Matthew 13:31–32 (NIV)

IT WAS 90 DEGREES FAHRENHEIT that July day when I first contacted Larry's church to talk about Christmas. As a volunteer for Operation Christmas Child, I invited churches in my county to pack shoeboxes of gifts for kids around the world. With over a hundred calls to make, I started early in the year.

Larry accepted the challenge for his small church and felt they could possibly do twenty-five boxes. He picked up a few supplies from me to promote the idea among fellow members. During National Collection Week in November, he arrived at the drop-off site with a carload of festive packages. "I'm sorry, Becky. We tried, but we only filled eighteen shoeboxes."

"Larry, eighteen is *wonderful*! That's eighteen kids who will learn about Jesus," I said. Volunteers gathered around Larry and me. I prayed for Larry's church and the children who would receive the shoeboxes. Like Larry, some might focus on the boxes that didn't get filled, but I believe every box is provided by Jesus.

Like a tiny mustard seed can become a full-sized tree, eighteen gospel opportunities can grow to reach many more. When kids hear the good news, they often share Jesus with their parents, grandparents, siblings, and friends. All work for the Kingdom is eternally important, no matter how small. —BECKY ALEXANDER

FAITH STEP: *Start big—or small. Spread hope through a shoebox or another act of service this season.*

TUESDAY, DECEMBER 3

In everything I did, I showed you that by this kind of hard work we must
help the weak, remembering the words the Lord Jesus himself said:
"It is more blessed to give than to receive." Acts 20:35 (NIV)

AT THREE YEARS OLD, MY niece, Hallie, packed her first shoebox for
Operation Christmas Child and learned it was more blessed to give
than to receive.

She spread a bag of gifts on the floor and placed them one by one
in the box—finger puppets, princess Band-Aids, snowman pajamas, animal stickers. When she came to a sparkly purse, she paused.
"Mommy, can I have this purse?"

"No, sweetie. That's for the little girl who doesn't have very much,"
my sister reminded her.

"Can I keep these stickers? I *love* stickers."

My sister smiled. "That little girl across the ocean will love those
stickers too. Thank you for sending her such a special present."

The following morning, my sister noticed the shoebox lid was
raised a bit. *Did Hallie take something out?* She opened the box and,
instead, found one of Hallie's favorite baby dolls squeezed in among
the items inside.

The lesson Hallie learned at three took root in her heart. She
is now a caring young woman who blesses those around her with
unusual thoughtfulness and overflowing generosity. Kids naturally
think of themselves, but Jesus teaches everyone to think outside the
box: it is more blessed to give than to receive, even when a sparkly
purse is involved. —BECKY ALEXANDER

FAITH STEP: *Introduce any children or young people in your life to serving and*
giving in Jesus's name through a local church or ministry.

WEDNESDAY, DECEMBER 4

*Never be lacking in zeal, but keep your spiritual fervor,
serving the Lord. Be joyful in hope, patient in affliction,
faithful in prayer. Romans 12:11–12 (NIV)*

I DROVE EIGHT HOURS TO volunteer at Operation Christmas Child in Boone, North Carolina. I dreaded the long drive, but I was eager to work in the processing center. The large warehouse buzzed with smiling people, workstations, conveyor belts, and forklifts. Holiday music rang through the rafters. Crates of toys, school supplies, toothbrushes, and other colorful shoebox gifts filled the building with Christmas joy. It was like helping in Santa's workshop—only better—because the mission was sharing Jesus with kids around the world.

I took my position at station 14, checking shoeboxes for prohibited items, such as foods, liquids, and gels. Then I added extra surprises, if space allowed, before passing the boxes down the line to be taped shut and placed in cartons. After two hours, the music stopped and everyone grew quiet. A chaplain asked us to put our hands on the shoeboxes near us.

"Dear Jesus," he prayed, "You are the reason we serve and celebrate today. We pray for the children who will receive these gifts. May their hearts be open to Your offer of salvation, and may they discover the hope we have in You. In Your beloved name, amen."

Over the next five days, we prayed for shoebox recipients every two hours. I cried each time, touched by the magnitude of the mission. The experience enriched my Christmas with meaning and purpose. I can't wait to make the drive and serve again. —BECKY ALEXANDER

FAITH STEP: *Check out the ministry of Operation Christmas Child at samaritanspurse.org/operation-christmas-child. Join us in praying for the children of the world.*

THURSDAY, DECEMBER 5

For this is what the Lord has commanded us: "I have made you a light for the Gentiles, that you may bring salvation to the ends of the earth." Acts 13:47 (NIV)

AT THE PROCESSING CENTER, I opened a green shoebox marked: "Girl: Age 5–9." A bright note rested on top of the items inside. In a young child's handwriting, with some misspelled words, the message read: "Dear heavenly Father, please be with the receiver of this gift, and bless her for her entire life."

I'll admit, my eyes leaked a few tears. What a precious prayer, penned by a child in the US for a child living far away. I moved the note aside briefly to check the contents. A doll with purple hair and polka-dotted dress, an undersea puzzle, a rainbow Slinky, a jump rope, a hairbrush, Play-Doh and cookie cutters, markers and a coloring book. No candy or gum, lotion, or toothpaste. All good.

I handed off the box for taping and shipping to the destination of the day. Before I inspected another gift, I paused. The next person to touch that cute doll would be a little girl in Rwanda! And she would hear about Jesus from Operation Christmas Child volunteers there.

Salvation has been God's plan all along. Isaiah first wrote: "I will also make you a light for the Gentiles, that my salvation may reach to the ends of the earth" (Isaiah 49:6, NIV). Then, Paul repeated God's message in Acts 13:47. Now I get to send the hope of Jesus across the oceans and around the world through simple shoebox gifts of love. —BECKY ALEXANDER

FAITH STEP: *Choose a way you can share Jesus with a child this Christmas.*

FRIDAY, DECEMBER 6

The LORD does not look at the things people look at. People look at the outward appearance, but the LORD looks at the heart. 1 Samuel 16:7 *(NIV)*

EVERY YEAR, OUR FAMILY CUTS down a Christmas tree. We drive to the mountains, search for the perfect specimen, cut it down, and strap it to our car. This past year, my husband, Zane, took our perfect tree off the car and laid it on the driveway once we came home.

I went inside and started to heat up chili for dinner, when I remembered there could be Christmas cards in our mailbox. Excited, I decided to check. Because our mailbox sits at the end of our half-mile-long driveway, I jumped in my car and backed out. I felt a bump and heard a scraping noise. I had run over our beautiful Christmas tree. It was no longer perfect.

Zane suggested cutting another. "No, let's put it up as is," I said.

Jesus has been teaching me to let go of my tendency to strive to appear perfect to impress others. I'm not perfect. Jesus, of course, knows this. He desires my heart and doesn't care what my Christmas tree looks like. This was an opportunity to put my efforts at rejecting perfection into practice.

We put up our imperfect tree, and throughout the Christmas season, I was reminded to not emphasize the outward expressions of perfection—the perfect tree, the perfect meal, the perfect celebration—but instead to cultivate a heart that seeks Jesus. What could be more perfect than that? —JEANNIE BLACKMER

FAITH STEP: *Find an imperfect Christmas decoration and place it in a visible spot to remind you how imperfect yet precious you are to Jesus.*

SATURDAY, DECEMBER 7

*When they had seen him, they spread the word concerning what
had been told them about this child. Luke 2:17 (NIV)*

I HAVE SEVERAL MOVIES THAT I like to watch at Christmastime.
Among them are old-time favorites *White Christmas*, *It's a Wonderful Life*, and *Holiday Inn*, and the more contemporary *The Preacher's Wife*. However, my friend Lolita is a huge fan of Hallmark Christmas movies. She says there are few things better than snuggling under a cozy blanket while watching a wholesome "boy meets girl" story with a happy ending.

I've never paid much attention to Hallmark holiday movies, but after hearing Lolita's ringing endorsement, I decided to give a couple of her recommendations a try. Much to my surprise, I got hooked! Now I watch those Christmas movies every chance I get. They lift my spirits and make my world a little brighter. I never would have given them another thought if Lolita hadn't shared her love of them with me.

In the book of Luke, an angel tells shepherds in the field about the birth of Jesus. The shepherds were so amazed and excited that they rushed to Bethlehem to find the baby and tell others about what they had seen. They had a part in spreading the good news. I sometimes wonder how many people have come to know Jesus because of something I said or did.

Just as Lolita introduced me to Hallmark Christmas movies, I can introduce others to Jesus. Now that's a real happy ending—and beginning. —BARBRANDA LUMPKINS WALLS

FAITH STEP: *This Christmas, recommend a holiday movie to a friend and use the opportunity to tell her about Jesus too.*

Second Sunday of Advent, December 8

But do not forget this one thing, dear friends: With the Lord a day is like a thousand years, and a thousand years are like a day. 2 Peter 3:8 (NIV)

FOR MONTHS, A FRIEND AND her husband planned a family trip to Walt Disney World in secret. Their children didn't know anything until the morning of the trip, when they awoke to an elaborate "Surprise!" by their parents and were whisked to the airport.

An unexpected trip worked for them, but I have a different perspective. For me, the anticipation of a vacation is just as exciting as the trip itself, and my husband and I want our children to experience that hopeful expectation along with us. We love talking about our plans, researching excursions, and feeling the excitement build each day we grow closer to our getaway. We've found that our shared anticipation makes our arrival that much sweeter.

I try to remember this as the holidays approach. Since I was a child, waiting for Christmas feels as if it lasts forever, but rather than let that frustrate me, I remind myself how much joy I will have when my waiting ends. The longer I've hoped for something, the more I enjoy it when the time comes. What is Christmas if not the fulfillment of hope? The world longed for the Messiah, and Jesus arrived! Waiting is not something I *have* to do but something I *get* to do because I know Jesus is on His way. The hope I feel now is an investment into the joy I will feel when Jesus arrives again. My anticipation will make His arrival that much sweeter. —EMILY E. RYAN

FAITH STEP: *This Advent season, change your perspective from waiting for Jesus to anticipating Him, and watch your hope soar.*

MONDAY, DECEMBER 9

---

*Father, if you are willing, take this cup from me; yet not my will,
but yours be done. Then an angel from heaven appeared to him
and strengthened him. Luke 22:42–43 (NIV)*

WINTER TEMPERATURES IN ALBERTA SOMETIMES dip to minus 40 degrees Fahrenheit. Add a snowstorm, and conditions turn deadly. Such was the case one night long ago when my dad braved the elements for my sake.

I was in high school then, and my parents had agreed to let me attend a friend's Christmas party despite a foreboding weather forecast. By the time the party ended at midnight, heavy snowfall made roads nearly impassable. Dad managed to fetch me, but his truck got stuck on the return trip. He decided to walk the twelve blocks home, intending to return with a different vehicle. I prayed desperately for God to either turn Dad around or send help before tragedy struck. Moments later, an unknown snowmobiler appeared, picked him up, and drove him safely to his destination. I've always believed that the stranger was an angel sent to minister to one of God's children in need (Hebrews 1:14).

Angels are real. They saved Daniel's life in a lions' den (Daniel 6:22). They opened prison doors so the apostles could leave their cell unhindered (Acts 5:19). They strengthened Jesus after Satan tempted Him in the wilderness (Matthew 4:1–11) and when He faced crucifixion (Luke 22:42–43).

I may face hardships but not without hope. Help stands ready. Be alert. Perhaps the stranger who suddenly shows up to lend a hand is an angel in disguise. —GRACE FOX

FAITH STEP: *Read about Elijah's encounter with an angel in 1 Kings 19:5–8.*

TUESDAY, DECEMBER 10

I will instruct you and teach you in the way you should go; I will counsel you with my loving eye on you. Psalm 32:8 (NIV)

As CHRISTMAS DRAWS NEAR, I start planning which day I should make enchiladas. Growing up with a Hispanic grandmother, all special family gatherings included them. Twenty years ago, when Grandma Lita (short for *abuelita*, which means "little grandma") first moved in with me, she taught me how to make her delicious enchiladas. She didn't have a written recipe; instead, she taught me how to eye things.

She watched as I mixed chili powder, water, and tomato sauce for the enchilada sauce. Then she'd let me know if it was too thick or too thin and what other ingredients I needed to add to make it just right. Grandma Lita instructed me by watching and counseling me. She did so with love and joy. Even though I've gained experience in the kitchen and can make her special recipe myself, I always invite her to watch me.

While I've liked having cooking direction from Grandma Lita, there were times in the past when I didn't like the idea of Jesus's instruction. I pictured Him more as a police officer, waiting and watching for me to mess up or make a mistake. But the more experience I've had in my Christian life, the better I've learned to appreciate His counsel, instructions, and directions.

Jesus always has the perfect recipe for teaching me, just like Grandma Lita. —TRICIA GOYER

FAITH STEP: *Write down a task or tasks you need help with. Pause and picture Jesus's loving eye upon you as you ask Him to instruct and teach you.*

WEDNESDAY, DECEMBER 11

But God demonstrates his own love for us in this: While we were still sinners, Christ died for us. Romans 5:8 (NIV)

I LOVE TO GIVE. I look for excuses to bestow gifts on everyone from our mail carrier to our neighbor from Austria to Betty, the awesome lady who cleans our church (oh, how I love her).

Christmas shopping starts on December 26. For eleven months, I browse and plan, deliberate and ponder. I frequent sales and peruse catalogs. When I discover a shirt that says, "Hello, Beautiful," I know that's for my coauthor, Beth, since that is the name of our first book. Anything with cats goes to my son, Ron, or my friend Laurie. My daughter, Marie, gets every purple item I can find.

Not only at Christmas do I relish gift giving. This penchant for blessing lasts all year.

While it takes me a lot of effort to find just the right gift, from the beginning of time, God planned to give the world the greatest gift of all. When I read Romans 5:8, I think of what a huge, generous heart Jesus has, to lower Himself for thirty-three years as a human. To show us the Father's giving nature. And finally to lay down His very life so we might become children of God.

Did Jesus deliberate, ponder, and think about the perfect gift we needed? No. He said an immediate yes to God's plan to save all of us. Jesus is the gift. The perfect one. —JEANETTE LEVELLIE

FAITH STEP: *If you haven't given your heart and life to Jesus, pray now to accept His gift of forgiveness and eternal life. Trust Him as your Lord and Savior.*

Thursday, December 12

So prepare your minds for action and exercise self-control. Put all your hope in the gracious salvation that will come to you when Jesus Christ is revealed to the world. 1 Peter 1:13 (NLT)

My husband, Ted, and I invited a friend for dinner whom we haven't seen in years. I'm excited but have a long list of things to do to get ready. The living room needs dusting, and the rugs by the entrance need to be shaken out. Chicken needs to go in the slow cooker. Preparing for a visitor gives me new eyes on things I can improve in our home so he will feel welcome.

Prepping for someone's arrival opens my eyes to my surroundings in new ways, and I think that's also true of readying my heart for my Savior. I know He's coming, so I'm ready. But as I set the table today, I realized that preparing can be an ongoing and active choice.

Because a friend is coming over, I look around and make sure everything is in order. Because Jesus is returning, I can look at my life choices and put new effort into being ready. I want to prepare my mind by focusing on Him, directing my thoughts toward gratitude and praise and remaining connected to Him throughout the day. I want to offer Him my best, just as I want to make a favorite recipe for a friend's visit.

The hope of salvation fills me with anticipation like a friend's visit brings. In a sense, my whole life is a preparation for eternity. I can live with enthusiasm, excited for what is to come. —Sharon Hinck

Faith Step: *Invite a friend over and spend some time preparing for her visit. Ask Jesus to prepare your heart for Him.*

FRIDAY, DECEMBER 13

Suppose one of you wants to build a tower. Won't you first sit down and estimate the cost to see if you have enough money to complete it? Luke 14:28 (NIV)

I'VE HEARD ABOUT COUNTING THE cost of following Jesus all my life. Recently, I've come to have a new understanding of the concept. Last night, Ted and I had a friend over for dinner. Because of my health challenges, extra exertion—even conversation—can cause bad flares. We had a lovely time laughing and chatting. But afterward, the physical crash hit. I've lived with this for many years now, and I hope that after a few days of extra rest, I'll feel better.

Knowing the cost to my body, would I do it again? In a hot second! The evening filled my emotional and spiritual bucket. And beyond that, I felt Jesus's hand in the conversation as Ted and I were able to connect with and encourage our friend.

Jesus knew all about counting the cost. He understood the pain ahead on His path, and He knew He had ample resources of love to cover the cost. Following Him means a clear-eyed understanding that there will be challenges. Chronic illness has taught me that when I know there will be a cost, I can prepare to spend my strength and energy on what matters. Through His sacrifices, Jesus gives me the hope of every resource I need. As I walk with Him, the blessings far outweigh the sacrifices. —SHARON HINCK

FAITH STEP: *Ask Jesus to help you count the cost of following Him and list them on a sheet of paper. Look honestly at some of the sacrifices ahead and ask Him for eyes to see that they are more than worth it.*

SATURDAY, DECEMBER 14

Most important of all, continue to show deep love for each other,
for love makes up for many of your faults. 1 Peter 4:8 (TLB)

OUR GORGEOUS TEENAGE DAUGHTER, Zoe, tends to procrastinate when it comes to celebrating special occasions. She has a great heart, but because of poor planning, birthday cards and Christmas gifts often arrive late, if at all. This past holiday, I decided to "help" her with early text reminders and suggestions of token gifts she could give her dad, whom she adores. I checked her progress and even sent links to web pages with gift items. A week before the holiday, I got desperate. I messaged her in all caps (which means yelling): TOMORROW IS THE LAST DAY TO ORDER PACKAGES GUARANTEED FOR DELIVERY BY CHRISTMAS EVE. But she took no action.

I know I was being overbearing, but I was upset. Her father and I take joy in delighting her and buying her gifts, and I hoped she'd see the importance of doing the same for her dad. I decided to let Zoe experience the awkwardness of not having anything to give him on Christmas morning. That would be a good lesson, right?

As I surveyed the tree sans gifts from Zoe on Christmas Eve, the Holy Spirit gently spoke to me: *Cover her youthful error. Put her name on the tag for one of the gifts you bought your husband. Let it be from her.*

Jesus covered me when I fell short. After all, isn't Christmas gift-giving an expression of love and grace? My daughter, just like me, needed both. That year, I was reminded what Christmas is all about. A good lesson—in fact, a gift—for us all. —PAMELA TOUSSAINT HOWARD

FAITH STEP: *Today, take the opportunity to cover someone's error. Consider your kindness a gift.*

THIRD SUNDAY OF ADVENT, DECEMBER 15

Show me, LORD, my life's end and the number of my days;
let me know how fleeting my life is. Psalm 39:4 (NIV)

AS THEY'VE GOTTEN OLDER, MY parents have become increasingly difficult to buy gifts for. If they want something, they simply get it, so it's hard to think of nice things they'd like but don't already have. After exhausting all of our usual ideas one Christmas, my husband and I decided to give them something they could only get from us—a night out with our family.

The evening began with burgers at a casual diner downtown, then we tested our wits at a nearby escape room. It was something none of us had done before, and we had a blast searching for clues, solving riddles, and working together as a team. At the end of the night, my parents thanked us and said it was one of the best gifts ever.

The evening reminded me of a lesson I'd learned before. Some say you spell *love:* T-I-M-E, so the best way to show someone you love them is by giving them the gift of your presence. It's what God did when He sent us His Son, Jesus. He loved us so much that He wrapped His presence in swaddling clothes and made a way for us to spend all of eternity with Him.

That act of love is overwhelming. I find myself wishing I could show my love for Jesus with grand gestures, epic feats of will, or lavish donations of riches. Instead, I follow His example. The best way to show love is to give Jesus my time. —EMILY E. RYAN

FAITH STEP: *This Advent season, show Jesus you love Him by giving Him the gift of your time.*

MONDAY, DECEMBER 16

Looking unto Jesus . . . who for the joy that was set before him endured the cross. Hebrews 12:2 (KJV)

KNOWING HOW IMPORTANT THE WORD *hope* is to me, a friend sent me a small, heart-shaped cotton pillow with HOPE in crimson cross-stitching. It's no larger than 4 by 5 inches. It has hung by a cord in our family-room window for years now, and it lifts my spirits every day.

As I gazed at it today, I caught the deeper meaning the gift giver (and the Gift Giver) may have intended. Beyond its beauty and one-word message lies the story of its construction. To spell *hope*, the fabric artist created 130 tiny, crossed stitches. The needle went up, down, up, down for every single crimson cross. That's more than 500 actions to produce one word.

How fitting that on this ornament pillow, *hope* isn't penned with ink or paint but with crossed threads. The crimson thread of Christ's sacrifice that paid for the hope of the world is woven throughout the Bible's story. The cross of Jesus spells it out for us—our only hope lies in Him, His birth, His death, and His resurrection.

How fitting that the effort to create all those stitches on my tiny pillow was a test of endurance. Sometimes I toss around the word *hope* as if it were a mere word. But hope changed everything and cost Jesus His very life.

Now that I've taken note of the details that went into the gift that hangs in my window, I'll never see it the same again. Hope, like Christmas, came at the price of a cross. —CYNTHIA RUCHTI

FAITH STEP: *Consider using braided red embroidery thread as a permanent bookmark in your Bible. Think of the symbolism it would represent.*

TUESDAY, DECEMBER 17

There are friends who pretend to be friends, but there is a friend who sticks closer than a brother. Proverbs 18:24 (RSV)

MY PRAYER AFTER MOVING FROM Ohio to Texas was, "Jesus, help me to establish relationships with neighbors and make friends." I wanted to get to know the people who lived near me and develop some close relationships, but after almost five years, I came up short. Neighbors were quick to wave and say hi when I met them on the street, but I still hadn't made inroads into developing the real sort of friendships I wanted.

On Christmas, I whipped up a giant batch of homemade fudge and hand-delivered it to our neighbors' doors. When new folks moved in, I'd bake a batch of chocolate-chip cookies. Everyone seemed to appreciate the gestures, but I still felt as if I'd only made acquaintances and didn't really share a common bond. *A little help here, please, Jesus!*

It was about that time I noticed one common characteristic most of our neighbors shared. They owned dogs. In fact, the canine population of the area was so large that I affectionately dubbed our neighborhood "Dog Town." Our family hadn't had a dog in years, but seeing all these bundles of furry cuteness made me yearn for one of my own. And so a new puppy topped my Christmas list that year.

The moment I took our Yorkie, Sam, on his first stroll around the neighborhood, I became instantly popular. Who doesn't love a tiny puppy? Thanks to Sam, and Jesus, I've finally made lasting friendships. —SUSAN DOWNS

FAITH STEP: *If you own a dog, walk it today and be open to the possibility of a new friendship. If not, pray that Jesus will put something new in your life in order to attract friends.*

WEDNESDAY, DECEMBER 18

But about that day or hour no one knows, not even the angels in heaven, nor the Son, but only the Father. Be on guard! Be alert! You do not know when that time will come. Mark 13:32–33 (NIV)

ONE CHRISTMAS WHEN OUR KIDS were elementary-school aged, my husband and I decided to make the long drive from our home in Washington State to my parents' home in Alberta, Canada. We confirmed our plans with my dad and asked him to keep them a surprise for Mom.

Dad knew the date we intended to arrive, but he didn't know the hour because much depended on road conditions. Unsure about whether we'd be there in time for dinner, he went grocery shopping and stocked up on food and snacks, supposing Mom wouldn't get suspicious. He did his best not to glance at his watch throughout the day. His anticipation built until he nearly gave away our secret, but he managed to subdue his excitement until we showed up.

Jesus is coming soon. No one knows the day or the hour, but it's important to prepare for His arrival. I do that by spending time reading His Word and conversing with Him in prayer. I also try to keep short accounts—not harboring unforgiveness or letting anger linger in my heart. I make it a point to share His love with others and help those in need.

Unlike my family's Christmas surprise, Jesus's anticipated arrival isn't to be kept a secret. I'll broadcast it far and wide, telling as many people as possible so they, too, can prepare and share the excitement. —GRACE FOX

FAITH STEP: *List what preparations you would make if you knew Jesus would arrive today.*

THURSDAY, DECEMBER 19

The LORD has done great things for us, and we are glad.
Psalm 126:3 (NKJV)

I'VE ALWAYS FELT BADLY FOR people whose birthdays fall on or near Christmas. I think they often get the short end of the stick because everyone else is swept up in holiday preparations and celebrations, not paying much attention to them. And I am sure that some of the "Christmas babies" probably receive birthday gifts that double as Christmas presents. To me, that just isn't fair.

I shared those thoughts with my friend Charlene, whose son was born on Christmas Eve. Charlene told me that she always tried to make sure Jeremiah didn't feel like the Christmas hoopla overshadowed his special day. So, in addition to putting up family Christmas trees (yes, more than one tree!), she decorates a "birthday tree" that is decked out in Jeremiah's favorite colors and ornaments collected over the years of his life. All his birthday gifts are placed under the tree, and the family celebrates him on Christmas Eve. The next day, he receives more gifts on Christmas. By no means is Jeremiah forgotten.

I wonder if I sometimes lose my focus on Jesus because of my shopping, party-going, and keeping a jam-packed schedule. Yes, I hear the familiar catchphrase "Jesus is the reason for the season," but do I need to slow down and celebrate Jesus more? I figure I can never celebrate Him too much. As the psalmist wrote: He's done great things for me, and I am glad. So instead of saying "Merry Christmas" to everyone, I think I'll use a new greeting: "Happy birthday to Jesus!" —BARBRANDA LUMPKINS WALLS

FAITH STEP: *In what new, creative ways can you celebrate Jesus's special day? Consider singing "Happy Birthday" or having a birthday cake for Him on Christmas.*

FRIDAY, DECEMBER 20

For God so loved the world that he gave his one and only Son, that whoever believes in him shall not perish but have eternal life. John 3:16 (NIV)

"LET ME SHOW YOU MY new sweater," my sister Nan said during one of our evening phone chats. A text message popped up with a photo of a smiling, bespectacled llama decked out in a sparkly green Santa hat and a matching collar adorned by multicolored pom-poms.

Nan planned to wear her purchase to an Ugly Sweater Christmas party, which has become all the rage during the holidays. I laughed when I saw the photo—the sweater wasn't something I would wear anywhere, and paying money for an ugly sweater seemed silly to me. But Nan had a specific purpose in mind for her newest possession.

God had a specific time and purpose for His only Son to be born here on earth. I usually think of John 3:16 as an Easter verse, but the words are especially dear to me at Christmas. If Jesus had never been born, He couldn't have died. And I wouldn't have a Savior to pay for my sins and reconcile me with God the Father. Without Jesus's birth and death, I would have no hope in my present life or the promise of a future life with Him in eternity.

While ugly Christmas sweaters can seem frivolous, they have their place and purpose, just as Jesus has His place and purpose in my life. The only cost is my love, faith, and devotion to Him—a small price when I consider all Jesus has done for me. —BARBRANDA LUMPKINS WALLS

FAITH STEP: *Place a cross near your Christmas crèche to celebrate Jesus's birth and death. Praise Him for fulfilling His purpose on earth and in your life.*

SATURDAY, DECEMBER 21

Let the word of Christ dwell in you richly, teaching and admonishing one another in all wisdom, singing psalms and hymns and spiritual songs, with thankfulness in your hearts to God. Colossians 3:16 (ESV)

I WAS EXCITED TO ATTEND a Pacific Northwest Ballet rendition of *The Nutcracker.* Even though the ballet is a Christmas classic, it was the first time I had ever seen it. A few weeks before the performance, I read the story of young Clara, who receives a Christmas Eve gift of a wooden nutcracker that comes to life and takes her on a journey into a magical land of sweets.

Although I was a *Nutcracker* newbie, I was surprised how familiar Tchaikovsky's beautiful melodies were to me. I found myself humming along to the "March of the Toy Soldiers" and swaying to the "Dance of the Sugar Plum Fairy."

I knew the music like I know so many scriptures I associate with Christmas. Many I learned as a child while memorizing my parts for our church's annual holiday play that told the story of Jesus's birth. "For unto us a child is born, unto us a son is given" (Isaiah 9:6, KJV). "Blessed are you among women, and blessed is the child you will bear!" (Luke 1:42, NIV). "Glory to God in the highest, and on earth peace, good will toward men" (Luke 2:14, KJV).

Those words dwell deep within me, reminding me of the wonderful blessing of Jesus's coming. Like the music of *The Nutcracker*, the good news of the Savior brings me joy and hope. It even makes me want to do a happy dance! —BARBRANDA LUMPKINS WALLS

FAITH STEP: *Write out a few of your favorite scriptures that point to Jesus's birth. Recite them as you prepare your heart for Christmas.*

FOURTH SUNDAY OF ADVENT, DECEMBER 22

But the angel said to them, "Do not be afraid. I bring you good news that will cause great joy for all the people. Today in the town of David a Savior has been born to you; he is the Messiah, the Lord." Luke 2:10–11 (NIV)

OUR SON SOLOMON FIRST PARTICIPATED in our church's annual children's nativity show when he was four. He played a wise man, complete with a purple robe, silver cape, and kingly crown that sat crooked on his blond hair. I had to console him backstage and bribe him with treats before he reluctantly walked on stage bearing his gift of gold. The next year, he traded his royal costume for that of a peasant as he and his cousin played Mary and Joseph. This time, he walked more confidently onto the stage, holding his cousin's hand and leading her to the manger, where they sat beside a baby doll and listened as the story unfolded.

Two years later, they needed someone to fill a role at the last minute, so they asked Solomon to play Gabriel. As the "experienced actor" in the group, he wanted to play the part authentically and was frustrated that the angel didn't get to deliver his own lines. "It's good news, Mom!" he said. "This is how it should be done." His eyes grew wide and a huge smile spread across his face. "Hey!" he cried with delight, pumping his fists into the air and jumping with joy. "Unto you a child is born! Now, go! Go! GO!"

Whenever I celebrate the birth of Jesus, I remember my son's example and let my whole body react with joy. —EMILY E. RYAN

FAITH STEP: *Listen to upbeat praise music this Advent season and jump for joy as you sing along.*

MONDAY, DECEMBER 23

In their hearts humans plan their course, but the LORD establishes their steps. Proverbs 16:9 (NIV)

OUR FAMILY STARTED MAKING CHRISTMAS plans in October. Our oldest daughter and her husband said they would drive to our place in British Columbia, a distance spanning five hours and one mountain pass. She would bring gifts that I'd bought online and had shipped to her address in Washington State to avoid paying international postage. Our youngest daughter lived near us, so she offered to host everyone on December 24, beginning with brunch and ending with dessert following our church's candlelight service. She and I set the menu and then shopped, baked, and cooked as Christmas approached.

The couple from Washington headed our way on the morning of December 23. Three hours later, they suffered a minor collision on the icy mountain pass. They called to say they were not injured, but their car was damaged and would be towed back home.

The news upended our plans. This mama shed a few tears of disappointment, but I reminded myself that Jesus rules over the circumstances of our lives. Nothing happens that takes Him by surprise. I also meditated on the truth of His character: Jesus is wise, and He is good. I couldn't understand why He allowed an accident that damaged our kids' car, rattled their nerves, and canceled our long-awaited reunion, but I knew I could trust Jesus because He established our steps. —GRACE FOX

FAITH STEP: *Commit Proverbs 16:9 to memory and say it each morning. As you make plans this holiday season, thank Jesus for establishing your steps, even if circumstances change.*

CHRISTMAS EVE, TUESDAY, DECEMBER 24

But you will receive power when the Holy Spirit comes on you; and you will be my witnesses in Jerusalem, and in all Judea and Samaria, and to the ends of the earth. Acts 1:8 (NIV)

HOMEMADE BISCUITS WITH CHOCOLATE GRAVY is a breakfast tradition at my house on Christmas morning. I looked around the table at my precious family enjoying every bite. Most of them had helped with our Operation Christmas Child packing party. Daughter Cassie had shopped all year long for toys and clothes on clearance. Niece Sophi folded carton after carton of flat cardboard into ready-to-fill shoeboxes. Truck driver Tim, my husband, had hauled whatever we needed, wherever we needed it. Six-year-old Sadie, my granddaughter, had served as my faithful sidekick each step of the way.

"I've been following the route of our ninety-three boxes online," I said. "They went from here to Atlanta and then on to the Port of Charleston. From there, they shipped on December 6 to West Africa. Now they're across the Atlantic Ocean in Burkina Faso!"

"I hope the kids like their gifts," Sadie said. "And the notes I sent."

"What did you write in your notes?" Sophi asked.

"Jesus loves you. From Sadie," she said, a soft smile on her lips.

Acts 1:8 records the last words of Jesus before He returned to heaven. Those words challenge me as a believer to share His message of love everywhere—from my hometown of Decatur, Alabama, to the ends of the earth, in Burkina Faso. —BECKY ALEXANDER

FAITH STEP: *Maybe you can travel to other parts of the world and be a witness for Jesus. If you can't go, find another avenue and send the good news about Jesus to the ends of the earth.*

CHRISTMAS DAY, WEDNESDAY, DECEMBER 25

Give thanks to the LORD, for he is good; his love endures forever.
1 Chronicles 16:34 (NIV)

"LOOK AT ALL THE STUFF I got this year," my eight-year-old grandson, Reed, says gleefully as he surveys the brightly wrapped boxes and gift bags of all sizes that surround him. On this Christmas morning, he is beside himself with excitement as he tears off wrapping paper and ribbon while our family watches with amusement.

Reed's mom tells him to first announce who gave him the gift before he opens it. But he's so consumed with finding out what's inside that he forgets to say who it's from. She further directs Reed to take a moment to thank the giver before moving on to the next present—instructions she must repeat more than once. It's a hard lesson in gratitude for a kid who just wants to get his loot as fast as he can so he can play to his heart's content.

The exchange between Reed and our daughter makes me think about how many times I've failed to pause and thank God for each of the amazing gifts He has given me in my life—family, friends, His Word, and the freedom to worship. But the greatest gift of all is Jesus, who came to change the course of humankind and offer salvation from our sins. Might I greet Him this day with the same excitement as a kid on Christmas morning. —BARBRANDA LUMPKINS WALLS

FAITH STEP: *What wonderful gifts have you received from Jesus? Take a moment to name them and thank Him with childlike exuberance for each one.*

THURSDAY, DECEMBER 26

But he was pierced for our transgressions, he was crushed for our iniquities; the punishment that brought us peace was on him, and by his wounds we are healed. Isaiah 53:5 (NIV)

THE FOUR OF US STARED at each other with confused looks on our faces. When I'd called the now-dark-and-empty restaurant to make reservations, a sweet voice on the other end assured me it would be open on Christmas Day. Now it looked as though my husband, two children, and I would have no Christmas dinner.

My husband, Kevin, suggested we drive home to formulate a plan B. Inside, we brainstormed possible meals we could throw together with Spam, frozen corn, and cottage cheese. Suddenly, our daughter Esther remembered she had an entire ham dinner that someone had given her. She drove home and got it.

Within an hour, we were feasting on a yummy meal, thanking Jesus for my quick-thinking daughter and her generous friend. Plan B was delicious!

When God formed His plan to save the human race, Jesus's sacrificial death was His only option. There was no plan B. If Jesus had refused or had given in to the temptation to come down from the cross, we wouldn't be part of God's family. It seems unthinkable, but for Jesus, there was only one plan—to die for our sins. And that was the purpose of His birth, as well.

No plan B was a beautiful Christmas gift. —JEANETTE LEVELLIE

FAITH STEP: *Thank Jesus for obeying God's only plan to rescue and redeem mankind, including you.*

FRIDAY, DECEMBER 27

GOD's loyal love couldn't have run out, his merciful love couldn't have dried up. They're created new every morning. How great your faithfulness! Lamentations 3:22–23 (MSG)

MY HUSBAND, DAVID, AND I received the diagnosis, and it left us shaken. A tumor encased David's carotid artery at entry to his brain. Both of us listened, without hearing, as the doctor explained possible treatments and the likelihood of success. We went home to digest the news, and over the next few days, our lives trudged forward. The fragility of emotions threatened to overtake our powerful faith.

But as the shock wore off, fear failed to freeze our hope. We knew David's situation would challenge us, but we also knew we could depend on the Great Physician for guidance. We'd lived through cancer, a brain tumor, and a traumatic brain injury together. And we—and our trust in Jesus—remained. As Paulo Coelho said, "God always offers us a second chance in life."

David and I bowed our heads together often, opening our hearts and baring our souls to Jesus. One morning following fervent prayer, I raised my gaze to meet David's face. His eyes were illuminated with hope, and the light of Jesus's love reflected on his face.

At that moment, I knew he'd be all right, no matter what the future held. He'd been touched by Jesus and healed, whether he got well physically or not.

I continue to pray for David each day and remember the verse above, thanking Jesus for His loyal love. —HEIDI GAUL

FAITH STEP: *Mark a small rock with the words "Lamentations 3:22–23." Keep it handy as a reminder that Jesus's loyal love never runs out.*

SATURDAY, DECEMBER 28

She will give birth to a son, and you are to give him the name Jesus, because he will save his people from their sins. Matthew 1:21 (NIV)

TRAVELING IS NEVER EASY, BUT doing so during a worldwide pandemic was challenging. Months ago, my husband, John, and I wanted to travel to Central Europe to meet our newest grandson, born to our missionary daughter, but the ever-changing rules of who was allowed in (and through) various countries caused us to plan and replan our visit, which was a problem since our passports were close to expiring. Then, a few weeks before the trip, I came down with COVID-19. It seemed impossible that I'd receive the negative test necessary for travel, that our passports would be accepted, and that all the countries would be open for travel. Still, we dared to hope. Thankfully, every piece fell into place, and we were able to hold our grandson a week after his birth.

So much hope and prayer went into our trip, yet it pales in comparison to the generations of prayers and hope that culminated in the birth of Christ. Jewish priests and patriarchs, kings and commanders, peasants and prisoners all looked forward to their Rescuer, their Messiah. Then, one day, an angel announced His coming through a dream. The promise given to Joseph—that Jesus would save His people from their sins—is a promise for us too.

The hope of generations fell into place with the birth of Jesus. This is our hope, too, when we put our trust in Him. —TRICIA GOYER

FAITH STEP: *Write down something you've been hoping for and take it to Jesus in prayer. Thank Jesus for His salvation from your sins and offer Him all you hope for.*

SUNDAY, DECEMBER 29

And he will be called Wonderful Counselor, Mighty God, Everlasting Father, Prince of Peace. Isaiah 9:6 (NIV)

LATELY I'VE BEEN NOTICING HOW part of my brain remains alert for the sound of my name in a roomful of people. It's as if I have an antenna tuned to the "Suzanne" frequency. I probably learned to listen for my name as a child because I got in trouble if I didn't come when I was called.

I was called Suzi as a child, but I don't hear that much anymore. Only my husband, Mike, and close family members who live far away call me by that name. Now that I've been ruminating on this, I've realized that Mike rarely calls me Suzi or Suzanne. Since I'm lost in thought much of the time, not hearing my name means I miss the first few words of anything he tries to tell me.

As a nurse, I learned that something happens physically when we hear our name. As early as the first year of life, functional MRI studies show that certain areas in the brain react or light up and hormones are released when we hear our name spoken. Ironically, this happens even when a person is sedated or sound asleep.

Jesus would have experienced this too. He lived in a human body and would have heard Himself called "Yeshua," the Hebrew word for Jesus. It was the name His parents obediently gave Him when an angel appeared to Joseph (Matthew 1:21). But long before Jesus's birth, scripture recounts Jesus's many names: Messiah, Wonderful Counselor, Mighty God, Everlasting Father, Prince of Peace.

But I call Him my Savior. —SUZANNE DAVENPORT TIETJEN

FAITH STEP: *On a note card or piece of paper, inscribe your favorite name for Jesus. Put it in a prominent place and ponder its meaning.*

MONDAY, DECEMBER 30

Kish said to his son Saul, "Take one of the servants with you and go and look for the donkeys." 1 Samuel 9:3 (NIV)

I USED TO BE A fun person: up for adventure, flexible in spirit, ready to laugh. The deeper I journeyed into motherhood, however, the heavier the weight of responsibility became. Having three teenagers now means saving for college, worrying about them behind the wheel, battling to get them off their screens. That fun person is just a memory from my past.

Last Christmas, I decided I needed to resurrect her. I bought five Nerf guns and wrapped them as gifts. Oh, my goodness, did we have fun! We created rules, broke into teams, and established home bases. For hours, we raced around the house, up and down, defending our teammates and conquering our foes.

That fun and joy lingered for days, wrapping around us, drawing us close. In retrospect, I could see that although I'd lamented over the loss of my fun side, going in search of it led to more than just joy. It deepened the bond I have with my family.

In 1 Samuel, Kish loses his donkeys. On the surface, this seems like a terrible situation. Yet when Kish sends his son Saul out in search of them, not only are the donkeys found but Saul also comes back anointed by Samuel to be the very first king of Israel.

Both examples remind me that nothing is ever lost with Jesus. When I search out what I'm missing, seeking Jesus's grace as I do, I always find far more than I'm looking for. —CLAIRE McGARRY

FAITH STEP: *See if you can resurrect an aspect of yourself you thought you'd lost. Watch in anticipation for how Jesus blesses you beyond what you expect.*

NEW YEAR'S EVE, TUESDAY, DECEMBER 31

You will seek me and find me when you seek me with all your heart.
Jeremiah 29:13 (NIV)

IN THE PAST, I'VE APPROACHED the new year as a blank canvas I needed to fill. Usually, this involved an ambitious to-do or not-to-do list. The year yawned before me, a gaping chasm of *shoulds*. I *should* get more fit. I *should* write that book. I *should* stop picking my nails. I *should* read through the Bible. I *should* stop yelling at my kids.

None of these goals were bad. In fact, they were all good by most anyone's standards. Sometimes I achieved my goals. Often I failed. And then I realized there was one important element lacking: Jesus. Now, don't get me wrong. I prayed for help, stamina, and direction for achieving my goals. That's the point—they were *my* goals. My goals, however good and godly, were mine. And since they were *mine,* I was trying to attain them on my own.

Almost invariably, I'd find myself working really hard to achieve them. When that happened, I felt good. When I failed, I felt bad. Regardless of the outcome, the process was tiresome, worrisome, and burdensome. Not Jesus's easy yoke at all. I definitely got weary and heavy-burdened (Matthew 11:28–30).

The last few years, I've sought Jesus instead. No goals, resolutions, or *shoulds*. I put my focus on Him and His will for me. "Yes, when you get serious about finding me and want it more than anything else, I'll make sure you won't be disappointed" (Jeremiah 29:13, MSG).

I can't wait to see what Jesus has planned for me next year!
—ISABELLA CAMPOLATTARO

FAITH STEP: *Try setting aside your resolutions and resolve only to draw closer to Jesus next year.*

About the Authors

Becky Alexander teaches for the International Guide Academy and leads tours to Charleston, Savannah, New York City, Washington, DC, Niagara Falls, and other destinations. She even works on cruise ships from time to time. Before her travel adventures, she was a children's minister for twenty-five years. Now she invests in kids by volunteering year-round with Operation Christmas Child, a ministry of Samaritan's Purse.

Besides *Mornings with Jesus,* devotions penned by Becky also appear in Guideposts' *Inspiration from the Garden* and *Pray a Word a Day.* Her story, "Connected by Kindness" in *Chicken Soup for the Soul: Miracles & Divine Intervention,* received first-place awards from the Carolina Christian Writers Conference and Southern Christian Writers Conference.

Becky loves to write about the colorful wildflowers and singing warblers on her family farm in Decatur, Alabama. She collaborated with her biologist brother and teacher sister to create *Clover's Wildflower Field Trip,* an award-winning children's book that supports elementary science units on plants and natural habitats. You can meet Clover, the book's character, and say hi to Becky at happychairbooks.com.

Susanna Foth Aughtmon is an author and speaker who loves to use humor, scripture, and personal stories to explore how God's grace and truth intersect with our daily lives. Susanna lives in Idaho with her funny, creative husband, marketer/pastor Scott Aughtmon. She is mom to three fantastic young men, Jack, Will, and Addison, who bring her a whole lot of joy.

Susanna likes to connect with her readers through her blog, *Confessions of a Tired Supergirl,* and her *Good Things* newsletter. You can catch up with her on Facebook and her website, sfaughtmon.com.

Jeannie Blackmer is passionate about using written words to encourage women in their relationships with Jesus. Her most recent books include *Talking to Jesus: A Fresh Perspective on Prayer* and *MomSense: A Common Sense Guide to Confident Mothering.* She's been a freelance writer for more than thirty years and has worked in the publishing industry with a variety of authors on more than twenty-five books. She's also written numerous articles for print and online magazines and blogs.

She loves chocolate (probably too much), scuba diving, beekeeping, a good inspirational story, her family, and being outside as much as possible. She and her husband, Zane, live in Boulder, Colorado, and have three adult sons. Find out more about Jeannie on her website, jeannieblackmer.com.

ISABELLA CAMPOLATTARO is a longtime Guideposts contributing author who cherishes the opportunity to transform her mayhem into messages of encouragement for struggling people. In addition to writing for *Mornings with Jesus,* Isabella has written for *Guideposts One-Minute Daily Devotional, Pray a Word a Day, Every Day with Jesus, God's Comforting Ways,* and *Daily Guideposts for Recovery.* An active blogger and speaker, Isabella is the author of *Embracing Life: Letting God Determine Your Destiny,* aimed at helping women navigate challenging life events.

She and her two boys live on Florida's lush Suncoast, where she enjoys Jesus, traveling, cooking, writing, reading, running, arts and culture, random adventures, deep conversation, the beach, and music. Connect with Isabella at isabellacampolattaro.com and on Instagram, Twitter, and Facebook.

SUSAN DOWNS took her first job as a proofreader at age nine, when her small-town-newspaper-publisher father would pay her a nickel for every error she could find in the typeset proofs before they went to press. In the many years since then, she's worked as an editor for several Christian publishers, including Guideposts. She has served alongside her minister husband throughout their fifty-plus years of marriage, as well as worked as an international adoption program director, a social worker, and, while serving as a missionary in South Korea, a compassionate-ministry coordinator.

Susan and her husband, David, have five children, five grandchildren, and two Yorkies.

PAT BUTLER DYSON is a freelance writer living in the sun-drenched Gulf Coast Texas town of Beaumont. She shares life with Jeff, her husband of forty-one years, who teaches business at Lamar University and toils in the family hardware business. Pat has written for Guideposts publications for twenty-seven years. She especially enjoys writing for *Strength & Grace,* Guideposts' magazine for caregivers, and is a contributor to the website prayerideas.com. She likes cycling, exercising, reading, and sunsets at the beach. Most of all, she relishes spending time with her large, crazy family. All her grandchildren call her "Honey," except for three-year-old Jameson, who calls her "Hot Cheese."

Pat frequently uses humor in her devotions, because how can you live in this world without a sense of humor? She is delighted to contribute devotions to *Mornings with Jesus* for her fourth year. Readers may connect with Pat on her Facebook page.

GRACE FOX has contributed to *Mornings with Jesus* for ten years. Once a stay-at-home mom and daycare provider, she's now the author of thirteen books, including her latest devotionals *Keeping Hope Alive: Devotions for Strength in the Storm* and *Fresh Hope for Today: Devotions for Joy on the Journey*. She's also a devotional blogger, a member of the First 5 writing team (Proverbs 31 Ministries), and co-host of the podcast *Your Daily Bible Verse*.

Grace serves alongside her husband, Gene, as co-director of International Messengers Canada, a missionary-sending agency with nearly 300 staff in thirty-one countries. She trains church leaders in the Middle East, and she and Gene lead short-term mission teams to Eastern Europe annually.

In 2018, Grace and Gene moved aboard a 48-foot sailboat moored near Vancouver, British Columbia.

Connect with her at gracefox.com and on Facebook, and learn more about her at gracefox.com/books.

HEIDI GAUL lives with her husband in Oregon's Willamette Valley, where she gardens, hikes, and seeks new adventures. An ex-Bible Study Fellowship group leader, she's contributed to ten Guideposts' devotionals, including *Every Day with Jesus, Mornings with Jesus, Guideposts One-Minute Daily Devotional,* and *Pray a Word a Day*.

A Cascade Award winner for devotionals, she has written pieces that have appeared in *The Upper Room,* as well as in eleven *Chicken Soup for the Soul* anthologies. She has final-judged for major Christian writing competitions and enjoys speaking, leading workshops, and mentoring groups.

She'd love to hear from you at heidigaul.com or on Facebook.

TRICIA GOYER is a speaker, podcast host, and *USA Today* bestselling author of over eighty books. Tricia writes in numerous genres, including fiction, parenting, marriage, and children and teens. She's a wife, homeschooling mom of ten, and a mentor to writers through her Write That Book club (triciagoyer.com/write-that-book). Tricia lives near Little Rock, Arkansas.

SHARON HINCK is an award-winning novelist whose stories celebrate ordinary women on extraordinary faith journeys. She recently released a new three-book series called *The Dancing Realms*. She continues to work as a part-time writing professor, a freelance speaker and teacher, and an author and editor. She cherishes her roles as wife, mother, and grandmother. Most of all, she is grateful to be called beloved by Jesus and hopes to encourage others who need reassurance of His grace and faithfulness.

Sharon loves interacting with readers; explore the fun things she's posted at her website, sharonhinck.com.

PAMELA TOUSSAINT HOWARD is a native New Yorker who currently lives and works in Atlanta, Georgia. She developed a love for the written word and the confidence to become a writer from her dad, a printing plant supervisor. Pamela pursued a degree in journalism from Fordham University and won a coveted summer internship at *Essence* magazine. She went on to become the magazine's associate editor and subsequently a trade newspaper reporter, nonprofit media spokeswoman, and coauthor of five published books, including *His Rules* (Waterbrook/Penguin Random House). Also a licensed minister, Pamela is a host of *Church around the Corner*, which airs on WGNM-TV in Georgia, sharing practical biblical principles.

She and her husband, Andrew, have enjoyed traveling together since their honeymoon in Tokyo, Japan, five years ago. The couple ministers to the homeless and to the formerly incarcerated through their informal backpack outreach, which provides toiletries, snacks, socks, and a New Testament to encourage hearts and hopefully reduce prison recidivism. To learn more, message her on Facebook.

JEANETTE LEVELLIE, a former history teacher and newspaper columnist, loves the color orange, strong tea, and Jesus. She is the author of five books and hundreds of articles, stories, and devotions. A popular humor/inspirational speaker and an ordained minister, she offers her relatable blend of fun and biblical encouragement to every audience.

When Jeanette isn't preparing messages or writing, she enjoys gardening, watching black-and-white movies with her pastor husband, Kevin, and discovering new ways to avoid housework. Her favorite people besides Jesus and Kevin are her two grown children, three grandchildren, and four rascals in cat suits.

She enjoys life in the rural setting of Paris, Illinois, where people graciously help their neighbors. Find Jeanette's splashes of hope and humor at jeanettelevellie.com.

Ericka Loynes first fell in love with words as a child in Chicago, performing speeches under the guidance of her mentor, civil rights activist Mamie Till Mobley, the mother of Emmett Till. Seeing her own mother publish works for a Christian company sparked the idea in Ericka that she, too, could be a writer.

Ericka has written in spaces ranging from college journals to corporate training. She contributed to the book *Blessed Is She: The Transforming Prayer Journeys of 30 African American Women* by Victoria Saunders McAfee and is a coauthor of *The Ashes Have Voices: Stories to Motivate, Inspire and Ignite Healing*. As one of the 2018 Guideposts Writers Workshop winners, Ericka is thrilled to be writing devotions for *Mornings with Jesus*.

Currently, Ericka is a director of organizational design and development. She enjoys encouraging others through career coaching, motivational speaking, and, of course, inspirational writing. Born and raised in Chicago, Ericka currently lives in Memphis with her husband and young adult son.

Erin Keeley Marshall has enjoyed writing for Guideposts Books for many years and counts her opportunities to contribute to *Mornings with Jesus* among her favorite career blessings. Her work spans numerous genres as an editor, and she is published in both fiction and nonfiction. Visit her at erinkeeleymarshall.com and on Facebook (@ErinKeeley MarshallAuthor) and Instagram (@erinkeeleymarshall).

Dianne Neal Matthews attended her first writers' conference (with great timidity) in 1999. Since then, she has written, cowritten, or contributed to twenty-four books, including *The One Year Women of the Bible* and *Designed for Devotion: A 365-Day Journey from Genesis to Revelation* (a Selah Award winner). Dianne has also published hundreds of articles, guest blog posts, newspaper features, stories, Bible studies, and one poem. Since 2012, her favorite writing project each year has been sharing her faith journey with some of her favorite people in the world, the wonderful readers of *Mornings with Jesus*.

Dianne and her husband, Richard, have been married since 1974 and live in west Tennessee. When she's not writing, Dianne enjoys volunteering at her church, trying new recipes, reading, soaking up nature, and FaceTiming with her three children and four grandchildren. She loves to connect with readers through her Facebook author page or website, diannenealmatthews.com.

CLAIRE MCGARRY is thrilled and honored to contribute to *Mornings with Jesus* again this year. She is a maker of lists, mistakes, brownies, and soups. Dirty laundry is her nemesis as she tries to focus more on creating a loving home, rather than cleaning it. Claire is the author of *Grace in Tension: Discover Peace with Martha and Mary* and the family Lenten devotionals *Abundant Mercy* and *With Our Savior*. A regular contributor to *Living Faith* and catholicmom.com, her work has also appeared in *Chicken Soup for the Soul* books and numerous devotionals. A former lay missionary and founder of MOSAIC of Faith, Claire endeavors to bring people to God through her retreats, women's groups, and writing.

Claire lives in New Hampshire with her witty husband and three spunky kids, who always keep her laughing and humble. She can be found via her Facebook author page and her blog, shiftingmyperspective.com.

JENNIFER ANNE F. MESSING is thrilled to be a contributor to *Mornings with Jesus* this year. She's a Cascade Writing Award winner and five-time finalist ("Published Short Story" in 2018, 2019, and 2021), an author of four books of short fiction and poetry, speaker, graphic designer, and worship leader. A past president of the Oregon Christian Writers, she earned a bachelor's degree in journalism. She has over 250 short stories, articles, and poems published in sixty magazines and books, including *Woman's World, LIVE, Purpose, Seek, Glittery Literary,* and *Nudges from God.* Her latest book, *Love's Faithful Promise: Heart-Stirring Short Stories and Poems of Romance and Faith,* was named winner of the 2020 American Fiction Awards "Christian: Inspirational" category.

Originally from the Philippines, Jennifer Anne has been married to Michael Messing for thirty-one years. They are the parents of three grown children and grandparents of three young boys, and reside in Oregon. Connect with her on Facebook, Twitter (@JennyAnnMessing), and her website, jenniferannemessing.com.

CYNTHIA RUCHTI has earned a reputation as a carrier of hope. She tells stories hemmed in hope through her novels, nonfiction, and devotional contributions to books such as *Mornings with Jesus,* as well as speaking events for women and writers. Many of her more than thirty-six books have received a variety of industry honors. For thirty-three years, Cynthia wrote and produced a scripted radio broadcast that offered hope over the airwaves. That experience helped prepare her heart and skillset for the books she writes today.

Keeping her eyes open for ways Jesus is working hope into the fabric of life accompanies her occupations as a wife, mom, grandmother of six, author, speaker, and literary agent with Books & Such Literary Management. She and her grade-school sweetheart husband live in the heart of Wisconsin, not far from their three children. Her tagline is: "I can't unravel. I'm hemmed in Hope." Her website is cynthiaruchti.com.

EMILY E. RYAN is a minister's wife and mother of four who loves writing devotions because it helps her see Jesus in everyday moments. In this season of life, most of those moments involve pouring into the lives of teenagers, both as a mom and as a public school English teacher, and she is challenged and humbled by the call to share Jesus across generations. Her books include *Who Has Your Heart? The Single Woman's Pursuit of Godliness* and *Guilt-Free Quiet Times: Exposing the Top Ten Myths about Your Time with God.* In addition to *Mornings with Jesus*, Emily's devotions also appear in Guideposts' *God's Comforting Ways, In the Arms of Angels,* and *Inspiration from the Garden,* and she has been writing and speaking at conferences, retreats, and women's events for over twenty years.

Emily and her family live in the great state of Texas, but you can avoid the heat and humidity by visiting her online at emilyeryan.com. She loves hearing how God is working in the lives of her readers, and her virtual door is always open.

KAREN SARGENT's first submission to Guideposts was published in *Angels on Earth* in 2017. Since then, she has enjoyed writing devotions for *Strength & Grace, Pray a Word a Day, Mornings with Jesus,* and more. She is the award-winning author of *Waiting for Butterflies* and *If She Never Tells* and leads book launches for authors. She and her husband enjoy retirement in beautiful Southeast Missouri.

CASSANDRA TIERSMA is a self-confessed messy-a.n.i.c. (messy, absentminded, normal-ish, imperfect, creative) woman of faith. She's also an author, poet, and former reporter/journalist whose articles, photography, and poetry have been published in multiple newspapers. Her book, *Come In, Lord, Please Excuse the Mess!,* is a guide for spiritual healing and recovery for messy-a.n.i.c. women who struggle with clutter bondage. Blessed with a sense of humor, Cassandra's not afraid to be a fool for Christ, whether writing and performing comedic monologues and song parodies, working with children, or singing and playing her antique autoharp. With a colorful history as a performance artist, writer, speaker, workshop presenter, and ministry leader, it is Cassandra's mission to bless and encourage women in their faith so that they can become the full expression of who God created them to be.

Cassandra lives with her husband, John, in a small mountain California town, where she serves as women's ministry director at the historic little stone chapel that is their church home. Cassandra loves to hear from her readers. You can connect with her by sending an email to cassandra@cassandratiersma.com.

SUZANNE DAVENPORT TIETJEN is the author of *The Sheep of His Hand* and *40 Days to Your Best Life for Nurses,* in addition to writing for *Mornings with Jesus.* She and her husband, Mike, have lived on his family farm in Illinois, in a cabin deep in the Hiawatha Forest of Michigan, and now on the high plains of Wyoming. Suzanne was a longtime shepherd and currently keeps bees. She is a retired neonatal nurse practitioner who cared for sick and tiny newborns in ambulances, helicopters, and hospitals of four states for more than twenty-five years.

BARBRANDA LUMPKINS WALLS is a writer and editor in northern Virginia, where she fights traffic and gets inspiration daily for connecting God's Word to everyday life. Barbranda is the lead essayist for the photography book *Soul Sanctuary: Images of the African American Worship Experience* and serves as the editor for her church's annual Lenten devotional booklet. The former newspaper reporter and magazine editor has written for a number of national publications, including *Guideposts, Our Daily Bread, Cooking Light,* and *Washingtonian.*

Barbranda and her husband, Hal, enjoy spending time with family, especially their adult son and daughter, son-in-law, and beloved grandson. Connect with her on Twitter @Barbrandaw and Instagram at barbl427.

BRENDA L. YODER is a licensed mental health counselor, school counselor, speaker, writer, and former teacher. She is the author of *Fledge: Launching Your Kids without Losing Your Mind* and *Balance, Busyness, and Not Doing It All* and has been featured in Guideposts' *Evenings with Jesus* and *Chicken Soup for the Soul* books. She's the co-host of the *Midlife Moms* podcast and the Midlife Moms Facebook community.

Brenda is a wife, mom of four adult kids, and grandma. She and her husband, Ron, also host an Airbnb and raise Bernese Mountain dogs, goats, cattle, and chickens on their farm in northern Indiana. When she's not working or writing, she loves gardening, antiquing, camping, sitting outside with a cup of coffee, and traveling the back roads. Connect with her at brendayoder.com or on Instagram or Facebook.

TOPICAL INDEX

A NOTE FROM THE EDITORS

WE HOPE YOU ENJOYED *Mornings with Jesus 2024,* published by Guideposts. For over 75 years, Guideposts, a nonprofit organization, has been driven by a vision of a world filled with hope. We aspire to be the voice of a trusted friend, a friend who makes you feel more hopeful and connected.

By making a purchase from Guideposts, you join our community in touching millions of lives, inspiring them to believe that all things are possible through faith, hope, and prayer. Your continued support allows us to provide uplifting resources to those in need. Whether through our communities, websites, apps, or publications, we inspire our audiences, bring them together, and comfort, uplift, entertain, and guide them.

Visit us at guideposts.org to learn more.

We would love to hear from you. Write us at Guideposts, P.O. Box 5815, Harlan, Iowa 51593 or call us at (800) 932-2145. Did you love *Mornings with Jesus 2024*? Leave a review for this product on guideposts.org/shop. Your feedback helps others in our community find relevant products.

Find inspiration, find faith, find Guideposts.

Shop our best sellers and favorites at
guideposts.org/shop